'I first interviewed Oscar when he was fifteen ye[...]
ing, and Oscar is still winning in many more w[...]

'Phenomenal read on a lifelong passion, achi[...]
determination to live!!'   – Earl Evans, joint CEO of Shaw and Partners,
EFG Group

'Oscar has proven his incredible talent with decades of awe-inspiring
victories; now he is going to beat the unbeatable.'
– Miles Dally, former CEO RCL Foods

Oscar Chalupsky was born in 1963 in South Africa. His long list of
accomplishments includes twelve-times World Molokai Surfski Champion;
ten-times winner of the Texan Challenge, considered the world's toughest
kayak race; triple winner of the big white-water Umkomaas River Marathon;
Spain's famous Sella Descent; as well as a multiple Surf Ironman champion.
Currently living between Portugal and South Africa, Oscar is CEO of Nelo
Surfski, a kayaking coach and co-founder of NuMobile in South Africa.

Graham Spence is the co-author of the bestselling trilogy *The Elephant
Whisperer*, *Babylon's Ark* and *The Last Rhinos*, which he wrote with conser-
vationist Lawrence Anthony. A former journalist and editor from South
Africa, he now lives in England.

NO RETREAT, NO SURRENDER

TO BRUE

KEEP POSITIVE

NO RETREAT, NO SURRENDER

The inspiring story of a world-champion
sportsman and cancer warrior

OSCAR CHALUPSKY

WITH GRAHAM SPENCE

PENGUIN BOOKS

No Retreat, No Surrender

Published by Penguin Books
an imprint of Penguin Random House South Africa (Pty) Ltd
Reg. No. 1953/000441/07
The Estuaries No. 4, Oxbow Crescent, Century Avenue, Century City, 7441
PO Box 1144, Cape Town, 8000, South Africa
www.penguinrandomhouse.co.za

Penguin
Random House
South Africa

First published 2022
Reprinted in 2022, 2023 (twice) and 2024

5 7 9 10 8 6

Publication © Penguin Random House 2022
Text © Oscar Chalupsky and Graham Spence 2022

Front cover photo: Lucas Tozzi; back cover photo: Anthony Grote

PUBLISHER: Marlene Fryer
MANAGING EDITOR: Robert Plummer
EDITOR: Dane Wallance
PROOFREADER: Bronwen Maynier
COVER DESIGNER: Ryan Africa
TYPESETTER: Monique van den Berg

Set in 11 pt on 14.5 pt Minion Pro

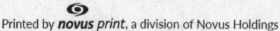

Printed by **novus print**, a division of Novus Holdings

MIX
Paper from
responsible sources
FSC
www.fsc.org   FSC® C022948

ISBN 978 1 77639 020 5 (print)
ISBN 978 1 77639 021 2 (ePub)

This book is dedicated to Clare, Luke and Hannah, the Chalupsky and Ellis Brown families, friends, and the true unsung heroes – the medical professionals at the forefront of saving countless lives from cancer.

Contents

Author's note

I am not a big social media user, but on 29 November 2019 something made me log onto Facebook. A message popped up on my screen. It was short – just five terse words. 'Big O has big C.'

I read it several times in disbelief. Oscar Chalupsky, the toughest, most competitive and arguably the most successful watersport competitor in the world has cancer? The guy who takes positive thinking and self-belief to stratospheric heights; the guy who has defied every imaginable athletic axiom regarding age, stamina and endurance has been stricken by a killer disease?

I shook my head. No – it couldn't be true. Oscar is indestructible.

Oscar contacted me later to confirm the dreadful news. His voice boomed over the phone, vibrant and laughing, hardly the voice of a sick man. 'It's multiple myeloma,' he said. 'Incurable. So we'd better start writing that book.'

I have known Oscar for close on forty years, although for much of the time we have lived in different towns or countries. Whenever we meet up, it's as though we're resuming a conversation we had yesterday. We had talked before about doing a book, but never got around to it, probably because Oscar is one of those people in perpetual motion and I didn't think it was possible for him to sit still long enough for lengthy interviews.

But things had now changed, faster than any of us could have imagined. As Oscar said, now was the time to start writing. However, Murphy's law predictably came into effect as I had moved to England and was about to ghost-write another book with a tight and contractually enforceable deadline. I couldn't start working with Oscar for at least another six months.

But when someone has incurable cancer, deadlines take on a far more significant meaning. I asked, as delicately as possible, how much time did we have to write the book? Oscar laughed. 'Plenty – no rush at all.'

'But your cancer is incurable,' I said.

'That's what the doctors say. Not me. I'm just hanging in until they find a cure. No problem.'

Once I was free of contractual obligations, we started the book. Much of what we wrote I had witnessed first-hand, beginning in 1983 with Oscar winning the 250-kilometre offshore surfski race between Port Elizabeth and East London that was then called the Texan Challenge. A year or so later, I spent two weeks living on a shoestring in Hawaii accompanying him when he won his third successive Molokai to Oahu ocean race. For the next decade and a half, I would get phone calls from around the world at various inhospitable hours updating me on whatever race he was competing in. Every call was upbeat, as a chat with Oscar lifts the gloom no matter what time he rings. And for me as a journalist, the bonus was that many of those calls resulted in front-page stories for the various newspapers I worked for. Oscar is what we in the trade called 'colourful copy'.

If anyone can beat multiple myeloma, one of the deadliest strains of the globe's most lethal disease, it is Oscar. At the time of writing, he has valiantly defied modern medicine, not only by living a full and vigorous life, but by doing so with grit and optimism that many of us would consider insane. The initial doomsday diagnosis was that he had perhaps six months to live, and – even more alarming – he'd probably contracted the cancer eating at his spine two years beforehand. Consequently, at the time of writing, he has flouted the grim reaper by almost five years. As he says, he is 'hanging in' until a cure is found.

Oscar's idea of 'hanging in' is simple. No retreat. No surrender. He is still out there paddling oceans, cycling, swimming, playing golf, keeping fit. He still lives the endless summer lifestyle and must be one of the oldest cancer warriors doing so. His innate, irrepressible cheerfulness, his unconquerable will and sheer appetite for life is still as indomitable as ever.

Oscar is donating a portion of his royalties from this book to Campaigning for Cancer, or C4C, as the overwhelming majority of cancer fighters in Africa are not wealthy. It's a sad fact that without expensive medication, life expectancy is short, sharp and painful. For those on this continent unable to get treatment – unable even to make their voices heard – there is no more powerful ally than Oscar Chalupsky. (If you would donate directly, please visit https://campaign4cancer.co.za/wp/getinvolved/.)

While working on the manuscript with Oscar, two of my immediate family members also contracted cancer. To say Oscar's story was inspirational for them is an understatement. It also suddenly became far more personal for me than merely being a wordsmith.

I hope this book on a truly larger-than-life character, who can laugh in the face of both adversity and triumph, will also be an inspiration to others.

GRAHAM SPENCE, JUNE 2022

Acknowledgements

I would like to thank the following people who have contributed so much to my life. The list grows with the more people I meet, so inevitably some will slip through the net. But you all know who you are – and you have my eternal gratitude.

Firstly, thanks to my sponsors over the years: Gavin Varejes, who provided my first ever sponsorship to Hawaii and for being a great friend for more than fifty years. Paul Naude from Gotcha beachwear, a great businessman and friend. John Barnes and Paul Larche from Merc A Rama, who provided me with an upmarket vehicle during my 'beachbum' days. Car sponsors Mark Conway from CMH, and Richard Corfield and Michaela Chalupsky from KIA Motors. Richard Downey from Thule roof racks and luggage, a life-long friend who was in the army with me and lived in our home in Westville. I recently made the speech at his sixtieth birthday. Maui Jim sunglasses. Braca-Sport Paddles, who supply me with the best paddles in the world. Alberto Chiaranda, former CEO of Wild Coast Sun, Sun International. Golf-ing maestro Ernie Els, who sponsored me in my tenth Molokai win. I have stayed with Ernie and Liesel all over the world, and I am very proud to have once been mistaken for his brother at a major US tournament. Earl Evans and Allan Zion of Shaw and Partners for playing a major role in the growth of the sport of surfskiing.

I would also like to thank friends who have helped me and my family: Gordon Rowe, my godfather who built my early kayaks and paddles. RIP. Lifelong friend and mentor Tony Dumas from Florida – special thanks for always providing superb hospitality whenever we were in the USA. Tony Scott and Andrew Sutherland, my mentors in Durban – and absolute legends. Bob Twogood, the first of many great friends in Hawaii. Mike Muller, who drove my escort boat in most of the Molokai to Oahu races and often put me up in his home on the island; and Chris Laird, escort boat skipper during my historic twelfth win. Kate Rose, also a great friend in Oahu whose hospitality to me and Clare is unsurpassed. Geoff Graf, who provided accommodation in Oahu, and Tom McTigue, who got me temporary membership at the Outrigger Canoe Club on Waikiki beach every year. Sean McCarthy, whose company SMG provided sponsorship, and who is also a valued family friend. We spent many fantastic holidays together. Former world surfing champion Shaun Tomson, my surfing inspiration. Thanks also for once getting me out of trouble in Hawaii! Sharon Blakeway, Clare's closest friend from school who came to our aid in tough times; and Richard Barrow, our generous neighbour in Lambert Road, Durban, who helped us in a difficult situation and also sponsored one of my Dusi races. Mike Pampallis for excellent legal advice and assistance. Dean Gardiner for tough contests on the water. Australian Ironman champion Ken Vidler, who always looked after me in Perth. Jim Hoffman in New York, a great friend and Mr Fixit. With Jim on your side, you can't go wrong. The Strydom family in Cape Town. It was Pierre who first told me we were about to be readmitted to the 1992 Olympics and his family were generous in the extreme, providing accommodation both during my training for the Barcelona Olympics and later when I got cancer. David Abromowitz for excellent golf and memorable boat trips. Paul Harris for superb accommodation and advice. Stuart Lowe for invaluable information regarding multiple myeloma. Ken Forrester, Craig Hathorn and Jeremy Thompson in the Cape. Brian Reardon, Yakoob Paruk and Robert Mauvis in Durban, for good advice and friendship. Dr Len Nel, my superb dermatologist. Dr Dave Gillmer, fellow paddler and heart specialist. Dr Willem Erasmus, my magnificent plastic surgeon. Andy Leith, three times K-3 winner of the Fish River Marathon with my brother Herman and me. Johan Marais, my friend and business partner. Stephen Miller, for always being ready to help us. Seth Koppes in Hawaii, my doubles partner in my last Molokai. Arjan Bloem in Amsterdam and Ivan Lawler in London, who are always loyal. Marketing guru Gavin Dickinson, who provided accommodation whenever we were in Dubai; and Rene and Babs Appel for providing accommodation in Hong Kong. Professor Tim Noakes for nutritional advice. Craig and Nicky McKenzie, who generously gave us use of their luxury home during the Covid-19 lockdown while I was undergoing debilitating chemo treatment. Nelo and Helena Ramos in Vila do Conde, Portugal, for invaluable assistance and friendship. Gary Roscoe and Garth Person, my golf coaches. Gary would meet me at the Royal Durban Golf Club at 4.30 in the morning. To all my loyal customers throughout my careers with Key Delta, Sanlam, Oscar

Chalupsky & Associates, Citadel, Epic, NuMobile and now Nelo Kayaks – my journey is thanks to you.

Thanks also to the photographers whose photographs appear in this book, and for those who gave up their valuable time to be interviewed. Special thanks to my co-author and master wordsmith Graham Spence. And finally, heartfelt thanks to the friendly and extremely professional Robert Plummer and his team at Penguin Random House for making this book happen.

OSCAR CHALUPSKY, JUNE 2022

Prologue

A shaft of agony shot down my back, like a spear being plunged into my upper spine.

It was excruciating. I had never experienced anything like it, even though my whole life as an endurance athlete had been dedicated to pushing the extremities of physical pain.

It happened while I was limbering up in the ocean for the start of the Shaw and Partners Doctor (previously called the Perth Doctor), a twenty-seven-kilometre race from Rottnest Island to Sorrento Beach in Western Australia. It's a highlight on the global surfski calendar, attracting many of the world's top paddlers. That year, 2019, there were 437 of us. I race it regularly and have been first across the line three times in a row.

The intensity of the spasm, rather than the pain itself, is what shocked me. I'd been nursing niggling injuries for the past two years, but this time the torment was so severe it was off the charts. I dared not admit it, even to myself, but I instinctively knew it was serious.

The race is named after the famed Fremantle Doctor, a refreshingly brisk onshore wind that brings relief to Perth residents on sweltering summer days. The irony of the name did not escape me – a doctor was exactly what I needed, but it wasn't the wind.

I decided not to compete. That fact alone shocked me to the core. It would have been the first time in my life that I retired before the starting gun fired.

I was about to drag my surfski back onto the beach when I looked at the sky. Despite the brilliant sunshine, clouds were scudding on the horizon. The wind was gusting up to twenty knots from the south-west – a solid Force 5 on the Beaufort Scale, and perhaps later peaking to a near gale in the fresher blasts. Perfect for a fast race, which was just how I liked it.

I am known as a big downwind paddler: the stronger the blow, the better. Even though I was fifty-six years old, in squalls I believed I was unbeatable not only in my age category but in the overall race itself. The wind is nearly always strong on hot Perth afternoons, which makes The Doctor one of the fastest paddling contests in the world. It's also, in my opinion, one of the most fun. This year could be an epic race.

Instinctively, my competitive character kicked in. I threw my flip-flops into the seconding boat that would be following the race.

'See you guys at the end,' I said.

The gun fired and we were off, the ocean churning to whipped cream as more than four hundred skis turbo-charged towards the Australian mainland.

I limped off the line in agony. It was one of my slowest starts ever. I needed my back to loosen up, then, hopefully, I would step on the gas. It may sound a contradiction, but the aches semi-crippling me for the past two years always lessened with exercise. That's why I considered strenuous workouts to be the best medicine.

Not this time. The pain intensified.

I am used to beating up my body. Weekend athletes call it 'hitting the wall', but it's far more profound than that. In fact, it's the secret of extreme sports. I discovered as a teenager that we all have a mother lode of innate mental and physical steel, but to find that secret source we have to burrow into the darkest depths of our inner selves. It's something few people wish to do, as it demands peaks of pain and exhaustion infinitely more intense than mere fatigue. The human body and mind can perform at far higher levels than most people believe. Once someone grasps that, they can do anything if they are willing to pay the price.

I certainly am not exceptional in discovering this. It's the same almost mystical *yin–yang* that Special Forces soldiers, the SAS or Navy SEALs nurture when going through superhuman selection courses specifically designed to destroy even the toughest warriors.

It's also what every world-class athlete knows. It's the Holy Grail of endurance sport. It's what makes us win. Coming second is just a blip, a rescheduling for next time.

But out there that day racing The Doctor with my back seized in agony, the price tag suddenly seemed too high. I decided to quit. All I needed was to signal the rescue boat to come and fetch me. I started making excuses, telling myself that I had nothing to prove. I had won the race twice, been 'robbed' of the title once, and invariably finished in the top ten. So why carry on?

I was about to raise my hand in defeat, but something stopped me.

Despite the distress, I was still in my natural element. I am happiest when surfing down fast-running swells with spray in my face and a howling wind at my back. The siren of the sea beckoned the day I got my first surfski as a young boy, and it's a call I can never resist. Now, after close on half a century of racing to extremes, I realised I could not give up.

I instinctively found myself starting to dig deep, getting into the easy rhythm of power and flow, milking the elemental energy of every surging swell. I started reeling other racers in, but then, as I didn't know how much harm the pain was doing to my body, I decided to throttle back and cruised to the finish.

I came fourth in the Over-50 group and thirty-fourth overall. My time was marginally over one hour and forty-five minutes, two minutes behind the category winner and ten minutes behind the overall winner. So, I wasn't far off the pace by any means.

Once beached, I was so sore I could barely get off my ski. I had seen an expert sports physiotherapist earlier that week who said the pain was merely a pinched nerve shrinking as I cooled down after extreme exercise, so I tried to shrug it off.

However, that evening on the flight back to Portugal, the pain intensified further. I could not sit still for a minute. Wave after wave of agony exploded along my spine, and I could only get some brief respite if I stood. An Emirates flight attendant, who took customer service to new heights, filled a plastic two-litre Coke bottle with boiling water, wrapped it in complimentary airline socks, and told me to wedge that against my back.

It worked – better than any of the legion of painkillers that I had been gulping down like sweets. The rest of the fourteen-hour flight was at least bearable.

Back in Portugal, I phoned my physiotherapist, Vitor Pimenta, and asked him to book me in for an MRI the following day.

As the radiographer wheeled me into the capsule, my body started writhing uncontrollably. I frantically pushed the emergency button to be pulled out of the tube and stood for a few minutes. This happened three times before I was eventually able to lie still long enough for the machine to finish scanning.

I could tell by the startled expression on the radiographer's face as she looked at the readings that something serious was going on.

'What's the matter?' I asked.

Somewhat hesitantly, she allowed me to have a look at the machine printout. 'I'm not a radiologist, so I can't say anything,' she said.

She didn't have to. Even I could see what looked to be a two-centimetre tumour on my upper spine.

'Vitor will give you a full analysis,' she said.

However, Vitor, who was now a close friend, was too distraught to give me and Clare the news himself. Instead he asked my business partner and former Portuguese kayak champion Manuel 'Nelo' Ramos to tell us the awful news. The spinal tumour was malignant. Ironically, it had been Nelo who first suggested when I returned from Australia that my problem could be cancer, but I had not taken it seriously.

I then sent the MRI images to Dr Erik Borgnes, an American radiologist who had diagnosed my long-time friend, writer and paddling enthusiast Joe Glickman a few years prior with pancreatic cancer.

Erik's diagnosis was even more frightening. 'The tumour is secondary cancer,' he said. 'Stage 3, going into Stage 4.'

In other words, it was most likely terminal. I looked at Clare, who was sitting beside me, stunned. I had been expecting bad news but not this bad.

It got worse.

'We have no idea where or what the primary cancer is. So we cannot effectively treat the secondary cancer stage until we know what we are dealing with.'

Erik also said that the cancer had been eating away at the vertebrae, and the punishing exercise I had been doing could have snapped the bone at any moment. That would have caused instant paralysis, and he remarked that it was a miracle the spine was still intact.

'How much longer have I got?' I asked.

He was silent for a moment. But he knew me, and he knew that there was no point in beating about the bush. There was no easy way to answer the question.

'Perhaps six months.'

As the shock subsided, I realised with cold clarity that everything in my life had crystalised to this point. I had a family that I loved more than any-thing else and a lifestyle that has no equal. I had everything to lose.

I am used to challenges. Contests are the essence of being an athlete. But this challenge was like no other I had faced.

At stake was my life.

1

Where it all started

I think my destiny was mapped the moment I took my first breath.

Not only is my zodiac sign aquatic – Pisces – but the first mass-produced ocean surfski in the world, which I designed with input from my father and Tony Scott, a Durban paddling legend, was named after me. At least 'Oscar' is what we called it in South Africa. The rest of the world called it a 'Chalup-ski'.

With a legacy like that, what else could I do?

I was born in Durban on 1 March 1963, to a German father and a South African mother. Paul Chalupsky came from Mannheim and immigrated to South Africa as a young man primarily to avoid being conscripted into the army. He grew up in the grim aftermath of the Second World War, seeing first-hand the destruction of his native country, and had no wish to be further involved.

A skilled mechanic, he soon found work in South Africa's booming economy. More significantly for the Chalupsky legacy was that he brought over from Europe another skill in short supply – kayaking. As the city of Mannheim straddles the confluence of the Rhine and Neckar rivers, young Paul was a top paddler, spurred on by my grandfather Franz, who made the kayaks. When Dad arrived in South Africa, he was way ahead of local paddlers, not just in skills but in every aspect of the sport. In a magazine interview, which I still have, he described the local kayaking scene in those days as a 'joke'.

'For a start, the kayaks here are too short and unwieldy,' Dad told the journalist. 'Although there are some exceptionally strong guys paddling them, not enough emphasis is placed upon river craft.'

He hit the nail squarely on the head. Never one to mince his words, Dad also put his money where his mouth was, and he and my grandfather started building their own brand of kayaks in the garage of our house in Westville, a suburb on the western periphery of Durban. I loved watching them as a young boy, helping when I could – so much so that at junior school my nickname was 'fibreglass' due to all the chopped strand mat particles in my hair.

The kayaks built by Paul and Franz were not only streets ahead of anything else produced locally, they were world class. Within a few years, Paul held the record for every major race except for the three-day Dusi marathon between Pietermaritzburg and Durban, which purists regard to be as much of a running contest as it is about paddling.

My mother Mercia was born in Cape Town and had a hard childhood. Her father died when she was young, leaving the family destitute, and for some time she and her younger sister Andy lived in a care home. She told my sister Alma that the highlight of those bleak days was when ships came into harbour, as they often donated excess food to charity, which was a welcome respite from the usual bland fare.

But Mercia was made of steel. She moved to Durban and got a job in a hair salon at the Claridges Hotel, where she worked her way up to become a highly skilled, sought-after stylist. She and Dad married and soon started a rapidly expanding family. In fact, all four children were born almost exactly fifteen months apart, and we still joke that was owing to my father's German precision. I was the oldest, followed by Herman and Walter, and finally Alma.

Durban has some of the best beaches and surf in the world, and many kayak paddlers are also surf lifesavers. As Paul had won almost every local river race possible, the ocean was a natural progression and he joined the Durban Surf Lifesaving Club. This had a massive impact on me, as almost overnight the beach became my second home. Dad did regular weekend lifesaving duties, but even when he didn't have shifts, I was dropped off at the club at 6 a.m. with my brothers and Alma during school holidays and told to have fun. Most of the day was spent in the water, only emerging to wolf down half a loaf of bread and polony and a carton of milk before plunging back into the surf. I was barely eight years old and was already swimming out to the backline, where veteran lifeguards showed me how to bodysurf, read the powerful rip currents swirling by the piers, and dive under monster breaking waves. I loved every minute of it.

Swimming was a key feature of my dad's fitness regime, and most mornings before work he trained at the Westville municipal pool. I was a big kid, and as I was fast in the water he asked if I wanted to tag along. This was my first lesson in sport discipline, as when Dad said he was leaving at 6 a.m., he meant exactly that. If I wasn't at the door when the clock struck, he left without me. I soon learnt punctuality as well as self-control.

At the Westville pool, I trained under Doreen Hill, a former South African swimming record holder who was also a superb coach. Her son Graham was one of South Africa's best swimmers and later also went into coaching, guiding Chad le Clos to become South Africa's most decorated Olympian.

Thanks in part to Doreen's excellent tuition, I became a Nipper at the age of eight, two years younger than the standard starting age. It's a fantastic institution, teaching youngsters surf skills as well as basic first aid, from CPR to treating bluebottle and jellyfish stings, a nasty fact of life when easterly winds blow on Durban beaches.

Nippers also taught me possibly the most valuable lesson of my early life, but it wasn't in the surf. It was about mindset. It happened when I was about to turn thirteen and asked my father to buy me a racing bike for my birthday.

He agreed. 'But only if you win the Iron Nipper,' he said.

The annual Natal (now KwaZulu-Natal) Nipper Championships were coming up, but Dad wasn't interested in that. He was talking about the national event. He said it casually, almost as a throwaway remark, but I knew he was deadly serious. No win, no bike. Despite what most people think, my stern father never pushed me. Instead, he used encouragement, and in this case it was that if I wanted a bike, I had to earn it.

The Iron Nipper is based on the Surf Ironman race but instead of the surfski leg, we used rubber Surfoplanes. It was also obviously shorter, with the swim and Surfoplane legs about 300 metres, depending on surf conditions. I thought I would easily win the provincial championships, but I was in for a nasty shock when I was convincingly beaten into second or third place – I can't remember which. But what I do remember is crossing the finishing line and hearing my father say, 'That racing bike is not looking too good.'

For me, that was a game changer. I was a fast board paddler and an even faster swimmer, but I was still a 'cruisey' type of competitor. I never worried too much about where I came in any race. Even though I usually won, it was no big deal if I didn't.

Suddenly it was. With some degree of shock, it dawned on me that the Iron Nipper was no cakewalk. They didn't use the word 'iron' for nothing. I had previously thought winning was easy because I was bigger than everyone else my age, but I didn't factor in the determination of those kids I was competing against, no matter what their size. I now knew that I had to want that sweet taste of victory even more than they did. Doubly so, with a racing bike at stake.

The South African Nipper Championships were six weeks away and I started training like someone possessed – swimming with Doreen Hill every morning, then going down to the beach after school, running on the sand and swimming in whatever surf was pounding that day. Not only did my skills improve dramatically, so did my fitness. I was starting to realise how important that was to any athlete. As the saying goes, 'The only easy day was yesterday.'

With all the hard training, as well as my newfound determination and mental grit, the race itself was an anti-climax. I won easily. But the spin-offs were fundamental – the most obvious being that with a new bike, I didn't have to rely on people giving me lifts to the swimming pool or beach. I could train when I wanted. As a result, I got even fitter and stronger.

However, I also discovered something far more profound. When I held the Iron Nipper trophy in my hands, it was a defining moment as I understood that I could push my body through more intense pain and fatigue barriers than I ever believed possible. Not only that, I now had the will to do so. I told myself that if anyone beat me, they were lucky, not better. Sure, I have been beaten in my career, but that mindset of supreme self-belief – irrational or not – has never left me. It's seared into my subconscious and has won me more races than anything else when all seemed lost. But when I lose, few will deny that I am among the first to congratulate the winner.

It was also about this time that I started to learn how to paddle, my father's speciality. It happened casually enough, as my father always did his kayak sprint training in Durban's harbour and kept his boats at a nearby garage. One day while driving past the garage he asked, 'Why don't you give this a go?'

The reason I had not started paddling seriously earlier was because I was playing so much other sport, including cricket and provincial water polo, that I never got around to it much. But somehow we both sensed that the time had come for me to continue the Chalupsky legacy. We stopped at the garage and Dad pulled out two kayaks and we walked to the harbour slipway.

I tried to keep up with him, but he was far too fast. Whenever we stopped to rest briefly, he showed me how to get the most power out of a double-bladed kayak paddle; how to stroke long and hard; which were the most efficient arm, wrist and shoulder movements to use; and how to control my breathing and maintain supreme balance. I didn't realise it at the time, but I was getting a masterclass lesson that was a privilege accorded to precious few. But even so, Dad never forced me to train. I went paddling with him, and also Tony Scott, if I chose. Neither man pushed me. As far as they were concerned, that was something I had to do myself.

Within a year I had won all Under-14 sprint events on the national racing calendar. The following year I won all Junior (Under-18) sprint races, often against paddlers three years my senior.

Not only was I learning from two maestros, but I also had the best equipment. As a family, we built our boats ourselves, but sadly my grandfather Franz – a master kayak craftsman – never saw me win in the boats and paddles he perfected. He was always pushing my dad to get me started and even made me a miniature kayak. However, he and my grandmother found South Africa's climate too hot and returned to Germany the year before I started racing.

As a teenager, I had little sense of the political situation plaguing South Africa at the time. All I knew was that we were banned from competing internationally because of the government's apartheid policies, and so we had to race among ourselves. Consequently, I had no idea if I was any good outside the country. I carried on doing the best I could in national races, whereas other athletes my age were going all out against the best in the world. Who knows what would have happened if South Africans had also been exposed to such quality international competition?

However, I do remember our swimming coaches comparing global results, and my Under-10 age group fifty-metre butterfly time was the third or fourth fastest in the world – just behind fellow South African Nicky Gray. So it seems that despite the boycott, we were still right up there.

One thing was for sure: my 'cruisey' days were over. I now wanted things to happen – I expected to win. Even in friendly table tennis or snooker games at the lifesaving club, I played with absolute determination. My sole aim was to beat the person I was up against, no matter what the contest was.

This new resolve was tested to the wire during my first year as a junior in the 1977 National Surf Lifesaving Championships.

I turned fourteen on 1 March that year and the tournament was in April.

That meant I had thirty days to pass the mandatory Surf Proficiency Award, which involved mastering surf and first-aid skills and memorising the contents of a 300-page instruction book. The last of these was far more challenging for me, but I managed.

I arrived in Port Elizabeth four years younger than almost all other junior contestants. But that didn't worry me for long, as I soon won the surfski race and was second in the Malibu board event. Most importantly, I won the Junior Ironman – unheard of for a kid who had just turned fourteen against a field of eighteen-year-olds.

It was the highlight of my young life. But, as I was soon to find out, it was a sideshow for the real confrontation looming ahead the following year: an event that would make sporting history.

LESSONS LEARNT

IT'S POINTLESS WORRYING about stuff you can't control – which in my case was politics. There was nothing I could do about apartheid and sports boycotts. Instead, I concentrated on doing the best I could against whomever I was facing.

INCENTIVES WORK. My father promising me a racing bicycle if I won the Iron Nipper not only forged a positive mindset and strengthened my attitude and determination – it changed my life. My father used encouragement rather than coercion, and today, at the age of fifty-eight (the time of writing this book), I am still doing the sport I love.

DISCIPLINE IS ESSENTIAL if you want to do well, not only at sport but at anything in life. My father never berated me when I was late for a swimming session; he left without me. I was only late once.

DON'T GET PUSHED by others into doing something that you don't want to do. My father resisted his father making me paddle too early, and he was right.

2

Winner takes all

They gave me two minutes to catch my breath. I had just won the Junior Ironman contest in the 1979 Natal Surf Lifesaving Championships. Now the starting gun was about to fire for the seniors.

It was unusual for a fifteen-year-old to compete in both age categories. There was no way someone in their early teens could square up against veteran surf swimmers, board paddlers and surfskiers in one of the most gruelling water events devised. It was physically impossible for a youngster to outswim, outrun and out-paddle fully grown men in peak condition.

Or so I was told. And merely by looking at the current reigning champion Andy Sutherland standing a few yards away, it was easy to see why. Supernaturally fit with a swimmer's powerfully sloped shoulders and a paddler's ripped arms, he was the prototype surf gladiator.

A lifesaving Ironman contest consists of swim, surfski and board legs raced out to the surf backline, around a set of turning buoys, and back ashore. Between each leg is a beach run around two flags, as well as a final sprint to the finish. Apart from being raced at full tilt, it is intensely exciting to watch as the lead can swap multiple times and more often than not is decided in the final few seconds.

As a specialist Ironman, Andy was not necessarily the fastest in any single leg, but his overall combination of strength, supreme stamina and unrelenting pace was almost invincible. Whoever won the swim, Andy whipped on the board paddle. Whoever beat him on the board, Andy thumped on the surfski. And if he was pipped on the surfski, Andy often salvaged victory in the final beach sprint. He never gave up. His quiet, unassuming manner hid a steely will to win and he was tipped to take the crown again that year.

The surfski was easily my strongest Ironman discipline, but I was a good big-surf swimmer and my board-paddling skills were also right up there. The weakest link was my running, but fortunately for me these were short and sharp sprints, so I always found a higher gear when I needed it.

But was that enough to beat Andy?

As a teenager, he was one of my heroes, as were other Durban Surf Life-saving Club legends, such as Lester Kitto, my father Paul Chalupsky, Tony Dumas, Tony Scott and Eric Carlson, who taught me the fundamentals of competing in the roughest surf. The debt I owe such people is unpayable. The only way to try to do so is by continuing to instil the same dreams and determination in future generations that they inspired in me.

The first stroke of luck that day was the thundering surf. I relish such conditions, using the energy of the booming ocean to give me an added edge. The next was the sequence of the three legs. These are decided by a random draw, and on that day it was to be a swim-paddle-surfski race. That's right up my street. If I was still in contention in the final leg, I would annihilate anyone near me. Perhaps even Andy Sutherland.

But maybe that was wishful thinking. Not only was I challenging one of my heroes, also against me was the fact that the Senior Ironman took place directly after the Junior. I emerged from the surf with barely a moment to gulp down a Coke.

The beach was packed with spectators as the starting gun fired. We were off, sprinting at full throttle into the ocean. I knew that in the swim I had to push myself to the absolute limit. If I didn't keep up, I would never regain lost time.

Despite still being tired from the Junior race, I managed to slipstream the leaders and then used every skill I had learnt in the sea to catch a fast-running monster wave and bodysurfed ashore. As a result, I was among the first ten competitors out of the water.

We sprinted up the beach and I grabbed my paddleboard, plunging back into the surf. By now I had a second wind, and again the big sea was my friend and I powered through breakers that were flipping other paddlers. As with the swim, I caught a beautifully curling set back to the beach and Andy, several other top contestants and I grabbed our surfskis at roughly the same time.

I paddled the race of my life, punching through walls of foaming water on the way out and riding a rodeo of white horses on the way in. Out of the corner of my eye I could see Andy about half a boat length behind.

All that was left was the final sprint to the posts. I expected Andy to come thundering past and dug into reserves of granite I never knew I possessed. The finishing poles were a blur as I hurtled past.

It only sunk in that I had won when Andy, one of nature's true gentlemen, came up and congratulated me. He was obviously disappointed but was such a fine competitor and man of integrity that he was genuinely gracious about losing to a teenage upstart. His sportsmanship is something I have remembered all my life and have tried to emulate.

In surf lifesaving circles, this was tantamount to Namibia beating the Springboks in rugby. However, shocked as everyone was, the pundits pointed out that this was only a provincial event. The nationals were a couple of months away.

I would have to do it all again.

*　*　*

The 1979 National Surf Lifesaving champs were held in Port Elizabeth, about 900 kilometres south of Durban. I had flown in the day before, and as I walked onto the beach that morning my heart sank.

I was hoping for big surf and turbulent seas. I wanted fast-rolling sets of combers that I could catch and ride like a dolphin. Breakers that would give me an edge against superior swimmers and quicker board paddlers. Anything to keep me in contention until the surfski leg where I could blow everyone else away. Or at least, that was the theory.

In short, I desperately needed conditions as big and brawny as they had been at the Natal championships. But that was hopeful in the extreme, as unlike Durban, which directly butts into the Indian Ocean, Port Elizabeth is protected from the full wrath of open seas by the half-moon indentation of Algoa Bay. So instead of thundering rollers, the ocean was like a mirror. I could have sent a stone skimming all the way to Australia.

Which was a fitting metaphor, as that's where the Ironman race was invented. The Aussies are among the world's finest lifeguards and specifically designed the contest to incorporate the four main disciplines of surf lifesaving: swimming, board paddling, surfski paddling and running. The exact distances for each leg would vary upon current, winds and wave conditions, but they were roughly about 800 metres for the surfski, 600 metres for the board, 400 metres for the swim, and about 150 metres for each run.

However, for reasons that elude me, in South Africa we got that totally mixed up, instead measuring all water legs at about 800 metres. This resulted in making one of the world's toughest multi-disciplined sprint races even more gruelling, as well as giving specialist swimmers a decided edge. Swimming was the most time-consuming leg, so the longer distance gave freestyle speedsters leads of a minute or more that were extremely difficult to claw back in the far quicker board and surfski time frames.

I was scheduled to compete in at least thirty contests during the two-day Nationals, but they paled into insignificance against the final race – the Senior Ironman. That's all I was thinking about.

Despite that, I had a good day on the water, winning several events including the swimming, single- and double-surfski, and paddleboard trophies. I had also won the Junior Ironman title for the second time in a row the day before.

Then, to my delight, a few hours before the start of the Senior Ironman, the surf began picking up. The wind started gusting and the waves got bigger. Conditions I loved. Maybe, just maybe, I was in with a chance.

Finally, the big moment arrived. I was hardly an unknown, as most had heard of the brash youngster who had won the provincial Junior and Senior Ironman crowns back-to-back in Durban recently. But even so, few thought I would do it again.

The race is a bit of a haze to me after all these years, so I will leave it to a former surf lifesaver and one of South Africa's most prominent businessmen, Gavin Varejes, to tell the story.

'It was an incredibly powerful line-up, including the best surf warriors of the era – Andy Sutherland, Trevor Strydom, Lee McGregor, Jacques Marais, Anthony "Bones" Barrett – all amazing competitors,' recalls Gavin. 'And there was this youngster standing among them, totally unintimidated.

'The first leg was the longboard, and Oscar – who had smoked everyone else in the Junior Ironman the day before – came in third or fourth. I was standing on the beach with some veteran surf competitors and we remarked that wasn't bad for the youngster, as it was quite a big day with waves running at one to two metres. But the general consensus on the beach was that Oscar was going to blow at any minute.

'Next was the swim. Several Springboks, such as Lee McGregor, were tipped to dominate this leg, but to my astonishment Oscar finished in second place behind Andy Sutherland. I remember clear as anything Paul [Chalupsky] jumping up and down at the water's edge, waving his arms wildly and screaming "Go, Oscar, go!" in his strong German accent. In fact, I think they could hear him in Germany. The atmosphere was as electric as a Rugby World Cup.

'However, Andy was about fifteen metres ahead of Oscar at the start of the surfski leg and it seemed he had the race in the bag. But we didn't know, as we couldn't see if Oscar was catching or not as both guys were semi-obscured by the surf.

'Then at the cans [buoys] we had a clear view as they turned and I noticed with some shock that Oscar was just a boat length behind. It was an incredible feat of speed. "Did you see that?" I said to the guys next to me. "The kid is right behind Andy."

'There was silence. I think we all knew we were witnessing something special.

'Then both Andy and Oscar caught the same "backie" [backline wave] and came storming in neck and neck. They jumped out of their boats at almost the same time and most thought Andy had the edge, as we all believed he was the faster runner.

'They sprinted up the beach, the sixteen-year-old and the veteran reigning Ironman. Both were straining every muscle, every fibre, every sinew in their bodies. This was a fight to the finish like I had never seen before, and never since.

'In a blur, Oscar crossed the line a fraction of a fraction of a second in front of Andy. He won that race on the beach, something all of us considered impossible.

'Even now, more than forty years later, I get goosebumps when I think of it. Without doubt, it's the greatest individual sporting experience that I have ever witnessed.'

Once again, Andy was gracious beyond belief in defeat. I don't think he ever realised how much he taught me that day. Throughout my sporting career, I have always made sure that when I lose, the frustration is directed at myself, not at the person who beat me. Andy showed me the way.

As I walked onto the podium to collect the trophy, it was the proudest moment of my young life. Not only was I the first person in lifesaving history to win both National Junior and Senior Ironman races in a single event, at sixteen years old, I was the youngest.

On the strength of that I was picked for the Springbok lifesaving team to tour the West Coast of America.

Technically, the tour was illegal owing to the international sports boycott, but as we were considered to be among the best lifesavers in the world, the Americans desperately wanted to test themselves against us. Consequently, when we arrived in California we were billed as a club team to keep the press off our backs.

At sixteen, I was the youngest Springbok along with Nicky Gray, but I had been chosen as a senior as the junior slots were taken by Nicky and his brother Andrew, both specialist swimmers. Even so, I had an absolute blinder of a tour, topped by winning the surfski race, which was a shock for most people, especially the Americans when told how old I was.

Not only did we beat the Americans, I also learnt a great deal from icons such as Tony Scott and John Woods, the renowned Eastern Cape waterman. They taught me not only how to compete at an international level but also how to train for it.

The tour wasn't all guts and glory though, as I met Michael Newman, the stand-in for David Hasselhoff in the wildly popular *Baywatch* television series. Newman was the behind-the-scenes star of the show, showing Hasselhoff and Pamela Anderson how to act like real lifeguards on the beach.

Then, on returning home, I got some bombshell news. I no longer held the record for the youngest person ever to win both Junior and Senior Ironman titles simultaneously.

Almost 11 000 kilometres away on the beach of Maroochydore in Queensland, Australia, a teenager called Grant Kenny, soon to become a global paddling phenomenon, also won both titles. He was three months younger than me. His feat was extolled on sports bulletins around the world. In stark contrast, my victory had barely merited a mention, even on South African television.

That started a personal obsession. I decided then and there that I wanted to race against Grant Kenny more than anything else. I wanted to challenge him face to face. That was the only way we could once and for all settle the question of who was the best.

What made it even more frustrating was that, thanks to sport sanctions, Grant had no idea who I was.

I had to find him – a fixation that would take me to ocean races around the world.

Nothing would stop me.

LESSONS LEARNT

NEVER BE OVERAWED by the challenges you face. Defeat in your mind will cripple you before you start. I grasped that as a teenager racing against surf legends more experienced and, at that stage, more physically powerful than I was. I later reversed that situation, regularly beating youngsters more than half my age. I did so for many reasons, such as training, right conditions, technique – but above all, it was because I believed I could.

ALSO, NEVER BE SCARED to feed your ambitions – as we shall see later when I eventually met Grant Kenny.

3

Sunny skies and rugby

My first school was Berea West Primary, where most would remember me as the worst-behaved kid in class. I was caned every other day, mainly for practical jokes that teachers did not find funny, such as 'accidentally' pushing the swimming coach into the pool.

I was incapable of turning down a dare, although it was always mischievous rather than mean. Thanks to a firm upbringing by my parents, I clearly knew the line between fun and maliciousness and never damaged school property, for example. My numerous misdemeanours were pranks more than anything else.

That changed the moment I went to senior school at Westville Boys' High. From an arch prankster, overnight I transformed into Mr Goody Two-Shoes, working hard to improve my grades, rarely stepping out of line, and doing everything by the book.

This was most noticeable in my maths results. I was terrible at all subjects in primary school, but maths was the worst. That too, like my new goody-goody image, did a full-circle flip when a young teacher called Miss Hattingh walked into the classroom. As she was drop-dead gorgeous, I decided to excel at figures to impress her. Suddenly I was top of the class, a far cry from barely scraping through at junior school. Thinking back, it seems that even in those days I always had a goal in sight no matter what the reason was. Trying to impress a teacher because she was pretty might not be the most honourable of motives, but it worked for me.

I also shied away from the smokers, truant players and other rebels among my classmates. I considered rebelliousness to be childish, so much so that I think my junior-school teachers would have scratched their heads wondering what had become of me.

However, despite meticulously walking the line, I never received any recognition for that or my sporting achievements. One may argue that accomplishments are not just for kudos, but we are all human. It galled me that even though I was a Springbok surf lifesaver and kayaker as well as a provincial water polo player, I seldom rated a mention at the school assemblies or named in any honours list. That would have been okay if it was applied across the board, but other sporting stars were granted instant hero status by the school's headmaster, particularly if they were rugby players.

There was a popular radio advert at the time that had a catchy jingle: 'We love rugby, braaivleis, sunny skies and Chevrolet', which summed up white South Africa's psyche at the time. *Braaivleis* is the Afrikaans word for barbecue, the country's national 'dish' (if one can call chargrilled meat a dish), and rugby was the national sport, almost a religion, among whites. Westville Boys' High was no exception. The guys in the first team were treated like demigods and also got the pretty girls. A guy who had a smoker's hack at the age of seventeen but could catch and kick an oval-shaped ball was regarded as far superior to someone who was merely a Surf Ironman.

I had to accept that. It was what it was. But the school's management further rubbed my face in it by not making me a prefect in my matric year – despite the fact that many people were openly saying I should have been head boy.

I cannot hide the fact that it was a bitter blow. It was the strangest 'defeat' of my life and was completely out of my control. My mom and dad were as far removed from the pushy modern-day helicopter parents as it was possible to be, believing we had to stand on our own two feet. But even they were surprised that a national athlete and model pupil was treated with such disregard. My dad shrugged. He advised me not to lose sleep over it as there was nothing I could do.

However, there was something I could do. I could prove them wrong. I resolved that I would not only make the school's first rugby team but also get my provincial colours. In other words, I would play the lopsided school sports system at its own game.

I remember that decisive day clearly. I was standing on the touchline mandatorily watching a First XV match with friends Trevor Stapelberg and Andrew Walsh when I announced, seemingly out of the blue, that I was going to play for the team. Trevor and Andrew looked at me, amazed, then burst out laughing. 'Oscar, you're not even in the thirds – how are you going to make the firsts?'

'No problem. Not only that, I'll be chosen for Natal Schools.'

At that time, no one from Westville Boys' High had ever made the provincial schools' team.

'Yeah, right. Dream on. How are you going to do that?' my friends taunted.

I knew exactly how I was going to do it – by applying the same determination that I had in winning the Ironman titles. At 1.95 metres (6'4") and weighing more than ninety kilograms (200 lbs), I was the biggest kid at school, so my obvious position was lock forward and lineout jumper. I started practising right away, using the roof rafters at our house as my target. Every day I jumped a few centimetres higher, until eventually I was able to touch the beams. In those days it was illegal for players to lift their jumpers, so with all that practice I was easily leaping higher than any other school lineout forward. Other teams learnt to throw the ball as far away from me as possible, while we never lost our own lineouts.

Also, most rugby teams only practised twice a week, with a match on Saturday. My training was non-stop. I wasn't just playing rugby, I was swimming, hurling water polo balls, running on the beach or paddling in the surf every day of the week. My fitness was at Olympic levels, and while others collapsed at the end of a training session – let alone a game – I was barely breaking a sweat. To me this was no big deal. It was what I had to do to be a top kayaker or lifesaver, and it spilt over into rugby.

Within a month, I was in the first team. Much as they might have liked to, the selectors couldn't leave me out without facing criticism. Schools were judged by how well they played rugby, and suddenly I was the poster boy for Westville. Being so big and fit meant I dominated matches physically, while the never-say-die mindset I had honed in intensely competitive surf races also gave me a mental edge. It was either that or coming second. As I could sprint for the entire eighty minutes of every game, if I was not scoring tries, I was setting them up.

Westville's war cry now included the chant 'Oscar! Oscar!' and the irony of that was beyond bizarre. The entire school was cheering for someone who couldn't even become a prefect! The headmaster must have been wondering what was going on. Unfortunately, I never got around to asking him.

It was a massive learning curve for me. The main benefit was that it reinforced my ironclad belief in being able to achieve any goal if I was prepared to work at it, but another spin-off was learning the various mentalities of competitive sport. I soon discovered that the mindset of top-level schoolboy rugby was far removed from that of my natural arena of the beaches and rivers. I watched astonished as some of my teammates banged their heads against the changing-room wall to get fired up and be in the right mood for the game. I was very aggressive when racing in the surf – you have to be or else you will be shoved or kicked out of the way – but on the rugby field I played strictly by the rules. Indiscipline loses more games than anything else and I was far more interested in winning matches than winning fights. Some of my teammates would even secretly punch me in a scrum or maul in an attempt to make me lose my temper and let all hell break loose, but I never rose to the bait.

Then came the best part of all. Making my critics eat their words, I was selected for the Natal Schools team. Not only that, I was chosen to take part in Craven Week, the most prestigious youth competition in the country. Named after legendary scrum-half Dr Danie Craven, it brings together emerging rugby talent in a festival that has no equal anywhere else in the world. Most of the country's top players cut their competitive teeth in Craven Week tournaments.

Surprisingly, Dr Craven knew about me as my dad had won the Berg River Canoe Marathon in Cape Town several years previously, something the great rugby guru was aware of.

I was also selected to take part in the 1980 Super C competition, where the country's twelve biggest-name sportsmen competed against each other. In the line-up were icons such as Rob Louw, who was among the best rugby players in the world at the time; John Robbie, a star player for the British Lions during their 1980 tour here, now living in South Africa and currently a Laureus Sport for Good Foundation ambassador; Marcello Fiasconaro, a 400-metre Olympic silver medallist; and national middleweight boxing champion Charlie Weir, known as the Silver Assassin owing to a white patch in his hair. I was the only schoolboy.

The event was avidly followed in the South African media, and suddenly I wasn't only known in water-sport circles. The competition involved a wide variety of disciplines and we had to compete in everything except our own speciality. I had to learn how to play tennis and was coached by Johan Kriek, one of South Africa's greatest players. He was a superb instructor and I grew to love the sport, later teaming up for doubles matches with my accountancy teacher Trevor Hall, who eventually became headmaster of Westville. I also had to learn how to throw a discus and even shoot a bow and arrow.

It was a brilliant experience, huge fun and highly competitive, and I came fifth overall, beating Rob Louw. I think I also beat the hugely entertaining John Robbie, but I can't remember clearly and suspect that he can't either. Overall winner was Damon Rahme, the national decathlon champion.

Today it would be unheard of for a sportsman to compete in so many different events. No Olympic coach would sanction it. In fact, I should not even have been playing rugby, as I risked injuries that would leave me unable to defend my Surf Ironman titles. But on the plus side, I ended up competing outside my comfort zone in contests I otherwise would never have dreamt of doing.

I passed my matric that year, and the time for youthful fun and games was over. Everything had to be put on hold as, like most other white South African males, I was called up to do military service.

But before reporting for duty, I entered the most gruelling race of my life. It was an ocean surfski race called the Texan Challenge – better known as 'the Texan'.

It would be the start of a new era for me.

LESSONS LEARNT

IGNORE NEGATIVE PEOPLE. I managed to prove wrong everyone who said I had no chance of making the first school rugby team. I went further, getting Natal colours and playing in Craven Week. Always set higher goals than you think you should.

BELIEVE IN YOURSELF – especially when no one else does. This is a cliché, but like most clichés it is true. My teachers and even the school headmaster showed little interest in any of my achievements, so I had to make my own way.

NOTHING WORTHWHILE is easy. I would never have succeeded in getting provincial rugby colours in such a short time without working twice as hard as everyone else. Practising lineouts by endlessly jumping at roof rafters was not merely an after-hours training session for me – it was a metaphor for my determination to be head and shoulders above the rest.

WHATEVER YOU DO, give it everything you've got, and the positive benefits will spill over into all aspects of your life. That's what I did with other sports like tennis – even ping-pong and billiards – and it not only sharpened my will to win but also strengthened my humility to lose without rancour. To take that into a broader context, never do anything half-heartedly because you are afraid of losing.

4

The Texan

The 250-kilometre, four-day Port Elizabeth to East London ocean surfski challenge is considered the toughest race in the world.

It's the equivalent of running a fast marathon for four consecutive days, with the obvious exception that if you collapse in the Texan, you're likely to drown. Also, there are no medics or seconds lining the route with refreshments and energy drinks.

As a result, it's raced every second year with stringent qualifying conditions and is only open to registered active lifeguards. That, according to sports doctors, is the sole reason why there have not been any fatalities in the race. Touch wood.

There truly is no other race like it. For several years, it was the only ultra-distance ocean paddling contest in the world. Even comparisons with the far more famous Molokai to Oahu race in Hawaii are apples and pears. If the fifty-three-kilometre Molokai, the world championship of surfskiing, was part of the Texan, it would be the shortest leg.

The idea originated as a bar bet between two legendary competitors, John Woods, one of the original hard men of the surf, and John Ball, the country's finest ultra-distance runner at the time. Woods said a surfski paddler would beat a runner in a race up the coast to East London. Ball disagreed, saying there was only one way to find out. The race was on.

No doubt that bet was sealed over several beers, but both men remembered it sufficiently clearly to be at the starting point on the steps of City Hall in Port Elizabeth at 3 a.m. on 7 January 1972.

Woods, bronzed and brawny from a life on the beach, and Ball, lithe as a mountain goat, headed off on their respective journeys, one by sea, the other by land.

Woods launched his heavy, home-made surfski with a thick wooden paddle into huge seas in pitch blackness. For the first couple of hours, he navigated by ear, keeping the roar of the surf on his port side to make sure he was heading up the coast. No one had paddled this rugged coastline non-stop before, and

Woods didn't have only the crashing ocean to contend with, but also blisters, sunburn, seasickness and an epic swim to avoid being gutted on a reef.

Despite this, three days and eight hours later he landed at East London's Orient Beach – a mere ninety minutes behind Ball. The runner's chief complaint was sunburnt ankles.

It was a superhuman feat by both men, but particularly for Woods, who had the elements as well as extreme fatigue to contend with. And most would have left it at that – a one-off epic achievement, to tell around the bar as stories of derring-do grow bigger and wilder.

But not in South Africa. This was instead an ideal excuse to stage a killer of a race, and the Port Elizabeth to East London (PE2EL) surfski challenge was born. The following year twenty-four lifesavers pitched up at Bluewater Bay, Port Elizabeth, for the inaugural race. Tony Scott was the winner, followed by my father Paul. John Woods, who started it all, came third.

The race soon gained a reputation as the craziest, most off-the-charts endurance contest ever devised, attracting sponsorships from cigarette companies that were big into adventure-sport advertising and car racing in those days. The initial sponsor was Lucky Strike. I competed in a double ski with my father in the 1978 contest. I was fifteen years old, and as a result my father held me back. He said I was too young to be pushed to the brink, and I think a lot of other competitors agreed. Even so, we were second across the line at every stop, just behind seasoned racers Bevan Warlock and Trevor McWade. I kept pestering my dad to go faster, and on the final day he decided to slam the hammer down. We were first in East London, but our overall time was not quick enough for line honours. To this day, my father regrets that we didn't go flat out from day one. If we had done so, we would almost certainly have won.

Perhaps the most enduring memory of the race was that in those days we didn't carry much in the way of liquid replenishments, and there was no such thing as energy bars. At one of the halfway stops, my grandfather met us on the beach and gave us something to drink from a plastic bottle, which was nice of him. Except the liquid in question was wine mixed with water. In the African summer sun, it was the temperature of tea! I have never tasted anything so vile in my life.

Three years later, having just finished school, I was at the starting line again, this time in a single surfski, the Oscar I had designed in 1976. This was roots racing in its purest form as there were no such things as factory-made skis – if you wanted to race surf kayaks, you had to build them yourself or know someone who did. During a competition, you could not get your hands on a spare one for love or money. As a result, there was always a motley array of vessels at the starting line, varying considerably in weight, quality, seaworthiness and aqua-dynamics. As most of us were also river racers, we were used to pencil-thin kayaks built purely for speed, and consequently our boats were as tippy as bucking broncos. This was bad enough on white-water rapids, but in dumping breakers surfskis were almost uncontrollable for many competitors. The fibreglass boats broke easily, and all racers in those days suffered major equipment failures. Also, paddles were feathered at ninety degrees with hefty wooden handles, often resulting in acute tendinitis. Despite that, none of us took such drawbacks seriously – it was part of the game.

The sponsor that year, 1981, was another cigarette brand called Texan, which was even more high-tar than Lucky Strike, if that was possible. South Africans called them 'coffin nails', something we know to be true today. The irony that super-fit, healthy athletes would win trophies from carcinogenic cigarette companies was lost on most people.

As the first shards of sunlight cut across the dawn horizon, I could make out the murky figure of one of my heroes, Tony Scott, standing not far from me. He had won the inaugural race in 1973, and many considered it a forgone conclusion that he would win this one. He was said to be unbeatable, especially by a teenage upstart like me.

I had won the Junior and Senior Ironman national championships in 1979, so I was not an unknown. But even so, no one seriously thought that a youngster barely out of school would have the strength, speed and stamina to take on tough-as-teak Scotty over four days along some of the most rugged coastline in the world.

Scotty was one of the most natural sportsmen I knew. However, he defied almost every stereotype of the modern endurance athlete. He smoked the sponsor's brand like a chimney, drank beers with the best of them, ate cheeseburgers and fries rather than kale and quinoa, trained when he felt like it – and yet still won almost every race he entered. He was also an exceptionally nice guy. I looked up to him more than anyone else outside my immediate family. He and my father had initially coached me when I started training in Durban's harbour. And here I was planning on whipping him, or at least giving him a serious run for his money.

Having said that, I was so much in awe of him that I didn't want to beat him by too much. Maybe a couple of seconds. Or if we crossed the finishing line together in a dead heat, that would be even better.

Both of us were in for a shock. From my side, I discovered that with the amiable Scotty, friendship ended abruptly at the water's edge – which is probably one of the reasons why he was the greatest endurance surfski racer in the world at the time. From the moment we hit the surf, this was a fight to the finish. Scotty no longer regarded me as a family friend or even a fellow Durban Surf Lifesaving Club member. For the next four days he saw me solely as someone who had better get out of his way. It was a salutary lesson in racing. Scotty taught me more in that epic dice than he will ever know.

From Scotty's side, the shock was discovering how tenaciously fast I was in head-banging endurance races. He knew I was a quick paddler in sprint events, but nobody – including me – knew whether I could keep it up day after day over cripplingly long distances. I had never specifically trained for ultra-distances because I didn't have the time with schoolwork and all the other sports I played.

The first day was a nightmare, paddling for a solid eight hours into a howling headwind. After seventy-five kilometres of hell, Scotty was first ashore at the Woody Cape overnight stop, beating me by close on seven minutes. I ran out of liquids, seriously underestimating the time it would take to battle into the teeth of a near gale. In surfski racing, that is not an excuse – it's a calculated risk, as carrying liquids (mainly Coke and water in those days) is unwelcome extra weight. In fact, I think we broke every modern rule in the book, as not only did we skimp on liquids, most of us didn't even wear life jackets. It wasn't as though we were trying to be tough or careless; it was just the way things were and we didn't query it.

However, despite being dehydrated, windblown and sunburnt, I was pleased to come in second to my hero. The fact that I had matched him all the way gave me hope.

On the negative side, I was still a little bewildered at the hostility in the water, and that night on the beach my naive perceptions of the super-competitive world of surfski racing did a complete U-turn. Camaraderie among elite contestants is strictly limited to after the race. On the heaving ocean, no quarter is given. Even less is asked. Unless you believe profoundly in yourself and are prepared to burrow into pain barriers that most people don't even know exist, you have no business being out there.

Day two was a repeat performance, with Scotty arriving first at the Port Alfred overnight stop just ahead of me, increasing his overall lead by a handful of seconds. Once again, despite the blistering pace, I was surprised at how good I felt. Scotty's lead did not worry me.

The third day, a 68.5-kilometre stretch, is considered the most gruelling as everyone by now is dog-tired and there is no end in sight. Also, there's monster surf. A point break at Hamburg can take you all the way ashore – but it can equally easily sweep you onto the reef and reduce your boat to splinters. The safer course is to veer wide of the rocks, unless you want to risk everything for a win. I took the point break.

But even so, Scotty was first ashore, once again by a couple of seconds. As far as the pundits were concerned, the fact that he had won day three meant the race was all over bar the shouting. There was no way I could claw back more than seven minutes on the last and shortest leg. No one could beat Scotty by that margin – especially not a seventeen-year-old wannabe. All he had to do was not sink.

For me, the final day was all or nothing. By now I wanted to beat my former idol so badly I could smell it. All youthful hero worship had vanished in the heat of battle. But could I make up seven minutes?

Sadly, it was a day of controversy with accusations of slipstreaming that rankled for many years. Slipstreaming is exactly what it says on the tin – riding the wake of the paddler marginally in front, harnessing their speed and conserving your own energy. It is not illegal, and it's done in many races, not only with surfskis. Cycling teams in the Tour de France regularly 'draft' their star rider to keep him fresh for the final dash of each stage.

In this case, the singles and doubles front-runners were in a close group, always in sight of each other. Leading the doubles charge was one of Scotty's best friends, Dave McCormack, partnered with Mat Carlisle, followed by my father Paul and Paddy Quinlan. So, in close proximity we had Dave, who wanted Scotty to win, and my father, who obviously was rooting for me.

Scotty then accused my dad of pulling me into his slipstream, which was true, but we had an equally strong case in claiming that Scotty was also being slipstreamed by Dave McCormack. However, both of us were soon dropped by our respective slipstreamers, and it was only after this that I started to claw back the race.

I was the first single to arrive at the Kidd's Beach compulsory halfway stop, and then went for broke, blasting across the final 25.5 kilometres of ocean to East London. But I could not celebrate once ashore as I had to wait agonisingly on the beach for Scotty, wondering if I had done enough to win. I cursed myself for not going faster in the first three days. It was a lightbulb moment for me, as I now knew with cold clarity that I could go even harder and faster than I ever believed. It is something I have never doubted since.

Scotty powered his way through the surf, and we stood next to each other as the timekeepers added up their tallies.

Eventually the announcement came through. I had beaten Scotty by seventy seconds. At seventeen, I was the youngest PE2EL winner, and I hold that record to this day.

Scotty still says he 'let me get away' and that I won because my father slipstreamed me.

Perhaps the final word on this should go to Mat Carlisle, who is one of the best paddlers South Africa has produced. Mat, a superb sportsman, is scrupulously honest in everything he does, and as he was Dave McCormack's partner in that race, I'm happy to take his word for it.

Says Mat, 'My recollection is that on the last day officials started the leaders of the doubles race close to or at the same time as Oscar and Scotty, so we were soon paddling together.

'I then remember the four surfskis bunched up – myself and Dave, Paul and Paddy, Scotty and Oscar – with Oscar on our wave. Then Dave started to move off and out from the wave with Oscar on the outside, and I could see that we were about to drop Oscar.

'As we started an "interval" – a short burst of intense speed – I stopped paddling but everyone else took off. So what happened was that Scotty fell off the wave and Oscar took off with Paul and Paddy.

'Dave and I had words and I told him I wasn't going to get involved in the singles race. Scotty was now on his own behind Oscar, Paddy and Paul – I have no recollection if they were together or who was pulling who – so I agreed to pull Scotty back up to Oscar and then paddle our own race.

'However, Scotty couldn't stay on our wave when we had to speed up to catch Oscar. I can't remember what happened after that, but I think we were close to the halfway stop [Kidd's Beach] and from there on we paddled our own race.'

As with all true sportsmen, despite his disappointment Scotty shook my hand on the beach, and we remained good friends. We still are – so much so that we later teamed up for other double-surfski races, and as a duo we never lost. In fact, in 2021 at the age of seventy-six, Scotty did a Miller's Run from Miller's Point to Fish Hoek with me, and even as a septuagenarian he was a great partner to have in the back of a double. As for slipstreaming, suffice it to say that Scotty never beat me again in a single surfski.

Interestingly, also competing that year was one of Australia's top life-savers, Murray Braund, who came fourth. He said he had never been in such a tough event, and back home he started a similar race called the Pye Challenge from Foster to Sydney, which was slightly longer than the Texan. The Aussies invited us to send over our best guy for the inaugural race in 1982, and the Lifesaving Association chose Scotty. I don't think a teenager beating an icon in the Texan went down well with the old-boy lifesaving network, something I later found to be even more prevalent in kayak-racing circles.

In any event, Scotty won the Pye, and I was happy for him.

The next Texan was scheduled for 1983 and I planned to defend my title. This started a legacy, not only for me but for the entire Chalupsky family.

But in the interim, I had a date with an institution like none other in the world: the South African army.

LESSONS LEARNT

RESPECT PEOPLE BUT don't idolise them so much that it stunts your own progress. Otherwise you will always stay in their shadow.

TAKE EACH DAY of a contest as it comes. Although Scotty beat me on the first three days, I always believed I would catch him. I never allowed myself to lose sight of that. The same applies to life: deal with issues as they are, not as 'what ifs'.

DON'T BEAR GRUDGES – they rot your core. Tony Scott and I fought a bitter four-day battle on the water. There was controversy. There was rancour. But both of us put that behind us, later teaming up to race in double skis together. As a result, we won lots of trophies. That would never have happened if we allowed petty squabbles to dominate. Friendships should and must endure much longer than contests. To top it all, Scotty was master of ceremonies on the day I got married.

5

Marching to a different drum

The first three months in the South African army were referred to as 'Basics', a harsh training model specifically designed to toughen new conscripts physically and mentally and remould them as soldiers.

For most, this involved more hardship and punishment than they had experienced before – lengthy runs in full combat gear, all-night marches, ferociously demanding assault courses, press-ups until collapse, sit-ups until stomach muscles screamed, heavy pole exercises, and anything else the more 'creative' instructors dreamt up.

Mental torment was through systematic sleep deprivation and continuous yelling, swearing and bullying that would be considered abuse by today's gentler standards. This was deliberate, of course, and few dispute that our Basic Training was one of the most demanding initiations into any army anywhere in the world, with the exception of Special Forces.

However, for someone used to extreme sports, this was no big deal. I'm not just talking about myself; any endurance athlete would find Basics tough but certainly not torture. In fact, I had no problem in leading the pack in most races and endurance drills. And as for being yelled and sworn at – try getting in someone's way during an Ironman race!

Instead, the biggest problem for me was that there was no ocean. Potchef-stroom, where I was sent, is 520 kilometres from Durban and I had severe withdrawal symptoms not being able to swim, surf or paddle. I realised then how much I loved the sea.

The army hierarchy was aware I was a national sportsman, but that made no difference to the hard corporals doing their best to make our lives an absolute misery. I was just another *roof*, which is what they called conscripts. It's the Afrikaans word for 'scab', and it crystallised what our instructors thought of us. Until we had passed Basics, we were nobodies.

I was happy with that. I had got no special favours as a sportsman at school, so why should the army be any different?

However, I never finished my Basics, even though I was cruising through the most gruelling of endurance tests. The reason was a freak accident that turned out in my favour.

It happened during an assault course when I jumped over a high wall and landed on a concealed steel-and-concrete pylon. I was in the lead and no one had thought to warn me about it. With a fully loaded backpack, I fell hard, the steel ripping through my kneecap and calf muscle. There was blood everywhere, soaking my trousers like a dishcloth. The instructors rushed me to hospital and it took thirty stitches to seal the gash.

It could not have happened at a worse time. The American Surf Life-saving team was due to arrive in South Africa for a three-test series, and as reigning national Ironman and victor ludorum, I was a key member of the Springbok team. While I personally was furious that I'd injured myself owing to the carelessness of others, I had no idea of the frantic ripple effects the incident caused in military circles. The instructors wet themselves, they were so terrified of the consequences – and with good reason, as the army's top brass went ballistic. South Africa was already banned from almost all international sport, and here in one of the few events actually happening, a prominent competitor was hobbling around with a leg sliced to the bone.

I was immediately given time off to recuperate. There was some doubt that I would heal in time, although not in my mind, as in those days I truly believed I was bulletproof. I was going to be in the team and nothing would stop me.

Sure enough, two weeks later I was at Clifton lining up for the first test against the Americans. Clifton is Cape Town's most famous beach, but because of the freezing Benguela Current welling up from Antarctica, the water is bitterly cold, barely eight degrees on the hottest of days. I hoped that chill would numb my leg.

It didn't. In fact, the stitches ripped open on the first kneeboard event. Doctors sewed up the wound once more, but I tore through the sutures again in the second test. My knee could not take the pressure of direct contact during the board events, but as that is one of the key legs in the Ironman, I had no option but to take the risk.

In the third test I semi-solved the problem by covering the gash with a neoprene sheath, which at least prevented excessive bleeding.

Despite that, I had a fantastic tournament, winning all the Ironman contests and surfski races. But best of all, the Springboks won convincingly and showed that despite isolation, we were still among the best surf lifesavers on the planet. The only other contenders were the Australians, but many believed that we had the edge on them at the time.

The upshot of all this was that the army decided I could do far more for the country as a sportsman than as a soldier, and they didn't want to risk injuring me further. I was moved from Potchefstroom to Pretoria and given a cushy desk job in the personnel services department. Several months later, I was again transferred, this time to Natal Command in Durban and back to the sea. I couldn't have asked for anything better, spending more time training and competing than I did doing army work. After checking in for duty, I would officially be given time off to surf, kayak or play water polo.

Thanks to that, my stint in the army coincided with some of my most successful years in water sports. I was the first person in the history of lifesaving to win both Junior and Senior victor ludorum titles; the youngest kayaker to win Springbok colours; a member of the victorious Junior Springbok water polo team's tour of Israel; and winner of the 1981 South African Junior Sportsman of the Year award.

Winning both Junior and Senior victor ludorums was a particular highlight, as these are presented to the athlete with the most overall wins in a tournament. Although the Surf Ironman race more vividly captures the public's imagination, among elite athletes the victor ludorum is more prestigious.

However, I also prided myself on being part of a squad and would compete in everything I was asked to. In lifesaving, I was always involved in team events such as the squad march pasts, reel and line swims, and rescue and resuscitation exercises. In fact, the only contests I did not enter were the beach runs, flags – a series of twenty-metre beach sprints for flags buried in the sand – and surfboat races. In some competitions, I would be at the beach at 6 a.m. and by lunchtime would have competed in the elimination heats of up to a dozen events. Consequently, I was at peak fitness and felt on top of the world. The guys dominating the surf lifesaving scene such as Tony Scott, Andy Sutherland and Lee McGregor were getting older, while I was getting stronger.

My two years of army service drew to an end – *min dae* (few days), as the conscripts called it – and I mapped out my next plan of action. As a schoolboy, I often scanned the newspapers to see what were the best-paying jobs in the business world, and it was clear that the biggest hitters were accountants. That's what I wanted to be, and I had already prepared for this, completing two university credits through a correspondence course with the University of South Africa (UNISA) while in the army. This gave me a running start for chartered accountancy through a Bachelor of Commerce degree, and I enrolled at the University of Natal in Durban.

As my parents were not wealthy, I applied for and got a sports scholarship – but not, as most would assume, for water polo, kayaking or surf lifesaving. It was for rugby, no doubt on the strength of playing for Natal Schools in a curtain-raiser at the 1980 Barbarians–British Lions test.

I wasn't that interested in pursuing rugby as it was strictly amateur at the time, and in any event, I far preferred water sports to anything else. However, to keep my scholarship intact, I played rugby for the Under-21s, and the coach watched amazed as I regularly pitched up for games with beach sand on my feet and salt in my hair, having, for example, finished a forty-kilometre surfski race an hour earlier.

My life seemed firmly on track. As a sportsman, I was competing and winning at the highest level. Academically, I was on course to become an accountant, not because I loved audits and figures but because that was where the money was.

Then, out of the blue, a chance conversation changed my life for good. An acquaintance in Hawaii, Ron Watson, phoned me about an Ironman contest that was about to take place in the islands. That alone would not have interested me, as we had beaten the Americans in two international tournaments and I didn't see much of a challenge in going all the way to Hawaii to do it again.

But something else grabbed my attention. Ron, who was a member of the prestigious Outrigger Canoe Club on Waikiki Beach, said that this was no run-of-the-mill Ironman contest. Grant Kenny would be there. The same Grant Kenny who had won both Junior and Senior Australian Ironman awards in the same year as me. I'd done it first, but he was the youngest.

I decided to drop everything, save every cent I had, sell every asset I could, and buy a ticket to Hawaii.

At last. I had Grant Kenny in my sights.

LESSON LEARNT

MAKE THE MOST of every situation, no matter how bad it seems. Instead of being two years of drudgery, my stint in the army turned out to be one of the most productive of my sports career.

6

Chasing Grant Kenny

No doubt Grant Kenny would have been mystified to discover that someone almost 11000 kilometres away and whom he had never heard of was chasing him.

He probably would have thought I was a stalker. Which I was, but purely on a competitive basis. We had both won the same surf lifesaving titles, albeit on different continents, and I wanted to see who was best in a head-to-head contest.

Apart from that, our competitive lives could not have been more different. While my only international experience was two surf lifesaving tournaments against the Americans and a little-publicised water polo tour of Israel, Grant was already a global paddling phenomenon, winning medals in both the junior and senior K-2 world championships. Back home he was even more famous, a superstar with eight Australian gold medals. Not only was he a superb athlete, he was also the country's best-known water sportsman, thanks to a lucrative sponsorship deal with Kellogg's Nutri-Grain. As a result, his face was featured on breakfast cereal boxes in almost every Aussie household. Conversely, I barely made our national TV sports bulletins, apart from a few surfski races and the Super C event. However, that's the way it was, and I didn't think much about it.

So our lives were taking vastly diverse trajectories. He was focused on being an Olympic champion, while I was barred from almost all international contests. Instead, I was playing rugby and water polo and doing local kayak and surfski races that had nothing to do with world championships.

But still, somewhere, somehow, our paths had to cross, and I decided the meeting place would be the Ironman contest in Hawaii. It wasn't much of a decision, as global athletes like Grant boycotted competitions in South Africa.

Ron Watson assured us that South Africans would be welcome in Hawaii and, as we were starved of international competition, we decided to get a makeshift team together. It consisted of me, my dad, my brother Herman,

Hugh Ross, and Springbok swimming stars Graham Hill and Julian Taylor. With our manager Des Collopy, we hopped on a plane, crossed twelve time zones, and landed at Honolulu's airport for what I thought would be a date with destiny.

We had barely checked into a motel when I realised I had been duped. Grant was nowhere to be seen. He had never even entered the event and had no intention of doing so. In fact, it was barely an international contest as we were the only non-Americans. Was this a ruse to get the Chalupskys to enter? I don't know, but I don't think I had ever felt so deflated. All this way, all this money – all for nothing.

As a result, the 'big event' was little more than a Natal championship raced on Waikiki Beach. Herman won it, so from a Chalupsky perspective the trip was a success.

I was resigned to going home and binning the failed Kenny showdown as another fiasco, when I discovered from a conversation with a group of local surfski paddlers that Grant was indeed scheduled to come to Hawaii. But only in October. I had arrived nearly six months too early.

'What's happening in October?' I asked.

'The Molokai.' It was said with reverence.

'What's that?'

'Molokai to Oahu. It's Kenny's race, *bra*,' replied one. 'He's won it four times in a row.'

'Can I enter?'

'Yeah, but it's no use. You won't beat Kenny. No one can.'

I asked around and discovered that the Maui Jim Molokai Challenge was the most iconic race among the hardcore global surfski fraternity, even though we had never heard of it in isolated South Africa. Starting at the former leper colony of Molokai, it's paddled across one of the most treacherous stretches of ocean in the Pacific, ending at Oahu fifty-three kilometres away. The bottleneck between the two islands is known locally as the Kaiwi, or 'Channel of Bones', with monster swells surging through a vortex churned by currents, riptides and gales. It's considered the pinnacle of open-water kayak racing. And Grant Kenny reigned supreme. He was not only a legend in his home country but in Hawaii as well.

Even better, according to the locals he would be back that year to make it his fifth consecutive victory.

That put me in a dilemma. I had spent every cent I had on this trip and was also due to resume studies at Natal University in a couple of weeks' time. I could not hang around for up to six months waiting for my elusive counterpart to arrive.

Or could I?

I had some serious thinking to do. The sensible option would be to go home and back to my studies. I am sure if I had done that, I would have ended up as a successful and well-paid accountant. It was how I had meticulously mapped out my life. It was my end goal. It was what I *should* do.

And yet ... something nagged. Here I was many thousands of kilometres away from home, chasing a dream. This was my chance – perhaps my only chance – to make it come true. Should I roll the dice on the ultimate gamble?

There was no halfway option. No half measures. I could either follow my well-mapped, sensible game plan – or I could follow my dream.

I chose the latter.

I put everything on hold and, despite my empty wallet, decided to stay in the islands for the fabled Molokai race. I would have to live like a beach bum, but I would be at the starting line.

To make sense of my decision, I reasoned that I could finish my degree and become an accountant at any stage of my life. It was not time-sensitive, even though it did mean I would lose my rugby scholarship. But my showdown with Kenny could no longer wait. I had spent five long years aching for an opportunity such as this. Now, at last, I finally had Grant in the crosshairs. This might never come my way again. I realised I would never be content if I didn't grab the chance with both hands.

The obstacles were enormous. Firstly, every Molokai racer has to have a personal escort boat to rescue them if they get into difficulties far out at sea. Because of the treacherous waters, these have to be ocean boats, not dinghies with putt-putt engines. Hiring big boats costs big money, something I didn't have.

I also had nowhere to live. Even a bug-infested doss-house was out of my budget. Equally worrying was that my ocean-racing surfski – somewhat essential in a race like the Molokai – was in South Africa and I had no money to fly it out to the islands. On top of that, I needed transport to get to the beach to train; a plane ticket to Molokai for the start of the race; and, of course, I had to eat. My food budget was a dollar a day, which was the price of a taco.

The big picture was too scary to contemplate, so I decided to take each step as it came.

The first issue was accommodation. I put the word out among the kayaking fraternity that there was a guy out from South Africa to race the Molokai and he urgently needed somewhere to stay. I struck luck almost straight away. Bob Twogood, an Olympic-hopeful kayaker, was looking for a training partner and reckoned I could come in handy as I would be doing nothing else but paddling. He offered me the couch in his lounge to sleep on, and he also had a pickup truck, so in one fell swoop my accommodation and transport problems were solved.

Bob was tall with a typical power-paddler's build: skinny legs and slab-muscled shoulders. We got on from the word go as he is incredibly friendly and hides his determination and iron will to win behind a laid-back, island-style *da kine* attitude. For the next six months I spent most of my time training with him and he also took me to club races, where I met local paddlers whom I quizzed about the Molokai. They were unanimous that Kenny was unbeatable, and even when I won all the warm-up races, they said it wasn't good enough. Kenny would have won by even further.

As a top paddler, Bob was also interested in marketing kayaks and his eyes lit up when I told him I built my own surfskis that had won races such as the Texan Challenge. However, as I thought I was only doing an Ironman event, I had brought over a Paul-ski (designed by me and my father), which is good for short sprints but wouldn't suit the Molokai. Somehow I had to find a way to get my own Chalup-ski out from South Africa. I knew Bob would love it, and I started thinking that maybe we could form some sort of business partnership. But first I would have to win the race, as that would be the ultimate marketing tool in the islands.

Bob also introduced me to Marshall Rosa, a Hawaiian who had come second to Grant Kenny for the past four years. Marshall was incredibly strong, with arms that rippled like mating pythons when he powered out into the ocean, but I felt I had a better technique. It no doubt galled him to lose to foreigners and he reckoned this year's race was his to win. He was immensely popular, and the entire island was rooting for him.

Fortunately for me, the chair of the Durban Surf Lifesaving Club, Tony Dumas, raised funds through Gavin Varejes and air-freighted my Chalup-ski to Oahu, so at least I would be racing a decent kayak. A Chalup-ski is fragile and built for speed, and my worst nightmare materialised when it arrived semi-smashed by rough handling on the plane. I frantically spent the next few days patching it up for the race.

Then another disaster struck. I was about to take Bob's truck to the beach, but a Japanese friend had parked me in, blocking the driveway. The keys were in the ignition so all I needed to do was move the car out of the way. However, she is short – barely 1.5 metres – and as the vehicle was a tiny Honda, I had to squeeze sideways into the cramped driver's seat and accidentally moved the automatic gear stick into neutral. The car immediately started sliding backwards and the lever jammed as I tried to shift it into drive. I was unable to get my legs under the dashboard to pump the brakes and crashed into the neighbour's wall, seriously denting the Honda.

Obviously I would have to pay for damages, which was a problem as I was flat broke. Bob, who had already advanced money for the escort boat and my race-entry fee, now had to increase the loan. A lot was riding on this race.

Despite the setbacks, we were training like crazy and I was in great shape. No doubt my training programme was fuelled by the increasing number of possibly exaggerated horror stories being told about the Channel of Bones separating the two islands. These ranged from swirling currents, crippling jellyfish stings, massive sharks, flying fish rocketing out the ocean and knocking paddlers off their skis, extreme heat, mountainous waves and gale-force winds. Yet the more I heard about the race, the more excited I became. Just as I had never heard of the Molokai before, these guys had never heard of the Texan Challenge, which possibly has even more embellished war stories. However, as the prevailing winds in Hawaii blow from the east, the Molokai is raced mostly downwind, unlike the Texan where howling headwinds are common. It seemed that bad conditions for the locals – gales and swells – were good conditions for me.

Locals also spoke in awe of the fabled China Walls, a rocky headland near the finish that more often than not has gnarly surf creating a barrier of foam impenetrable to small craft. More paddlers bomb there than anywhere else. I didn't know much about it as I hadn't been over the course, so I just had to hope for the best. Ideally, I would have flown across the Kaiwi Channel to study wave direction, reef locations, surf breaks and currents, but even without an expensive car crash to pay off, that was way out of my budget. I would have to play it by feel on the day.

Forty-eight hours before the starting gun fired, I arrived at the pre-race registration and briefing with the forty other contestants. I couldn't register as a South African so would be racing under the banner of the Kanaka Ikaika Canoe Club.

Then, to my intense dismay, I noticed that Grant Kenny wasn't there. My heart sank. Had I missed him again?

I frantically cornered one of the organisers who assured me Grant was indeed racing, but as a multiple-times winner he did not bother to attend briefings. He was instead relaxing in his luxury room at the five-star Moana Hotel while his helpers handled registration protocol. That was a far cry from sleeping on an old couch in Bob's small suburban house.

But even if Grant wasn't at the briefing, his presence dominated the room. There were Kenny posters everywhere, while big screens played back-to-back films of him in action, extolling the fact that he paddled at sixty-two strokes a minute – more than one a second. This was considered a phenomenal feat.

As dawn broke the next day, we boarded a small aircraft for the twenty-minute flight to Molokai, probably Hawaii's least touristy island, with no traffic lights and only six thousand inhabitants. The view from the plane was my first glimpse of the channel and I liked what I saw. The wind was gusting to more than thirty knots and the swells were peaking at six metres. It would, as predicted, be a fast downhill race for most of the way with the swell surging powerfully towards Oahu. After the disappointment of the Ironman 'non-event', the car crash, the damaged surfski and constantly being told that Kenny was Superman, I felt this was the first real break I'd had.

As the paddlers lined up for the start, I set eyes on Grant Kenny for the first time. A fellow paddler pointed him out, but he needn't have. Bronzed, blond, ripped with muscle and sporting film-star looks, he was instantly recognisable as the Aussie poster boy. He was a breakfast-cereal advertiser's dream. The only surprise was that he was about thirteen centimetres shorter than me.

I walked over to him and said hello. The moment had arrived. We finally met. He nodded and smiled, still having no clue who I was. I silently vowed that by the time we reached Oahu, every Australian on the island would know my name.

I noticed he was paddling a Spec-ski, a superlight craft used for fast round-the-buoy racing, while I was paddling my slightly heavier and longer Chalup-ski. It would be an interesting duel over this heaving expanse of ocean.

The starting gun fired and I stayed by Grant's side, shadowing him. The waves were too big to see where Oahu was, let alone which course to take, but one thing I was certain of was that four-times winner Grant would know the fastest way. We paddled neck and neck, our surfskis almost touching as I watched his every stroke, how he moved his shoulders and hips, how his boat glided in the water. Marshall Rosa was also with us, so I knew if I stayed with them, I would remain among the front-runners.

The three of us carried on with this cat-and-mouse game, shadowing each other for about an hour. By now I had worked out which course Grant was taking, what the currents were doing, how fast the swells were running, and how to exploit every scrap of energy from the fizzing ocean. The soaring waves throbbed with power, and I could feel my Chalup-ski champing at the bit like a pedigree racehorse as we surfed the crests on high-speed runs. But the big seas were not for everyone, and even in those early stages, paddlers were regularly being swept off their surfskis.

Then, as the jagged outline of Oahu emerged in the distance, I had to make a decision. I could stay with the leaders and then sprint to the finish in a do-or-die dice, or go off early on my own and drop them by accelerating the pace. I was probably the fittest I'd been in my life, so I slammed the hammer down hard, catching several mountainous swells in succession to surge ahead. It was a risk as I was now reading the ocean purely by instinct, whereas Grant and Marshall were seasoned Molokai veterans.

Oahu loomed large with big surf pounding against Portlock Point, a treacherous reef at the outer edge of the infamous China Walls. As I rounded the Point, I turned into the wind, and the shock after paddling downhill for three and a half hours was visceral. From long, incredibly fast runs, I was suddenly headbutting into thirty-knot squalls that punched like a prize fighter. Waves ricocheted off the Walls in bursts of spray, but even so, they were not as awesome as some of the breakers I'd raced in back home.

I finally broke through China Walls' so-called 'ring of foam' and headed for Hawaii Kai. Those final few kilometres were absolute hell, equivalent to the crippling Heartbreak Hill in the Boston Marathon. Eventually I crossed the yellow buoys marking the finish line, watched by a bemused crowd wondering who the hell I was. To further sweeten the victory, as I walked up the beach the organisers announced that I had smashed Grant Kenny's record by fourteen minutes and fifty-six seconds.

But where was Grant? Where were the other much-vaunted Australians? Where was local hero Marshall Rosa? These were the questions being asked on the beach.

The answer came several minutes later when a few furiously paddling figures were spotted rounding China Walls. Grant crossed the finishing buoys in second place, twelve minutes behind me and three minutes ahead of Greg Bennett, an Australian rugby league player nicknamed 'Tank' for obvious reasons. Marshall unfortunately took a wrong line in a squall near the end and finished in a disappointing seventh place. I really liked him and hoped he would have done better.

Grant was gracious and congratulated me, although he said he had not taken the race seriously as he was training for the 1984 Olympics in Los Angeles. Even so, he had beaten his own record set the year before by three minutes, so he had still been going fast. He and I became friends and I always visit him if I can when I go to Australia. Strangely, neither of us has ever mentioned to each other that we are the only two people in the world to have been crowned Junior and Senior Surf Ironman champions on the same day. I also never told him that I had been waiting for this day for five years. But that was all over the newspapers, so he obviously knew.

Physically and emotionally, I had achieved what I set out to do. But practically, that victory was even more important as it got me out of a serious financial jam. Although there was no prize money, the fact that I had shattered the course record meant that my winning Chalup-ski was in big demand. I ended up selling it to a local paddler for a good price, paying off my car-crash debt and Bob's loans. Bob also did well out of the win as he secured the Chalup-ski franchise and started his own company, Twogood Kayaks, manufacturing my surfskis in Hawaii. Unfortunately, he missed selection for the US Olympic paddling team by a split second, so he never made the Los Angeles Games.

However, sometimes it seems that even a convincing win isn't convincing enough. In various paddling circles, the story circulated that something must have happened to Grant out in the ocean and I had fluked my way across the line.

I shrugged, saying no problem, let's do it all again, and I returned the following year to win once more, beating second-placing Marshall Rosa by nine minutes. Grant Kenny didn't race, but this time there was no more talk of 'flukes'.

After beating Grant, an obsession that had stalked me for half a decade was at last exorcised. It had well and truly been put to bed. But what would I do next? Should I go back to university, even though I had now lost my rugby scholarship? Or should I get a job to finance my passion for kayak racing, something that provided adrenaline-fizzed contests and an endless summer lifestyle that I loved?

I chose the latter, reasoning once again that I could always return to university and finish my degree, but I would not be able to race forever. Ageing muscle tone and gravity are the enemies of all sportspeople, and I vowed to defy them for as long as possible.

LESSONS LEARNT

DON'T ALLOW YOURSELF to be intimidated. The locals seemed to delight in saying that Grant Kenny was much better than me, no matter how fast I was paddling. I only had myself to believe in. That belief never wavered.

WEIGH ALL OPTIONS, then go for the one that suits your dreams. Looking back over several decades, my decision to roll the dice and stay in Hawaii for the Molokai was the best one for me at the time, rather than the safer choice of pursuing a desk job as an accountant.

In fact, it was one of the best decisions I have ever made.

BE GRACIOUS IN VICTORY. Grant Kenny and I are still friends. Need I say more?

7

Meeting Clare

I was in Hawaii when I got the shock of my life. My father phoned to say that my mother Mercia had been diagnosed with breast cancer. She had, at best, a few months to live.

Although she'd had a mastectomy as well as chemotherapy and radiation a couple of years earlier, the cancer had returned and was spreading so aggressively that the doctors were unable to do anything further.

After my return, she went down fast. Thanks to magnificent care from the Highway Hospice, she spent her last weeks in her own bed surrounded by her family and friends. As she had managed to get up to celebrate my youngest brother Walter's birthday with a glass of champagne the week before, we were hoping she would make it to her forty-eighth birthday on 30 November. She died the day before.

The funeral was at St Elizabeth's Anglican Church in Westville. Every pew overflowed with mourners, and people stood in the side and back aisles. Mom not only had a large and loyal hairdressing clientele, but all our sports friends also adored her. In fact, our car was known among lifesavers and paddlers as the 'chuck wagon' as she always had heaps of delicious food ready for everyone. She was the most loving and generous person I have known, which I think was a throwback to her days in a Cape Town care home as a lonely young girl.

The void in our family was immeasurable. My mother was such a stalwart that we took her gentle, unassuming presence for granted. She drove us to the start of races and training sessions, picked us up many miles away afterwards, and made sure that we had packed lunches and refreshments, no matter where we were. Every birthday she baked my favourite cake, a real sugar-bomb concoction of Marie biscuits with thick layers of mint and chocolate. She was always doing something special for us, and it could not have been easy for her in a household of four sports-obsessed males. Chalupsky men, as my wife Clare will attest, are not very domesticated. After Mom's tragic passing at far too young an age, my wonderful sister Alma stepped into the breach and without any fuss took over the many household chores. She was only sixteen, and the debt we Chalupsky men owe her is incalculable.

In February 1984, not long after the funeral, I met Clare Ellis Brown. I noticed her the moment I set eyes on her – dark-haired, slim and lovely. But I'll let her tell the story …

'My sister Tessa and I went to the Beach Baths to watch her boyfriend Douglas Dowell, son of the legendary Barbara Dowell, playing in a water polo match. Barbara was one of Oscar's swimming coaches, and as the Durban Surf Lifesaving clubhouse was nearby, we decided to go for a drink afterwards.

'Oscar was there, and someone told me his mother had recently died. He came up and started chatting, then handed me his business card – as if I was the one to phone for a date!

'The next time we met was at a pyjama party, but some woman in a negligee took all of Oscar's attention. Finally, we went on our first date, which was lunch at a restaurant called the Press Club.

'At first I had no idea who he was. In fact, I knew nothing about water sports, and when Oscar mentioned Surf Ironman races, bodyboarding or surfskiing, I hadn't a clue what he was talking about. The only sports I knew a little about were cricket and rugby.

'But he was so different from other men I knew. Enthusiastic, fun-loving, exuberant and always so cheerful – he was a real breath of fresh air.

'Then I started going to kayak and surfski races with him, not realising that meant I would have to be the driver. This resulted in not only a lot of driving – and I mean a lot – but also hours and hours of waiting. Many of the races started in the morning and only ended in the afternoon. I was either waving goodbye at the beginning or waving frantically at the end to show him where I was. The Texan Challenge was even worse, as that was four days of long waits on windy beaches staring at an empty ocean. I suppose I was lucky in that he was almost always the first paddler to finish. Imagine the girlfriends of the guys who came last!

'But there was also plenty of fun. We did some mixed-doubles paddling events together and he is an excellent coach. I always knew if my timing was slightly off.

'The end result is that we got married on 9 July 1988, at the Holy Trinity Catholic Church in Durban's Musgrave Road. It was the same church where Oscar had been christened, which we thought was a nice touch. We have been together ever since.'

When Clare and I first met, she was working for a finance company and I was a car salesman. As mentioned, I had ditched my university education to earn money and compete on the paddling and lifesaving circuits. Professional sport was still some way off into the future, but I sensed that I could hopefully one day make a living doing what I loved. However, until that happened, I needed a day job to pay for it. The opportunity came from a fellow Durban Surf Lifesaving Club member, Joe Emmanuel, who owned a car dealership called Key Delta. It was my first lesson on how crucial a network is, whether personal or professional.

Not only was selling cars my first proper job, but it also came with a steep learning curve. Joe was a great guy and excellent businessman, as was his son Paul, but at the lower levels I discovered I was mixing with people whose sole objective seemed to be to do as little as they could for as much pay as possible. This was a complete eye-opener – I didn't know such unmotivated people even existed. In the circles I moved in, everyone gave everything their best shot.

In retrospect, I have been a businessman for as long as I have been a sportsman, starting out at fourteen when I began designing and selling surfskis from the garage of our Westville home. Some I made with my father, some on my own. I didn't earn a lot of money as there was a limit to how many surfskis I could turn out, but it gave me a solid grounding in basic economics. I knew exactly how much resin and fibreglass to order; how many boats needed to be sold to break even; how much to charge; and that if I put my name on something, it had to be good. It instilled a deep-rooted entrepreneurial streak in me, and throughout my life I have preferred to be paid purely on performance.

The best thing to happen at Key Delta was that Paul Emmanuel recommended I buy a set of motivational tapes by sales guru Tom Hopkins called *How to Master the Art of Selling Anything*. They weren't cheap for someone on a novice salesman's commission, but I splashed out and it was the best investment I've made. I still consult them to this day. Basically, Hopkins's message is that nobody is born a salesman and success only comes from mastering the basics. Grandiose visions on their own are a waste of time; one has to painstakingly perfect skills from the ground up. Hopkins is talking about selling, but his lessons relate to every aspect of life, including – or perhaps especially – when aiming to be a sports champion. If you don't put in the training, you won't get the results. I have listened to those tapes more than a hundred times, and so has my family as I played the cassettes whenever we drove to kayak races or lifesaving events. So while other kids in cars had pop music on the radio, my children Luke and Hannah were listening, involuntarily or not, to Tom Hopkins.

My stint as a car salesman was short-lived. Like many South Africans, I was made redundant when the economy tanked in the mid-1980s after global companies disinvested in protest against apartheid. Chevrolet was one of them, with devastating effects for their South African dealerships. As Key Delta's policy was 'last in, first out', I was the first to be laid off.

Without a job, my desire to become a professional sportsman became even more intense. I wanted to make a living out of doing what I loved best, but in those days there were few professional opportunities, and even token prize money didn't exist. The best I could hope for was sponsorship in the form of a free car or travel expenses. But even at that young age, I found ways to make the most of the situation. I told companies backing me that I would pay my own way to races such as the Molokai, but that if I won, they should reimburse my costs. Fortunately, I usually won. My three prime backers were Gotcha, the beach-fashion label founded by Michael Tomson; surfer-businessman Paul Naude, who started South Africa's first surfing cult magazine *Zigzag* and is now CEO of the global clothing brand Vissla; and Yashica cameras. The Yashica sponsorship was thanks to fellow Durban surf lifesaver and businessman Gavin Varejes, who has helped more athletes than anyone I know.

However, sponsorships on their own weren't enough to live on, so I started looking for work again. My next job was as events coordinator for Sun International, southern Africa's largest hotel and casino group, then owned by Sol Kerzner. Sol, nicknamed the Sun King, was as famous for marrying former Miss World Anneline Kriel as he was for being a global business mogul.

The deal with Sun International was part salary, part sponsorship, and although the money was not great, the lifestyle certainly was. One of my biggest successes was founding the Wild Coast Sun Classic. It's unique – if there is any other kayak race incorporating a dice up a tidal estuary, a beach sprint along the famously rugged Wild Coast, a portage through an iconic golf course and finishing on a lagoon, I have yet to hear of it.

However, the core aspect of my job was promoting the Sun International brand through mass media visibility. To do this I merely carried on with what I was already doing, racing extensively, training hard and spending plenty of time keeping fit on the beach. The only difference was that this time I did so wearing a prominent Sun International logo. I didn't answer directly to any bosses, so I lived in shorts, a T-shirt and flip-flops. It was close to an idyllic endless-summer lifestyle.

Sun International was a glamorous brand to be associated with, but equally classy was another of my sponsors, a Mercedes-Benz dealership called Merc-A-Rama owned by John Barnes and Paul Larche. Seeing a perpetually broke, sartorially challenged athlete driving around in a millionaire's car of choice certainly caused some hilarity among my beach-bum friends. I think I started a trend of athletes getting car sponsorships.

That year, against all expectations, I won a high-profile event called the Denim Man. It was a type of adventure challenge where competitors had to ride off-road motorbikes, clamber over obstacle courses, zipline over lakes and even paddle out in a canoe to rescue a damsel in distress. It might sound gimmicky, but there was a big cash prize as well as a car and an all-expenses-paid holiday in Mauritius.

I was suddenly flush with money. Unfortunately, there was a pyramid scheme on the go called the Vegetable Lady, and as the owner of the company was the girlfriend of a local lifeguard, many of my friends at Durban Surf invested. The initial dividend payout was spectacular, attracting a bunch of new 'get-rich-quick' investors that included me. I even sold the Denim Man car I had won to plough into the venture. Then, in typical Ponzi fashion, the company went belly up. I lost everything.

I couldn't recoup the money in South Africa, but as it was obvious that professional sport was taking off big time in the rest of the world, I needed to look elsewhere. A prime example of this was Australia, where the breakfast-cereal giant Kellogg's was sponsoring an Ironman series with the equivalent of half-a-million-rand prize money up for grabs. The circuit consisted of eight contests culminating in the Coolangatta Gold, a forty-two-kilometre race that originated from a popular movie featuring my Molokai rival Grant Kenny. This was exactly what I was looking for, so I cashed in every remaining cent not swallowed up by the Ponzi scheme and headed off to the land down under.

This time the superstar was not Grant Kenny, although he would be competing in the series. Instead, it was Guy Leech, a twenty-year-old long-distance Ironman specialist who had stunned the surf lifesaving world with consecutive wins of the Coolangatta Gold. However, Grant was still right up there in the rankings and now had added an Olympic medal to his impressive résumé. He had won a 1000-metre K-2 bronze in the 1984 Los Angeles Games.

It was uphill from the word go – even before the contests began. I had to enter as a German as the Australians refused to allow South Africans to compete, but they also refused to recognise my Surf Proficiency Award (SPA) (now called a Surf Lifeguard Award). This was a major irritant as South African lifeguards were among the best in the world.

Consequently, as I stepped off the plane in Sydney, I had to pass a gruelling lifesaving test in the surf to get my Bronze Medallion – the Australian equivalent of an SPA – then do three hours' active lifeguard duty. This was the day before the first Ironman race on Wanda Beach, so with no time to rest and still suffering from jet lag after a thirty-hour flight, I was not at my best.

I expected to do well in the remaining races, but the series was a humbling experience for me. I was used to the short but intense Ironman races in surf lifesaving, but the Kellogg's Nutri-Grain series was a completely new format with contests lasting up to two hours. I was not prepared for this, and even worse, as far as I was concerned, beach running was now as important as surf events. Some courses had runs of up to six kilometres, contested at close-on sprint speeds. At twenty-two years old, I was carrying more muscle than ever before and weighed about 100 kilograms, the size of a large rugby forward. The end result was that while I blew everyone away in the water, I was far too bulky to be competitive on the beach.

For the next eight weeks there was a race every weekend, and it was always the same story with me way ahead of the pack in the paddle section, only to lose it on the beach runs. I still usually ended up in the top five, but I wasn't making much money.

The Coolangatta Gold (briefly called the Manly Gold, as it was held in Sydney the year I competed) was especially disappointing. I took a public bet with Guy Leech that I would beat him in the twenty-three-kilometre surfski leg, which I did convincingly. However, Guy – who was at least fourteen kilograms lighter than me – hammered me on the 7.1-kilometre run on particularly soft beach sand.

But despite the frustrating results, those were brilliant days: the banter of superbly fit athletes living the dream, the intense rivalry of world-class competitions, and the incredible fun of celebrating with friends after giving it your all in the ocean. I lived like a beach bum, scrounging food, hitching lifts from one contest to the next, and sleeping where I could. In fact, I was lucky to have a roof over my head for most of the time, as Marvie Sheehan, a Durban lifeguard who had been born in Australia, persuaded an uncle to let me use his Sydney house as a base. It was a real adventure. I wouldn't have missed it for anything.

More importantly, it got me focusing seriously on my future. The top Aussies I was competing against were all earning five-figure sums or more. Grant Kenny was already a millionaire, later owning an airline with his then wife, Olympic swimmer Lisa Curry, while Guy Leech was making a killing on the Ironman circuit. In contrast, I had a cabinet full of trophies and little else.

I also had to accept my limitations as a runner. My size was fine for top-level paddling, but I was too big and heavy to be a beach sprinter. Unfortunately for me, running was now an essential feature of long-course Ironman contests, and there was nothing I could do about it. However, I wasn't too worried about that as I was a waterman at heart. I simply needed to pick my contests more carefully.

To do so, I had to concentrate on my strength, which was indisputably paddling. Perhaps I was best known as a surfskier after winning the Texan and the Molokai, but I was also a Springbok kayaker. If I wanted to make a living as an athlete, paddling – in both oceans and rivers – could be the answer. Kayaking was a global sport, unlike Surf Ironman events.

Maybe that was an avenue to explore?

LESSONS LEARNT

WHEN MY MOTHER died, I learnt that acceptance is an essential part of grief. This was reinforced thirty-five years later when I was diagnosed with multiple myeloma. Life carries on. There is no use in brooding – you have to move forward. It also makes the burden infinitely easier.

IF YOUR JOB is purely a pay cheque and nothing else, you need to reassess your life. That is what selling cars taught me more than anything else. If possible, work in something you love.

DREAMS DON'T HAVE to be materially successful. I didn't make much money on the Aussie Ironman circuit, but the experiences and memories I have are priceless. It also helped me to focus on my strengths rather than lamenting my weaknesses. That made more of my dreams come true.

8

Running the rivers

One of Spain's most celebrated festivals is the San Fermín 'Running of the Bulls' in Pamplona. It lasts a week, and the highlight for most is watching hundreds of adrenaline junkies sprinting madly in front of charging *toros* to see who gets to the bullring first.

Obviously the fighting bulls don't see it that way and instead attempt to gore anyone in their path. At least sixteen people have died in these famous runs. However, more than a million tourists flock to the Pamplona festival each year to watch bullfighting, eat tapas, drink gallons of *rioja* and party like tomorrow never comes.

But equally famous among Spaniards is the 'running of the rivers', a hard-core kayaking festival in Asturias, the far north-western tip of the country. They don't call it the running of the rivers, but they should because the week-long festivities are as wild and colourful as anything that happens in Pamplona, and some of the races are as close to a blood sport as one can get.

The main race of the fiesta, the twenty-one-kilometre Sella Descent along the Río Sella traces its origins back to 1929. It's now the biggest kayak race in Europe, if not the world, attracting paddlers from across the globe and thousands of tourists. It starts in the town of Arriondas and close on a million people line the riverbank, letting off firecrackers, cheering, dancing and singing, while a train packed to capacity with revellers chugs down the tracks following the race leaders. The atmosphere is electric, fuelled with cider brewed from local apple orchards and imbibed at industrial levels, while Spanish guitars and flamenco music blare around the clock. It's truly an Iberian fiesta at its finest.

The race ends at Ribadesella on the Costa Verde Atlantic coast, and the party that has been in full swing all morning now ratchets up a gear, if that is possible. Every bar, bistro and brasserie is jam-packed with people dancing, singing and having the time of their lives.

So here I was in August 1981, standing on the banks of the Río Sella with Mat Carlisle, waiting for the starter's cannon to fire in my first international river race. This was the same Mat who had been unfairly dragged into the slipstreaming controversy when I had beaten Tony Scott in the Texan Challenge earlier that year. We were a great combination – both fast paddlers – but as I was only nineteen, Mat had the decided edge on experience. In fact, he had won the Sella Descent in 1978 with another top white-water kayaker, Jerome Truran, competing as a British team to sidestep sport sanctions. This time we were racing under the auspices of a Belgian club, but we were still part of an unofficial Springbok squad – and how I got to Spain is a story in itself.

The trials for the European tour that included Spain, the UK and Ireland had been held a few weeks previously on the Berg River in the Western Cape, and it was no secret that the largely parochial selectors favoured Cape paddlers. I was the youngest there, and most of the other paddlers considered me brash, to put it politely. The fact that to be a top competitor requires supreme self-confidence is a given, but if you showed that in those days, you were considered arrogant. More than anyone else, Muhammad Ali did sport a favour by revealing the true mindset of a global athlete, highlighting the self-evident truth that false modesty is hypocritical.

There were eight positions in the Springbok touring team and I was the third or fourth fastest, so I should have been a shoo-in. But that didn't stop the selectors from making me race every trial, hoping I would eventually bomb out. They were doing everything they could not to select me, and people I had beaten in previous races were being chosen while I was still battling for a position. I was so angry that I just went faster, throwing all the negativity back at them.

In the final trial, I was placed on one side of the river and Lance Park, also from Natal, on the other. I was easily the fastest, but I was so sick of the Cape paddlers blatantly 'pulling' their mates that I decided to help Lance. I cut everyone off to get to his side of the river and pull him along in my wake. Unfortunately, he couldn't keep up and finished third, not making the team. Lance, sadly, is no longer with us today.

What made it even more bizarre was that my father, one of the few selectors not from the Western Cape, couldn't intervene in the obvious bias, as it would be called favouritism. So having my dad there – a hugely respected paddler – actually worked against me. He never took sides, believing I had to fend for myself.

It got so acrimonious on the water that one of the older paddling 'legends' threw a punch at me. I ducked, then retorted, 'Hey, don't take it out on me because you're not fast enough!' That made him even more furious.

However, I was not interested in just beating my South African competition; I wanted the scalps of genuine global superstars. That was the key difference between me and some of the other paddlers. They wanted a Springbok blazer for a bucket-list tick, while I wanted to test myself against the world's best. For me, the Springbok trials were purely a means to an end.

Mat thought the same way, and as he and I knew each other well and were from the same province, we teamed up in the doubles and beat the favourites, Cape Town's Sunley Uys and Andre Collins. Our win was so convincing that the selectors eventually had no option but to select me or risk widespread criticism.

Our first race was the famed Sella Descent, a predominantly doubles race that has deep family connections for me. My dad, paddling with Kevin Culverwell, won the Sella in 1969, the last official South African team to do so in the apartheid era. His name is engraved on the Río Sella Bridge, as is every other winner. I wanted mine there as well.

What makes the Sella so exciting is that it is a Le Mans-style start, with paddlers running for their boats lined up on the riverbank. There is a haphazard draw, sometimes weighted in favour of Spanish racers, but if your boat is not near the front, you have a mammoth task clearing out the paddlers ahead. Like the Pamplona running of the bulls, chaos does not begin to describe the frenetic scene. For most racers, barging, shoving, clanking heads – even punching – is the only way to extricate oneself from the surging mob. As I said, this is a borderline blood sport and not for the faint-hearted.

But it certainly provides plenty of thrills and spills for spectators. The anarchy is also an integral part of the race's folklore, and I don't think any contestant would want it any other way. I was bigger than most other competitors and if anyone grabbed our boat to hold us back, I whacked them with my paddle. The Spanish press loved it, reporting extensively on the red-haired teenager with a combative will to win.

Mat and I were drawn in fifty-fourth position, which was far from ideal, and we had a horrible start. Despite smashing our way down to the bank, once in the water we were unable to turn in the fibreglass logjam, ending up on the far side of the river.

But we soon got our rhythm and started threading our way up the field fast. After about forty minutes, we had the lead boat, paddled by Olympic medallists Herminio Menéndez Rodríguez and Luis Ramos Misioné, in our sights. We were quicker than the two Spaniards on the straights, but they knew the narrow stretches of the river intimately and whenever we tried to pass, they forced us onto the bank. As the water was so shallow, we couldn't get around them.

We were almost touching one another as we neared the finishing line and the spectators were going crazy. At the final rapid we were right on their wake, and I thought the race was in the bag as we were obviously the faster boat. I loved the energy from the hugely excited crowd and briefly waved back at them as we swept past. But as fate would have it, that was the exact instant Mat decided to charge for the lead. That split-second lapse of concentration on my part took the edge off our acceleration, and then a small island split the river in half. The Spaniards went one side, and we the other. We finished half a second behind them. So, so close.

Andre Collins and Sunley Uys, the top Springbok team in the minds of the selectors, finished a few boats behind us. As this was the key race of the fiesta, Mat and I were bitterly disappointed not to have won. Thanks to me, it seems we snatched defeat from the jaws of victory. However, there were races every day of the festival after that, and Mat and I won almost all of them, getting some satisfaction in beating the Spanish Olympians. However, instead of celebrating this, it caused some tension with our team members who seemed to resent our victories. In one race, Mat got a cut above his eye from a flashing paddle that was possibly accidental as we passed a fellow South African boat. There was also some friction stemming from the fact that we were from Natal, whereas most of the others were from the Western Cape. This was a pity as we were all South Africans, and the tension definitely detracted from an overall team effort.

We then went to Scotland to race the Loch Tay, which was a singles race, and South Africans took the top three positions. Then we were off to Ireland for the thirty-two-kilometre Liffey Descent from Straffan in County Kildare to Islandbridge in Dublin.

Another member of the Springbok team, seemingly tired of us winning all the time, decided to split us up and announced that he and Mat would race the Liffey together. This was incredible from a national team's perspective, as in top-level sport no one deliberately breaks up a winning combination. But as he was a senior member of the squad (and also outranked Mat and me in the army), we had no one to complain to. Fortunately, he and Mat won to give us a clean sweep of trophies apart from the Sella. But if I had been allowed to race with Mat, I possibly would have been the youngest paddler ever to win the Liffey.

Despite everything, the tour was a pivotal milestone for me as I gained invaluable experience, not only from paddling with the superb Mat Carlisle but also from the white-hot cauldron of international kayaking. No one survives the Sella's Le Mans start without getting a healthy reality check on what global racing is like.

However, there was no denying that the fact we hadn't won the race bugged me. Intensely so.

It was unfinished business and I knew I would be back.

LESSONS LEARNT

POSITIVE AGGRESSION can be good. The chaotic Le Mans start is an integral part of the iconic Sella Descent. Without positive aggression, you will not win. This is true in many aspects of life, and the stress is primarily on the word 'positive' rather than 'aggression'. Always be forceful if there are no other options.

DON'T WORRY WHAT other people think. I still blame myself for spending too much time fretting over selectors who made it clear they didn't approve of me. They made it even clearer that they didn't want me in the team. There is nothing you can do to make the staid old guard suddenly like you. Also, the reality is that it is extremely difficult to get rid of 'legends' – in my case, established kayakers not necessarily still in their prime. You instead have to show that you are indispensable. Mat and I did this with such convincing wins over the selectors' favourites that they had no option but to include us.

The same thing happened in water polo where selectors hated picking youngsters over veterans who were past their sell-by date. All I could do was score more goals. In other words, never give in – if you do, the old guard will win once again.

DON'T COUNT your chickens. This is an old chestnut, but that doesn't make it less true. I was waving at the excited crowd at the end of the Sella Descent thinking we would overtake the leaders at any moment. Both Mat and I know that cost us the race.

9

Blood brothers duel

In 1983, I returned to defend my Texan Challenge title. I never for a moment thought it would be as intense or controversial as the win over Scotty two years previously, as that was a race in a million.

But what did I know?

I did, however, know it was going to be a milestone for the Chalupskys as almost the entire family was racing. It was also, sadly, the last Texan that my mom watched. Fifteen-year-old Alma was in a double surfski with my dad and made history as the first (and youngest) woman to enter, while my sixteen-year-old brother Walter teamed up with another Durban Surf Lifesaving member, John Whittle. Herman was racing with Paddy Quinlan, who had partnered my father in the previous Texan Challenge.

The race turned out to be one of the most gruelling for me, but not because of any fierce competition on the water. Instead, it was with officialdom.

On the first sixty-seven-kilometre section from Port Elizabeth's Bluewater Bay to Woody Cape, I broke the course record by thirty minutes and was twenty-five minutes ahead of the second paddler, Mark Lewin. But rather than celebrate the new record, race officials decided I had cheated.

It happened like this. On the Woody Cape leg, all paddlers have to keep inside a clearly visible boat moored 800 metres offshore to stop them from going too far out to sea and taking a short cut. However, once my time was announced, another racer claimed I had gone outside the boat, which he said was the reason for my record-smashing run. This was total rubbish as, although far in the lead, I had clearly seen the official marker boat moored at the buoy and deliberately paddled inside of it, well within the legal route. I was convinced they had also seen me. The officials, however, didn't believe that and penalised me thirty minutes. As a result, I was now downgraded to third position, a couple of minutes behind Mark Lewin and another Natal paddler, Shaun Rice.

I have never been so angry. No one had seen me go outside the buoy – because I hadn't – but race officials still took the side of hearsay against fact. They didn't want to believe anyone could paddle that fast, I guess.

At the start of day two, I got into my boat without speaking to anyone. I decided to throw the race officials' penalty back in their faces and win every section of the next three days by at least thirty minutes. Normally I keep just ahead of the pack if I can, gauging distance and increasing speed to win, but this time would be different. I didn't only want to win: I wanted to smash the rest of the field and shame the officials for their baseless decision. In short, I wanted to prove my point beyond any doubt.

That's exactly what I did each day, except for the third leg from Port Alfred to Hamburg that was cancelled as surf conditions were considered too horrific.

On the fourth day I arrived at East London nearly an hour ahead of second-placed Shaun Rice. In fact, I was only eight minutes behind the winning doubles team of Tony Scott and Dave McCormack.

But even so, I nearly made a serious mistake that day. As the early morning was cool and overcast, I set off without a water bottle. The sun soon burned off the cloud and it was a scorcher. I arrived at the finishing line dehydrated, and when medics weighed me, I had lost four kilograms.

That was one of my hardest races, but the pain was self-inflicted. I was racing against myself to prove a point. Few people afterwards disputed that the official decision to penalise me was ludicrous.

However, I was now the acknowledged Texan Challenge champion. I had beaten old-guard legends such as Scotty, and even the younger paddlers like Shaun Rice were two or more years older than me. There was no one else on the horizon.

Or so I thought. In fact, there was – and it was as close to home as one could get. My brother Herman. He had come third in the Texan doubles race and now had a serious taste for this unique, physically crushing event. He had me in his sights and smelt blood. But the next Texan Challenge was only in two years' time, so he had a long wait ahead.

In the interim, I won the National Surf Lifesaving Ironman and victor ludorum contests again, and on the strength of that, as well as winning the Texan, I was voted the 1984 South African Junior Sports Star of the Year. It was against a quality line-up featuring opposition such as Daryll Cullinan, who later became one of the country's greatest cricketers, and Evette de Klerk, who would become a double-medallist in the 1993 African Championships in Athletics after the sports boycott was lifted.

Then, one day while doing lifeguard duty on the beach, I noticed that the Natal Bodyboarding Championships were about to take place. I love bodyboarding, although I do it purely for fun, as it's a great way to catch and read waves at grass-roots level. In those days I always had a board – often called a boogie board – in my car to play around with when not training. So I entered, not thinking it would take me anywhere.

It certainly did, and somewhere I never expected. I surfed my heart out, unrestricted by any expectations but still determined to do well. As a result, I was selected for the four-man provincial team to contest the national championships in East London.

I drove down to Nahoon Beach, a famous reef break where the nationals were to be held, and my first stop was John Pollock's surf shop. John had a pile of bodyboarding videos and I binge-watched them, taking note of the more radical manoeuvres and spectacular acrobatics. I then rushed off to the beach and practised hard, stunning everyone – myself included – by winning the championships later that week. First prize was a trip to Hawaii to compete in the world championships, but it unfortunately coincided with a Springbok lifesaving test series. However, I had fallen in love with the islands after winning the Molokai and decided to fly to Hawaii instead.

That did not go down well with the lifesaving selectors, but I went anyway. World surfing champion and fellow South African Shaun Tomson was in Hawaii at the time, and he became my handler, driving me to various beaches, and we generally had a great time riding waves together. We surfed Waimea, which only breaks at twenty feet, as well as Pipeline, which has among the most dangerous waves in the world as heavy walls of water explode on a shallow volcanic reef. If you wipe out, you have to belly flop to avoid being mangled on the coral. It was monster surf, and suffice it to say that riding those thundering breakers on your belly results in your manhood literally rattling in the water.

Bodyboarding entails catching rides using fast-accelerating flippers. On one occasion at a break called Rabbit Island, a couple of surfers catching the same wave dropped in on me. This was blatant bad manners and I took offence, resulting in some argy-bargy in the water. Fortunately, Shaun was nearby, and as he has huge status in Hawaii, he managed to calm everything down before it escalated into a beach brawl. Localism is rife in the islands, and it's not a good idea to tangle with the Hawaiians.

The championships were held at Haleiwa Beach, which is more sheltered than most North Shore surf spots. The surf was small that day, which seriously hampered me, and I was up against professional bodyboarders. In the end, I came twelfth overall. The fun far outweighed my performance on the day, however.

Then, in 1985, it was back to the Texan Challenge. This time it was going to be a real blood-brothers' duel. And if people thought the contest with Scotty was exciting, the dice with Herman would rival even that for drama.

The race started the day after New Year in hellish conditions – a howling, head-on easterly wind and dumping surf that could, and did, snap surfskis like matchsticks. Usually it takes the leaders six hours to cross Algoa Bay, and Herman and I were neck and neck all the way. But in that blasting headwind, it took us eight hours to reach the Woody Cape beach. When we posed for photographers on the shore, we were almost holding each other up through sheer exhaustion. Close on fifty paddlers, all experienced lifeguards, pulled out of the race on that torturous first day.

To our utmost relief, the wind swung west that night. We would be paddling downwind to Port Alfred. But disaster soon struck for me, as I had barely passed the surf backline when my paddle broke. I swam my boat ashore to get another. But I couldn't pick up any paddle, as although I am right-handed, I kayak with a left-handed blade. Very few other paddlers do this, and in this race there were only four – Herman, my father, Tony Scott and another Springbok, Robbie Stewart. If I couldn't get a replacement from one of them, for me the race was over.

I could count Herman out for obvious reasons, but fortunately my father, who was paddling in the doubles section, hadn't set off yet. He hurriedly handed me his paddle and I was back in the water. However, Herman had gained ten minutes, which had me seriously worried. Ten minutes might not sound like a lot over 250 kilometres of raging water, but with someone of Herman's calibre it could be unbeatable. Still, I managed to claw back some of the clock and reached Port Alfred four minutes behind.

The westerly was still blasting on the morning of the third leg to Hamburg, the toughest and longest section of the race, and I decided to go for broke. I used the fast-running conditions as expertly as I could and was first ashore at the Great Fish River halfway checkpoint.

By now I had almost eliminated Herman's overall lead and was surging down the powerful swells making good time when a guy on a ski boat following the race said the wind was even stronger out to sea. I headed further offshore, only coming closer in at about five kilometres from the finishing line. Suddenly I noticed someone ahead of me. I was stunned. Was it another paddler who had set off early?

I then got an even bigger shock. It was Herman! I couldn't believe my eyes. I thought I had dropped him at the checkpoint, and there he was ahead of me.

Displaying masterful tactics, Herman had not followed me out but stayed close inshore, making skilful use of the tidal currents and outthinking me. The reason I hadn't seen him pass was due to the big waves, and at that moment I realised how stupid I was to have blindly followed the well-meaning advice from the ski-boat skipper. Adrenaline surging and arms scything like a windmill, I came in as fast as a white-water sprinter. This was potentially dangerous as there is a reef adjacent to the shore that most paddlers are correctly advised to steer well clear of. It has rogue waves appearing from nowhere and can chew boats up without spitting them out. But it is the shortest and quickest route home and, just as I had done two years ago against Scotty, I willingly took the risk. Catching a surging roller, I skirted over the jagged rocks with centimetres to spare and hit the beach mere seconds ahead of Herman. However, he was still the overall leader.

The blood-brothers' duel was the main topic of conversation around campfires that night, but I think that superb, superhuman effort by Herman using the inshore currents took more of a toll on him than he would admit. His face was a grimace of pain as we stumbled up the dunes, and for Herman, the most taciturn of the Chalupskys, to show emotion was almost unheard of.

On the final day I powered ahead, breaking the singles' course record with an overall time of twenty hours and fifty-eight minutes, seven minutes ahead of Herman. There is no doubt that two brothers pushing each other to the absolute extremity resulted in such a fast time – particularly as the first day was paddled into a gale-force headwind. Scotty and McCormack also broke the doubles record with an outstanding time of twenty hours and thirteen minutes.

Over the years, I won a total of ten Port Elizabeth to East London surf marathons. But none were as gripping as the duels with Scotty and Herman – or as frustrating as my fight with officialdom in 1983.

It also marked the start of an intense but friendly lifelong rivalry with my brother. That, as much as anything else, shaped me into the competitive sportsman that I still am, all these years later. I can thank him for that.

LESSONS LEARNT

DON'T BE DISCOURAGED by obstacles in your way. Not all people see your successes as achievements – they see them as their own failures.

ALWAYS FIGHT BACK. The only way to show the Texan Challenge race officials the error of their ways when I was penalised was to go even faster.

BE PREPARED, NO matter how short the notice. I did my 'cram' homework for the national bodyboarding championships by binge-watching videos and practising manoeuvres. However, to be realistic, it was a stretch too far to think I would repeat that against global professional bodyboarders – but it was great fun trying.

10

Back to Spain

Six months after our classic duel in the Texan, Herman and I teamed up to race the 1985 Sella Descent, a race that was still unfinished business for me.

This was not unusual. Herman and I would often metaphorically fight to the death in one contest, then join forces to race another as best of friends.

The Springbok selectors now had some new blood in their ranks, and I didn't come up against the same hurdles I had faced in getting selected for the 1981 tour. This time Herman and I easily made the team, although of course none of us would be officially competing for our country of birth. However, that year the Sella was once again destined to remain unfinished business as we landed in Madrid, hired a car and drove to Asturias only to be told that the race had been held the previous weekend. So much for the efficiency of our organisers.

I was bitterly disappointed as I believed Herman and I had stood an excellent chance of winning. This was confirmed by the fact that we won all the other races in the festival week, beating the Sella winners in each event. But it seemed the Sella Descent itself would be as elusive for me as chasing Grant Kenny several years previously.

It was also blatantly obvious to both Herman and me that if we wanted to race internationally, we would have to do so under a different flag. South Africa was barred from all sports, but we were still able to exploit certain loopholes. In our case, it was through our German-born father. I already had a West German passport as I needed it to race on the Australian Ironman circuit, so I decided I would try out for the paddling squad training for the 1988 Olympics in Seoul. Ultimately, I wanted to be a professional sportsman, and if German nationality was the only way to go, so be it.

I could already speak passable German thanks to my father and grandfather, so I picked the language up quickly when I arrived in Munich, flat broke but ready to do what it took to make the Olympic team. One of the German coaches, Karl Kaiser, had been to South Africa and heard of me, and through him I got rudimentary accommodation at a sports clubhouse.

By rudimentary, I mean exactly that – a mattress and tatty sleeping bag on the floor. It was so basic that I started having fond memories of Bob Twogood's sofa in Hawaii. My budget was a Deutschmark a day (this was before the euro), which meant I could eat oats and not much else, while the rest of the triallists were on high-energy diets and carbo-loading. Fortunately, I got odd jobs painting the sports clubhouse and Munich's Olympic stadium hall, as well as fixing bunkers at a golf course, which brought in some spare cash. The German paddlers were not friendly by any stretch of the imagination, and I was never invited to anyone's house, or even for an evening drink. In fact, they barely spoke to me. I suppose it may have been because they regarded me as an outsider, but there is no way the South Africans I knew would have treated a fellow triallist like that.

The competition was brutal, as flat-water sprinting is not my strongest discipline and the Germans are among the best in the world. Still, I made the finals of the 1 000-metre, but not the cut-off, and was third in the 10 000-metre race. The 10 000-metre is not an Olympic event, which meant I would possibly be included in the World Marathon Championship squad to compete in England, but I would miss my ultimate goal of racing in the Olympics.

After I had spent two months living like a hobo on a sports clubhouse floor in Munich, Herman arrived in Europe for the Sella Descent. He had won the Berg River Canoe Marathon a few weeks earlier, following in the footsteps of my father, who had won it exactly twenty years before in 1966. It's South Africa's longest river race, 240 kilometres of some wild stretches of river, so he was exceptionally fit. So was I, training with peak-condition Olympian hopefuls, and we would take some beating in the Asturias fiesta races. We weren't part of a Springbok team this time, instead competing under the colours of Munich MTV, a popular sports centre in the city and one of the venues for the 1972 West German Olympics. It was also within walking distance of Dachau, a sombre reminder of the country's tragic history.

From Munich, we drove to Spain with our uncle Franz, who would be our chauffeur as well as second us during races. Franz was a kayaking purist who loved the art of paddling and had been at the Sella when my father won in 1969, so it was great to have him in our team. He was also a fast driver, which proved invaluable, as we later discovered.

The Sella start was again a frenzied, no-holds-barred Le Mans bunfight on the riverbank. As mentioned, no one was seeded in those days and we had a terrible draw, way down the line. As a result, it took us about four kilometres of elbowing and barging down the river to blast our way through the pack and into the lead, which we held comfortably for the rest of the race. We won by about 250 metres and, at last, another two Chalupsky names were engraved in the Roll of Honour list on the Río Sella Bridge.

As we had done the year before, we won every other race in the fiesta. In fact, on one day we won a double-header, one in the morning and the other in the afternoon. The two events were about 150 kilometres apart, and Uncle Franz sped us quicker than a Grand Prix driver in his powerful Mercedes to the morning contest in Villaviciosa, then to the afternoon race on the Pisuerga River on the eastern Asturias border. Even so, we nearly didn't make it as a tunnel through the mountains was closed for repairs. I pulled out a newspaper with a prominent story about *los hermanos Chalupsky* (the Chalupsky brothers) and the construction workers were so impressed that they specially opened the road for us. My name is now engraved six times on the Pisuerga River bridge.

One of the biggest upshots of that week was that my fellow German Olympic triallists suddenly realised I was not some foreigner trying to muscle into 'their' team, but a well-known athlete on the international racing circuit. They'd barely acknowledged me in Munich, so they were mystified to see the Spanish crowds almost mobbing me and Herman after our multiple wins. They certainly looked at me in a new light after that, and some even became our friends.

Equally revealing to them was how much fun river marathons were. They were so hung up on grinding flat-water contests that they didn't know any better. To them, races like the Molokai or Texan Challenge were alien concepts, and it also made me realise how little I liked the dour monotony of flat-water sprinting. Big ocean swells and white-water rapids were my true home.

The next year, Herman and I decided to return to Spain and make it two Sella victories in a row. Once again we would have to pay our own way, and as Clare and I had just got married, I had to broach the subject 'creatively'. We had honeymooned in the Natal Midlands, so I hit on what I considered to be a brainwave.

'Why don't we go to Spain for a real honeymoon?' I asked.

Clare saw through that straight away when she noticed that it dovetailed exactly with the Sella Descent. My claim that this was merely a coincidence didn't hold much water.

'It was no surprise as I know Oscar never goes anywhere where there isn't a race,' she said later. 'But at least Spain is a lot more fun than a windy beach in Port Elizabeth.'

However, I was – with good reason – a little reticent in sharing too much advance information with Clare about our second honeymoon. While she knew Herman would be travelling with us, she didn't for one second think he would be sharing our hotel room in Madrid. To say she was surprised would be understating the case. But that was nothing compared to her shock when we arrived in Asturias to find that the 'honeymoon suite' was not some romantic penthouse in a five-star hotel but a hostel crammed with other Sella racers.

However, nobody doesn't enjoy the Asturias kayaking festival, and Clare was no exception. In fact, she seems to remember the size of the local gin and tonics more than the actual races. As anyone who has been to the country will attest, Spanish G&Ts have a tiny dash of tonic splashed into a large glass of gin. One sip is enough to dance the flamenco, voluntarily or not.

Herman and I had an even worse draw than the year before, compounded by the fact that we were up against a crack Australian team, Ramon Andersson and John Jacoby. Andersson was destined to become a bronze medallist at the 1992 Barcelona Olympics, while Jacoby is a four-times World Kayaking Marathon champion. Unlike us, they had a great draw, starting right at the front of the pack, and although we got close, we never caught them. We finished a disappointing third.

But once again, we cleaned up on the rest of the fiesta races, beating the Aussies in the process. Our only loss was during one no-holds-barred dice when we were banned after ramming another boat. It happened during the Villaviciosa race, when a Spanish team deliberately tipped us over as we were about to take the lead. At the end of the race, we saw them getting out of their boat and Herman, who was driving, aimed straight for them. As the engine-room paddler, I approved of what he was going to do and pulled as hard as I could. We T-boned them, smashing straight through their kayak. The partisan crowd on the bank were as mad as snakes, throwing stones at us, shaking fists and challenging us to come onto the riverbank for a fight.

The officials were not happy either, imposing a fine and ordering us to pay for the badly damaged kayak's repair. A photo of us ramming it appeared in the Spanish press, and once tempers had cooled, everyone had a good laugh. Kayaking is no sport for crybabies.

Later that year I finally got picked for the West German squad to race the first World Marathon Championship in Nottingham, England. However, my delight was short-lived. As I was boarding the plane, I was called off and told that British canoeing officials had refused to accept that I was a German national. My South African connections were too well known and I would not be allowed to race anywhere in the UK. The West German Canoe Federation had no option but to drop me from the squad. I was now blacklisted whether I raced for South Africa or Germany.

I had no idea what I was going to do next.

LESSONS LEARNT

DON'T WALLOW IN DISAPPOINTMENT. Mat and I didn't win the Sella on my first attempt. So I came back and won it with Herman.

NEVER LOSE FOCUS. Living like a hobo in Munich was hard. But I was there for a reason – to make the Olympic team. I didn't achieve that goal for the 1988 Games, but as we shall see, I did four years later.

NEVER EVER SWEAT the small stuff. Herman and I missed the 1985 Sella through bungling bureaucracy. Instead of throwing our toys out of the cot, we won every other race on the festival circuit instead.

11

The wilderness years

The shock announcement from the West German Canoe Federation was the start of my wilderness years. I was in the prime of my life, yet every door had now slammed in my face.

Except one. The Molokai. The Hawaiians, always an independent, free-spirited bunch, refused to shut me out. They accepted my German passport, and that was that. To a certain extent, I think this was due to loyalty, as I had done everything in my power to promote the event since my first race in 1983. It was now regarded as the pinnacle of surfski marathon racing, and wherever I went, I sang its praises.

This wasn't just PR hype, as I wasn't lying when I said the Molokai is one of the best contests of its kind in the world. The organisation is superb, the venue idyllic, and the race itself spans a beautiful yet hazardous stretch of the Pacific seething with currents and big waves. Best of all, it attracts the most tenacious of the arcane hardcore-marathon paddling community. In other words, my kind of people. Without even being aware of what I was doing, I became an unofficial ambassador.

In fact, for the 1985 race I even brought a journalist along with me. Graham Spence was a Durban-based freelancer, who usually reported on hard news but was also a water-sport enthusiast having grown up on the beaches of Mozambique. We were on a shoestring budget, and Graham was downgraded to the floor in Bob Twogood's lounge while I had the marginally more comfortable sofa.

He soon had plenty to write about. A week before the race I rescued two near-drowned paddlers who had been swept off their surfskis at Makapu'u Point near Diamond Head, Oahu's iconic volcanic cone. They were struggling against the riptide, so I got them to hold on to my surfski and paddled them ashore. Graham was on the beach, got the story on the spot and wired it home. He says he believes it was the first time in South African press history that the exact same story, written by the same guy 12 000-kilometres away, was simultaneously the front-page lead on the weekend editions of

Natal's two major newspapers. It was even splashed on both rivals' bill-boards.

However, we didn't have that much luck with a Hawaiian newspaper reporter who didn't believe I was German. He wasn't convinced about Graham either, who had a British passport as his parents were expats, but had as strong a 'Sarf Effrican' twang as me. Unfortunately, the reporter asked him a couple of questions as well, which Graham foolishly tried to answer in a cut-glass Brit accent. He sounded like a strangled turkey, and if the reporter had lingering doubts beforehand, they were now well and truly confirmed. The story was negative, calling me a sanctions-buster, but thankfully no one seemed to take any notice.

We arrived in Molokai on the night before the race, but we only had enough money to book a single room at the beachfront hotel. Fortunately it was on the ground floor, so as soon as I checked in I opened the window and Graham, Bob Twogood and a couple of other hangers-on climbed in. I commandeered the bed, Bob the only chair, and the others sprawled on the floor watching basketball on TV all night. I think I was the only one who slept.

Unfortunately, Grant Kenny wasn't at the starting line, but a much-hyped Aussie invasion arrived led by Chris Bond, an Olympic hopeful who had beaten Grant in a recent marathon. He was touted as the new 'ironman', but I had heard those stories before and instead regarded Marshall Rosa as the main challenger.

I was right. Despite a mid-ocean scare from my seconds in the *Maggie Joe* fishing boat claiming that Chris was taking a 'better downwind line', I led from start to finish, beating second-placing Marshall by several kilo-metres. Chris Bond came seventh and showed true grit by making no excuses. He told Graham he had gone too fast too soon and simply 'punctured'. Plain and simple.

The next day we were at the Outrigger Canoe Club when Tom Selleck, star of the megahit TV series *Magnum, P.I.*, walked in. No one paid any attention as the Outrigger prides itself on being the most exclusive and private club on the islands. Well, no one except Graham and me, who watched wide-eyed. Our hosts cautioned us not to hassle the actor, but I thought, to hell with it, this publicity for the Molokai was too good to pass up. As each *Magnum* episode started with a clip of Selleck paddling a surfski, I gathered he knew something about the sport. I walked up and introduced myself.

Selleck beamed that famous moustachioed grin and shook my hand. 'Say, you really blew 'em away yesterday,' he said. 'I was listening on the radio.'

We chatted for a few minutes and he mentioned he suffered from tendinitis aggravated by paddling, as well as a wrenched back from playing beach volleyball. I grabbed a paddle from another Outrigger member and gave 'Magnum' some pointers on how to grip the paddle in a way that would ease both injuries.

Fortuitously, I had the Molokai trophy with me and asked Selleck if Graham could take a picture of the two of us. He readily agreed – as long as no advertising was involved. This was a problem as my baggies, T-shirt and baseball cap were festooned with fluorescent Gotcha gear logos, so I had to strip off and borrow clothes. The photoshoot was cut short as Selleck was barefoot and the beach sand was hot, so Graham hit his camera's motor drive. Once again, we made the front page of many South African newspapers, which I think alone paid for Graham's air ticket. It didn't matter, though. Graham later told me that the bareboned trip was the most fun of any journalistic assignment he'd been on – and he's been on plenty of luxury expense-account junkets.

My sixth successive win in 1988 was a game changer. For the first time, the Molokai had prize money. The sponsorship came from Hawaiian property tycoon Tom Gentry, who holds the Blue Riband record for the fastest transatlantic powerboat crossing, previously held by British billionaire Richard Branson. Gentry, who died in a powerboating accident in 1998, loved water sports and put up $2 000 prize money, which at least paid my way for that year.

But the game changer was not the prize money. It was instead the vastly increased publicity. With Tom Gentry on board – albeit only for that year – the race featured far more prominently in newspapers and got prime TV airtime. As I won it, the spotlight fell squarely on me.

I didn't know it then, but I was soon to be a victim of my success. The next year the race got even more hype as Olympian Greg Barton entered with the expressed intention of ending my winning streak. This was no idle threat: Greg was a double-gold Olympic medallist and had also won the International Canoe Federation (ICF) Sprint World Championships three times by then (and would go on to win a fourth). So he was fast. In fact, he was an even bigger A-lister than Grant Kenny had been seven years previously.

To show how serious he was, Greg had a custom-designed, superlight boat built specifically for the race that took surfski innovation to new heights. While wary of Greg, I was convinced I had the edge as his impressive array of medals and world titles were predominantly for shorter distances. The Molokai is a marathon, and a treacherous open water one at that.

I decided to do my usual race – go as hard and fast for as long as I could, using my downwind experience to maximum advantage and sticking closely to the most direct route, the rhumb line. It paid off, and again I led from start to finish, beating Greg by more than fifteen minutes.

That was big news in the sporting media, but maybe too big. As with the Gentry sponsorship, a lot of attention focused on my South African roots, pointing out the irony that I had beaten a multiple-Olympic medallist but couldn't race in the Olympics myself. There was the usual knee-jerk outrage from some sections of the international media, and the Molokai organisers once more came under huge pressure to ban me. This time, with threats of sanctions from the ICF, the Hawaiians had little option but to yield and I was barred from the 1990 Molokai. Coincidentally or not, that year the race was won by Grant Kenny. The following year it was won by my previous nemesis on the Australian Ironman circuit, Guy Leech, whom I invariably beat in the water but who thrashed me on the beach runs.

So with the last international race now closed off, my international career seemed well and truly over. I was twenty-seven years old.

There was not much I could do except race locally. It was a huge blow, but we have great races on the South African circuit. The most fun for big river paddlers like me is the Umkomaas Marathon in southern KwaZulu-Natal, which is one of the wildest white-water contests anywhere in the world. The first six rapids are all Grade 4 if the water is high, which it usually is, so the dropout rate is larger than any other river race. I loved it, winning three times, once with my old friend Mat Carlisle and twice with Greyling Viljoen, a paddling pastor who later swapped the cloth for a psychologist's couch.

I also won the Fish River Marathon in 1985, which I raced 'blind', never having paddled the river before. It was a blistering contest, and on the first day the lead swapped several times between me, fellow Springbok Chris Greeff and Graham Monteith. I won by a single second. On the second day, Chris and I were neck and neck for the first half, then I dropped him, winning by eleven seconds. It was a victory that gave me intense personal pleasure, as without knowing the course I had to rely solely on innate river skills. As that year the Fish River Marathon was also the national title race, I was crowned South African K-1 champion.

The two other big races are the Dusi Canoe Marathon and the Berg River Canoe Marathon. The three-day Dusi is probably the country's best-known river race, as it was founded by world-renowned conservationist Ian Player. However, it is basically a biathlon as there are many gruelling portages, some several kilometres long. Consequently, the fast runners have a distinct advantage in low-water conditions. As mentioned, I am no runner, so the Dusi was not for me and my best result was third, paddling in a double with Mike Tocknell. However, one year the river was in flood, and Les Keay and I shot every thundering rapid in sight on the final day of the race. We held the record for the fastest time over that leg, arguably the most gruelling, for a decade.

The Berg River Marathon – the country's longest race, spread over four days – also eluded me. On three occasions, I won the first day but got lost on the second as it's a difficult course through a maze of channels. It's easy to take a wrong turn, so detailed local knowledge, which I didn't have, is vital. In fact, if a local paddler wins the first day – the fastest and most open stretch – they almost have to sink not to win the next three. My top position was second overall, so sadly my name is not up there on the honours board with my father and brother.

I was in peak physical condition, as apart from racing rivers, I was playing top-level water polo and competing in surf lifesaving championships, regularly retaining my Ironman title. But it all seemed to be of no avail, as I knew that with sanctions against South Africa I could never follow my dream of being a professional sportsman.

There was one sport that South Africans could compete in: golf. As it was professional, it was an individual contest, and players such as Ernie Els and the maestro Gary Player were legends on the world circuit. My handicap was twenty-four, which meant I was at best a weekend hacker and had a lot of work to do. I had to get it down to scratch as soon as possible, so I set myself a seemingly impossible target. I would have a zero handicap within a year.

To give my goal some spice, I walked into the Royal Durban Golf Club one day and told the Tuesday Group that I would be a scratch player in twelve months. The Tuesday Group are serious golfing enthusiasts, so named as they play nine holes every Tuesday afternoon come hell or high water, and if any gung-ho gang could spur me on, they could. Amazingly, they are still active today, thirty years later. As far as I and most other people knew, getting a scratch handicap in a year had never been done before and I got a load of good-natured ribbing for my 'arrogance'. So much so that the Tuesday Group took a formal bet with me that I couldn't do it. The bet itself was simple: I had to play at least three rounds under par within twelve months. I seldom need incentives to achieve targets, but the relentless good-natured needling from the Tuesday Group certainly added some extra motivation.

Time was not on my side, however. I was holding down a full-time job as an insurance broker, while also spending up to six hours a day training on the beach and rivers as well as at water polo sessions. There was not enough time in the day, so to squeeze in as much golf practice as possible, I was at the course before 4.30 a.m. every morning. It was too dark to practise driving on the fairways, so I concentrated solely on chipping and putting until coaches Garth Pearson or Gary Roscoe arrived for my lesson at 7 a.m. The Royal Durban is a unique golf course, situated inside a horse-racing track with some particularly gnarly bunkers and greens. As a result, my short game excelled, while my long game could have been better. However, one of Gary Player's most quoted quips is 'driving is for show, putting for dough'.

Twelve months later, I was a scratch player, much to the amazement of the Tuesday Group. My lowest score was two under par. Even though they lost the bet, their delight that I had done it was genuine.

Soon afterwards I was playing golf in Cape Town with Dave Abromowitz, a top ocean sailor whom I had met at a yacht race in Mauritius, and was introduced to Graham Beck, said to be one of South Africa's richest men at the time. Graham, a wine farmer, horse breeder and philanthropist, had initially made his money as a mining magnate. He watched me tee off with Dave and said that if I could play three under par at the demanding Clovelly Golf Club course, he would sponsor me and my family to live for a year in America and train under arguably the world's most famous instructor, David Leadbetter. That would pave my way to becoming a professional.

But until that happened, I had to concentrate on my day job.

LESSONS LEARNT

TAKE EVERY OPPORTUNITY YOU CAN. The Molokai was the only international contest open to me after 1986, so I grabbed it with both hands.

NEVER TAKE HYPE TOO SERIOUSLY. Greg Barton was on paper the most formidable foe I had faced. But I looked at the positive angle – no matter how many Olympic medals he had, I was the reigning Molokai champion. He had to topple me, not vice versa.

AIM AS HIGH AS YOU CAN. But be realistic in setting goals. I genuinely believed I could bring my golf handicap down to scratch, even though few others did. I would not have taken the bet if I didn't think I could do it.

HOW MUCH DO YOU WANT IT? This is the key question in anyone's life. To hold down a full-time job, train for six hours a day on other sports, and achieve what many thought impossible – a scratch golf handicap in a year – would never have happened if I didn't want it so badly that I could taste it.

12

Winning in business

Being unable to compete internationally meant that professional sport no longer seemed like an option for me. This forced me back to a day job and to focus more on building my career.

While I was happy with the freedom of my work with the Wild Coast Sun, I was not making good money. As Clare and I were about to get married and start a family, this was a major concern. I needed to boost my income.

I have always believed in the power of networking, and on the beach one balmy day, fellow Durban Surf Lifesaving Club member Etienne van der Westhuizen asked in a roundabout way what I was earning. He was shocked when I told him, saying I could at least double that at the insurance giant Sanlam, where he worked.

Etienne is an interesting guy and a legend for a uniquely South African reason. Because of international sanctions, our TV programmes were as exciting as watching weeds sprout, and as a result there was a whole industry devoted to producing photo-story comic books. They had an array of exotic titles such as *Grensvegter* (Border Fighter) and *Ruiter in Swart* (Horseman in Black), but the most popular was *Kid Colt*, which, as the name implies, was set in the old Wild West. However, it was somewhat different from Wyatt Earp at the O.K. Corral as the cowboys spoke Afrikaans. Kid Colt, the hero, was played by Etienne, and with a weightlifter's build, a surfer's tan and long sun-bleached hair, he was accorded Hollywood status by celebrity-starved South Africans. Teeny-boppers swooned at the sight of him.

In real life, Etienne was as far removed from a frontier gunslinger as one could get. He was, in fact, a corporate warrior, one of Sanlam's top insurance salesmen and far quicker with a pen than a Colt .45. He introduced me to the company's provincial manager, Tony Smith, and from there my career skyrocketed.

Tony was a marketing whizz and immediately took me under his wing, soon becoming my chief mentor. One of his trademarks was always being smartly dressed, and he seldom took his jacket off, which is quite a feat in the sweltering Durban heat. I was a bit dubious about swapping my baggies and T-shirt for a suit and tie, but if I wanted to make some serious money, it seemed the time for fun and games was over. Just before taking the job, I followed Tony's advice and visited a men's clothing store to buy the best suit I could afford. Unfortunately, I could only afford one, which I wore every day. And like Tony, I never took my jacket off.

I started off spectacularly, selling a top-drawer life-insurance policy to double Springbok surf lifesaver and swimmer Lee McGregor. Lee and I had some history and regularly competed against each other in lifesaving contests. He was as tough as they come, and like Etienne he had long blond hair and film-star looks, so he was also something of a poster boy for water sports. We were both considered by the media to be 'colourful copy', not least owing to a memorable punch-up on the beach in the 1985 Ironman championships. Lee says I swore at him in the surf, and as we emerged from the waves, he threw a punch. In the ensuing melee, we both lost the race. A photographer caught the exact moment that Lee's haymaker was about to land on my head.

But once the dust settled, we remained friends and two years later he signed me up as a crew member on his twenty-metre yacht in the Crystic Beachcomber Mauritius-to-Durban race. I am not an experienced sailor, but Lee knew I could read big swells in gale-force winds well and wanted me to work the mainsail sheets. We were second across the line in Durban, which is a reflection on Lee's remarkable captaincy as he was up against professional racing crews. Dave Abromowitz, my future golfing partner, was first.

Lee was also a successful businessman, running a plant-hire company, and he wanted to take out an investment policy over ten years. I sold him what I believed was the best on the market, but when my commission cheque arrived, I was horrified at the exorbitant amount. It was the equivalent of three years' salary! I started to query the ethics of that, wondering how I could justify such a large payment for a single relatively short-term deal. Lee thought he was buying a ten-year policy, but the payout was for a sixty-year investment. It appeared that was how the insurance market was structured.

I then started to delve deeper into insurance commissions and decided that the policies were massively skewed in favour of salesmen. A huge chunk of the payout went to costs, which I believed discriminated against the client. Embarrassed, I went back to Lee and told him that his policy had to be a proper ten-year deal and I restructured it accordingly, cutting down significantly on my commission.

This was a key moment for me and I decided that insurance and investments were two different policies, and had to be sold as such. It was wrong to sell life policies as insurance when they were thinly disguised investments – and not even good ones, given the exorbitant commissions charged.

What I did next was considered radical at the time. I ditched the lucrative deals that I considered unethical and instead concentrated on selling Professional Provident Society (PPS) policies that pay no commission. Most thought I was crazy throwing away easy money, and they regularly said so. I then took it further, telling clients exactly how much commission insurance salesmen were making on policies that were meant to benefit the holder's dependants. The industry didn't thank me for that, but clients loved it. They could now see how commissions compared to returns and could decide for themselves if they wanted insurance or investments. If it was the latter, they should not take out insurance unless it was a no-commission policy such as PPS. Conversely, if clients had a crippling bond on their homes, I suggested they pay that off as they could be saving up to 20 per cent, a sizeable return on any investment. I believed that by looking after my clients' interests, I would reap rewards in the long run.

My approach, that insurance and investments were separate issues, was different from the industry's norm. What I deliberately forfeited in high-commission sales, I made up for in client trust. Most of my clients were young professionals such as doctors, dentists, attorneys and architects who – like me – had just started their careers. I believed my business would grow as theirs did, and I started getting referrals from grateful customers who got full insurance payouts when they most needed them, such as times of job redundancy or family illness. I soon became one of the top guys in South Africa selling PPS policies.

It started to snowball. People I had sold to then started asking for other financial advice, proving my point that goodwill is far more important than lucrative short-term sales.

I also discovered that winning in sport had a lot in common with winning in business. The boardroom can be just as metaphorically bloodthirsty as a gladiatorial arena. And as in sport, success requires not only talent but also hard work, discipline and an iron will. But above all, you need to be organised. I always had a plan for a race, and losing the first day of a surfski marathon or the first leg of an Ironman contest necessitated adapting tactics. Being organised means that you are serious about winning, not just pitching up and hoping for the best. I soon found this to be crucial in the corporate world as well, and I changed much of Sanlam's time-management structure by developing a diary system using techniques I had learnt from sport as well as Tom Hopkins's book *How to Master the Art of Selling*. I initially used it personally to organise my own day, taking care of my work schedule, golf practices and kayak training while also making time for my family. I also listed the exact number of people I needed to phone, visit, and get deals or referrals from if I wanted to hit my increasingly ambitious targets. It is amazing how much can be done in a day if one has a rigid schedule. Mine started at 4.30 a.m. and finished at 10 p.m.

After a while many Sanlam salesmen were using my diary techniques for both time management and financial planning. It's all a numbers game, as increasing a customer base equals increased commissions, which is the essence of selling. The more constructive work you put in, the more you get out. But to be constructive, you have to be organised.

I also decided not to be scared to make large investments myself if that boosted my efficiency. As a result, I bought one of the first cellphones in the country. It was huge – so much so that I had to put the battery in the boot of my car. It was also way out of my budget, costing the equivalent of about $15 000 in today's terms. But my clients were blown away at how easy it was to contact me. There was no leaving a message with a secretary. I was picking up calls personally even when I was out of the office. That was considered radical then, but the phone soon paid for itself. Can you imagine a businessperson without a cellphone today?

Things were going exceptionally well. Clare was pregnant with our first child, Luke, and we bought a house in Durban's affluent Berea suburb over-looking the Indian Ocean. I was writing more business than most of my colleagues, making good money and exponentially growing my client base. I was a scratch golfer, having won my bet with the Tuesday Group, and was even contemplating the opportunity of turning professional. I had been awarded my Springbok Ocean Kayak colours the year before, not that there was anyone outside the country to compete against. However, that didn't worry me as it seemed like I was on the brink of becoming a professional golfer.

It never happened. The main reason was that on 11 February 1990, Nelson Mandela was released from prison after twenty-seven years behind bars. This was the beginning of a process that resulted in the country's first fully democratic elections in 1994. It was the most tectonic event in recent South African history and we were suddenly no longer the pariah of the world.

Then I got a phone call that was to change so much for me. It came out of the blue from a good friend who was also a top paddler, albeit more than ten years my senior. His name was Pierre Strydom.

'Oscar,' he said, 'are you still playing golf?'

'Yes,' I answered. 'Why?'

'Bad choice, my friend. We're sending a kayak squad to the 1992 Olympics.'

'What?'

'Ja. The IOC [International Olympic Committee] is going to send us a formal invite to Barcelona.'

Stunned, I said nothing.

'Pity you haven't been paddling for the past eighteen months,' Pierre added.

I took a deep breath and laughed. 'Don't worry about that,' I said. 'I'll be in that team.'

LESSONS LEARNT

TRUST IS PRICELESS. Always have your clients' interests at heart. Don't think only of the commission cheque – think of what is best for your client and most times you will be rewarded tenfold in the long run.

ORGANISATION MEANS WINNING. There was no way I could have handled family, work and sport in my life unless I had a schedule that I followed religiously. Being disorganised equates to lost opportunities – whether it's training for races or securing a business deal. The fact that most of Sanlam's salespeople followed my example proves my point. Challenge yourself to find ways or techniques to accomplish your tasks more efficiently. This applies to all aspects of life.

DON'T BE SCARED to do things differently. The way I sold policies for Sanlam – differentiating between investments and insurance – was considered revolutionary at the time and many thought I was mad to throw away lucrative commissions. But if I hadn't done that, I would never have increased my client base of young professionals.

13

The Barcelona Olympics

My hand shook as I put down the phone. I never thought that in my lifetime we would be readmitted to the Olympics. My pulse quickened.

If true, this was the biggest breakthrough for South African athletes in thirty-two years. And if anyone knew what was happening behind the scenes, Pierre Strydom did.

That alone was an anomaly, as Pierre lived in Benoni, which is in the heart of a rough mining area known as the East Rand and not considered the 'hippest' part of the world. Yet in that conservative backwater, Pierre was streets ahead of almost all other sportsmen and administrators. When he told me we would soon get the green light to compete in the Barcelona Summer Olympics, I took him seriously.

Pierre belonged to the East Rand Kayaking Club (ERKC), and in 1988 he and a few other members started a development programme for disadvantaged paddlers when the country seemed to be at an irresolvable political impasse. There were riots in the townships, and many black residential areas were considered no-go zones for whites. However, Pierre owned a bus-hire company and regularly travelled to surrounding townships to fetch aspiring paddlers, training them on Homestead Lake in Benoni's middle-class suburb of Farrarmere. Many thought he was crazy trying to introduce a distinctly European sport to township Africans, but Pierre was not only a brave man – he was way ahead of his time. However, even he didn't imagine for a moment the long-term repercussions of the ERKC's ambitious training scheme.

'We initially wanted to do some good, not for any other reason,' he recalls. 'There was no thought of us being readmitted to the Olympics – we did it because it was the right thing to do. In fact, we got a lot of flak from other members who were not that happy to see a busload of young blacks being bussed to the lake. But we persevered and got through that. So when the political situation started changing rapidly in 1991, we not only had a solid development programme in place but had also trained up a group of competent black paddlers.'

Pierre didn't know it at the time, but this was crucial for the future of South African kayaking. The new reality was that only sports that were making genuine attempts at racial integration would be allowed to compete in the Olympics.

'I then got a call from Sam Ramsamy, president of the National Olympic Committee of South Africa [NOCSA], and told him what we were doing at ERKC,' says Pierre. 'Not long afterwards, he arrived at the club with a delegation to check it out first-hand. They liked it. In fact, they liked it so much that we were the first sport to get the Olympic go-ahead after long-distance running, which was already dominated by black athletes.'

All this was thanks to Pierre's astonishing pioneering work in the townships during one of the most difficult, dangerous and traumatic times in the country's history. Other sports, such as water polo, which NOCSA deemed not to have integrated enough, weren't even considered.

Pierre was a national sprint paddler and had won several medals in the South African K-1 and K-2 Championships, so he was included in the initial Olympic training group. As the oldest guy there, he was also the mentor and squad manager.

Pierre and I have different recollections of that fateful call all those years ago that got me fired up about the Olympics. I remember it being more about him casually telling me that we would be competing and that I should get fit. He denies this. In fact, he didn't even think I would make the team.

'When I first phoned Oscar, he had stopped any form of kayaking, including surfskiing, for the preceding eighteen months and taken up golf,' says Pierre.

'All that considered, he now had to start from scratch and was not a flat-water sprint canoeist at all. I mentioned to him that I was sceptical whether he would be able to make the team, despite his claims that he previously did sprint training for lifesaving. Flat-water racing requires a different set of athletic skills and training methods, but in typical Oscar fashion, he dismissed these as minor obstacles and in no uncertain terms declared that he would be the best sprinter within a year. In retrospect, his prediction was not quite on target – after a year he was arguably the second-best 1 000-metre sprinter in the country. Anyway, I told him to come to the selection trials and we would take it from there.'

The trials were held in Johannesburg and I needed to make some hard choices. If selected, I would be away from home for at least a year while training full-time at high altitude. What further complicated this was that my career was skyrocketing, and going for Olympic selection meant I would have to take a long leave of absence from Sanlam. There was no way I could do this as a part-timer, and Sanlam agreed to hold my position open. But still, how would I support my family? I only earned by commission, so without selling I would not be making any money. To make the decision even tougher, Clare was eight months pregnant, so I would be leaving her at home with a new baby while training 600 kilometres away.

Just as I had done eight years previously for the showdown with Grant Kenny, I decided to go for broke. We rented out our posh house and Clare moved in with her mother, Norma. As always, Clare was there for me and realised this was a once-in-a-lifetime opportunity. But even so, to have to evacuate her comfortable home so I could follow my dream was a sacrifice not many would be willing to make.

Reality soon hit hard. Times were tough. I don't think I had ever been so poor since competing on the Aussie Surf Ironman circuit, so Clare approached several Durban businesspeople to sponsor me. I am still humbled by the kindness of people, and by three in particular: Charlie Good of Drum Services, Alan Burke of ARB Electrical, and Gavin Varejes, who had previously assisted me when I was down and out in Hawaii, were very generous.

But my Olympic dream was a voracious financial monster. Travel costs alone were in the region of R100 000, as apart from flying home most weekends, I also had to pay my own way to pre-Olympic training camps in Eastern Europe. Just considering how much in commissions I would lose that year was a rabbit hole I didn't want to go down. However, I believed my logic was sound. I could always make more money later, but to compete in an Olympics was an immeasurable opportunity – something I would never get again.

On 7 June 1991, Clare gave birth to our son Luke through an emergency C-section under general anaesthetic. At 4.45 kilograms, he was the heaviest baby born at Parklands Hospital, a record he held for a number of years. After the doctor, I was the first person to hold him and the bond was instant. A picture of that appeared on the cover of *Living and Loving*, and that particular issue was the magazine's best seller for several years. Perhaps it was fitting that Luke was born not only in one of the most crucial times of our lives but also in the most challenging. I think it's no coincidence that he has had a winning temperament from the word go.

To cut down on expenses, Pierre generously allowed me to live with his family while training, which at least took care of my accommodation situation. I flew to Durban to see Clare and Luke whenever I had time off, or else they came up to the East Rand.

However, I had barely arrived in Johannesburg when tragedy struck. We were paddling in a selection heat when one of the triallists, Gavin Cook, suddenly keeled over and fell out of his kayak.

Pierre was first on the scene. 'I was in the sprint lane next to Gavin,' he recalls. 'It was a very hard-fought heat, we were all racing neck and neck, and when I crossed the finish line, I turned and saw Gavin in the water holding onto his kayak. Although exhausted, I managed to paddle to him and dived in to grab him just as he let go and started to sink. Within seconds the rescue boat and Oscar were there and pulled us both aboard.'

It was obvious that Gavin had suffered a massive heart attack, and with the help of fellow Durban Surf Lifesaving member Grant Veckranges, I started CPR on the unconscious young man. We got him ashore and desperately phoned for an ambulance while Grant and I continued with resuscitation. When the ambulance arrived, to our dismay we discovered the defibrillator was not working.

Time was running out fast. Using my car phone we contacted Gavin's father, who was a doctor, and he called for an air ambulance. By the time the helicopter arrived, Grant and I had been doing CPR for three hours.

Sadly, Gavin died before reaching the hospital. It was a sobering reminder of what people are prepared to do to fulfil their dreams. A talented paddler, he was only twenty-two years old and had shown no previous symptoms of heart disease. In fact, he appeared to be supremely fit.

After that tragic start, the squad settled down to serious training. In particular, I had to put in some long hours as I had previously been concentrating on getting my golf handicap down to zero. Now my total focus was on paddling, and even though I had no doubt I would be selected, I knew that Pierre did.

However, Pierre now admits that his uncertainty didn't last long. 'My questions about Oscar making the team soon disappeared,' he says. 'He got very good very quickly. It was the first time I saw that side of Oscar where he clicks over into competitive mode. It's pure tunnel vision and he works extremely hard, putting in at least 20 per cent more effort than almost anyone else I know. He has the capacity to do a lot of work, way beyond what is normal, and that's part of his success. It's not just physical or his size; it's also the fact that he goes into everything boots and all. He pushed every training session to the absolute limit. Everything he did was at peak performance, and his single-minded belief in himself is phenomenal.'

Another key reason for the hard training was that we were so far behind all other international Olympic paddlers. We had a lot of work to do as this would be our first-ever Games against veteran Olympians who had been on the world stage for many years. In contrast, no South African had ever even competed in the Junior World Championships, where most paddlers are blooded at a young age. To say we were unprepared in every aspect is the understatement of the decade.

Also, given the local paddling circuit's preference for distance racing, very few of us were sprint purists. I had no illusions that this was going to be a big wake-up call for everyone. Perhaps I was slightly better prepared as I had raced on the world stage before, winning the Molokai seven times in a row. I had also trained with West German Olympic hopefuls in 1986 and remembered the endless sprinting sessions where no river skills such as reading rapids, currents or slipstreams came into play. It was just up and down lanes, pure and simple. And mind-numbingly boring. But I was prepared to do it all again for an Olympic slot.

The one thing that did bother me was that our coach, Nandor Almasi, considered weightlifting to be the most essential part of our fitness regime. Nandor is from Hungary and is highly respected in international kayaking circles, but his training methods were vastly different from anything I had experienced. We seemed to spend more time in the gym doing bench presses, dumb-bell repetitions and working out on machines than we did on the water. I grunted my way through infinite repetitions of sit-ups, pull-ups and push-ups, more than I'd ever done before and will hopefully ever do again. Nandor concentrated excessively on upper-body strength, which – to be fair – was the conventional wisdom among most Olympic coaches at the time. But I knew after countless miles of top league paddling that my thighs always took more strain than my arms as a result of the continuous rotation of big core muscles. Yet how much leg exercise did we do? None.

It all seemed a little old-fashioned, but I gave it my best shot, reasoning that a veteran like Nandor knew what he was doing. Maybe this was what kayak sprint training involved.

However, I hated doing monotonous exercise, which is why I kept fit for lifesaving by playing water polo rather than swimming up and down lanes. The same with paddling. For me it's far more beneficial working out in rivers or surf where you can refine your natural technique instead of just bulking up and mindlessly powering the boat. I preferred using brain as well as brawn.

The final squad was eventually cut down to six men and two women. I was selected for the K-4 event with Mark Perrow, Bennie Reynders and Herman Kotze. All were exceptionally strong paddlers by South African standards, and Mark would also race the 1 000-metre K-1, while Bennie and Herman were selected for the 500-metre K-2 as well.

The national team was announced with much fanfare and wall-to-wall press coverage. Sixty-eight men and twenty-five women were selected to contest eighty-seven events in nineteen sports. Every one of us was acutely aware that we were making history, and the buzz among the squad was extraordinary. The country was experiencing a surge of optimism after decades of gloomy apartheid. The release of Nelson Mandela and his genuine pledge of national reconciliation was an incalculable inspiration to every athlete as we moved towards the birth of a rainbow nation.

However, despite a rising sense of optimism, the country was on a political knife's edge. On 17 June 1992 there had been a massacre in Boipatong, where clashes between rival political movements resulted in the deaths of forty-five people. Nelson Mandela blamed the security forces, and Archbishop Desmond Tutu called for South Africans to be barred from all international events. With such political acrimony suddenly exploding, our invite to the Olympics was in serious jeopardy. That's how tense the reality was, and the country desperately needed a skilled behind-the-scenes diplomatic trouble-shooter to bring all sides together.

Fortunately, we had one. His name was Clive Grinaker, a top businessman and sports promoter who was fundamental in uniting all South African sport under a single non-racial banner. Clive personally knew Nelson Mandela, Steve Tshwete (who would become the country's first black minister of sport) and Sam Ramsamy, and his role in getting us to Barcelona cannot be overstated. How he pulled it all off is a miracle.

Just before we left for Barcelona, Clive organised a farewell function to bring the athletes, politicians and sponsors together. At the event, held in the plush Sandton Sun and attended by Nelson Mandela, the sponsors stood on stage stressing how proud they were to be associated with the Olympic team and showed the promotions they would be screening on national television.

It was a hugely inspirational evening, and I approached Clive saying how well everything was going. However, I pointed out that the sponsors were all thanking us, but it should be the other way around – we should be thanking them. Without sponsorship we would not be going to Barcelona. Someone from the team needed to get up and say that.

He agreed, and then said I should do it. I was somewhat taken aback, but I told him I would be honoured. He said he needed to clear it first with NOCSA and would get back to me.

I returned to my table, and not long afterwards Clive came up and said he had booked a slot for me to speak.

'Okay, when?' I asked.

'In five minutes.'

My mouth fell open. Five minutes? To give a keynote address at one of the most significant events in the country's sporting history?

It seemed like five seconds later that I was standing in the harsh glare of TV spotlights without a note in my hands about to say something that by its very nature had massive political overtones. Like most sportspeople, I am not a political animal, but I had taken a stance in 1986 when I signed the KwaZulu-Natal Indaba, a highly controversial document calling for majority rule in my home province. Apart from the obvious iniquities of apartheid, from a purely sporting point of view there was no way I could support a system that did not allow me to compete against other athletes because of different skin tones.

Speaking slowly and as clearly as I could, more to give myself time to think than anything else, I thanked not only the sponsors but also the brave people in the townships who had sacrificed their lives in the struggle to get us to where we were on this special day – a day on the brink of history. It went down well, and from that moment on, whenever there was a press conference or an official team statement, I was the guy facing the popping camera flashes. Unwittingly, I had become the unofficial spokesperson for the athletes, and even Olympic Committee officials treated me as such.

There was also some discussion about who would carry the flag at the opening ceremony, and it was decided that an athlete who had been disadvantaged by apartheid should do so. It was a decision I wholeheartedly agreed with, and the flag was carried by marathon runner Jan Tau. Even that presented some problems, as at the time the country's official banner was the orange, white and blue 'apartheid' flag, which certainly did not convey the spirit of the new South Africa. So we marched under a simple emblem consisting of a grey diamond representing the country's mineral wealth; cascading bands of blue, red and green representing sea, land and agriculture; the five Olympic rings; and the name of our country underneath.

As an emotional experience, the Olympics are unbeatable. What sticks out the most for me was walking into the opening ceremony in front of 80 000 spectators. For those involved in fringe or Cinderella sports like kayaking, it was surreal. Most of our races attract hundreds, not thousands, of spectators. The closest I had got to a Superdome atmosphere was running onto the rugby field at Kings Park Stadium in Durban to play the Natal Schools' curtain-raiser for the Lions–Barbarians match in 1980.

As unofficial squad leader, I suppose I was to some extent responsible for fostering team spirit, but I didn't need to. Every South African there was aware that we were caught up in something special. The camaraderie was more intense than anything I had experienced. When I trained with the German squad in Munich, I was very much on my own, shunned as an outsider. The difference this time around was truly astonishing as I was part of a family – and an extremely close-knit one. We were all in it for each other, and the genuine joy when anyone did well was profoundly moving. Apart from becoming friends with tennis player Wayne Ferreira, showjumper Peter Gotz, and world-class runners Elana Meyer and Zola Budd-Pieterse, I found the Olympic Village, with its welcoming ambience, to be a great place to mingle with sporting legends. I met Carl Lewis, once the fastest man in the world and who this time around won gold medals for both long jump and the 4 x 100-metre relay; the world's second-fastest man Frankie Fredericks; and Ben Johnson, the Canadian sprinter twice banned for failing drug tests. I bumped into Boris Becker, whom I surprised by greeting in fluent German. But the most embarrassing moment was getting into the lift with a lanky guy who introduced himself as Javier Sotomayor.

'What are you competing in?' I asked.

'High jump.'

'Are you any good?'

'I'm okay,' he replied. 'I hold the world record.'

Javier is Cuban and is still the only human ever to have cleared 2.45 metres, or fractionally over eight feet. Indeed, the strongest symbolism of the new South Africa was us sharing the same residential block as the Cubans. Barely five years previously we had been shooting at each other in the Angolan

Civil War, and many of my friends had been called up to fight in the bush. South Africa had been helping the guerrilla movement UNITA (the National Union for the Total Independence of Angola), while Cuba supported the Angolan government forces. This time the only 'combat' was an impromptu water fight amid much hilarity after a party.

Undoubtedly, the highlight for me was meeting Nelson Mandela. Sam Ramsamy introduced us and I expected Mr Mandela to shake hands briefly and move on, but he stopped for a chat. I told him how thankful I was for what he had done for all South Africans, and that the only reason we were in Barcelona was because of his magnanimity. I said that for us athletes, this was a dream we never thought would come true.

Madiba, as most South Africans called one of the world's most revered men, was a former heavyweight boxer and very competitive. He listened to what I said, then urged me to 'bring some medals home'. I said we would do our best, but equally important was that thanks to him the world knew that South Africa was back.

Unfortunately, from a kayaking point of view, our results were bitterly disappointing. In the K-4 we got as far as the semi-finals, as did Mark Perrow in the K-1, while Bennie and Herman did not advance from the initial K-2 stages.

Why did we do so badly is a question often thrown at me. There are plenty of reasons – our training, equipment and technique could perhaps have been better. But the real answer is that most of us had no idea of what being an Olympian actually involved. The cold, hard enormity of competing in the ultimate sporting crucible is not just about physical prowess. Passion and an indomitable mindset are equally crucial, and those are not things that can be nurtured overnight. Most of the people we were up against were already Olympians or had spent almost all their lives dreaming of becoming one. For them it was an obsession. For us, until recently, it had been a pipe dream. Consequently, the chances of fostering such a winning mentality and bringing home a sackful of medals with just twelve months of training were slim to non-existent.

Pierre agrees. 'Olympians are usually professional, full-time athletes with extensive support personnel and structures, not to mention funding. Our kayak team had none of this. Nandor, the coach, was paid by the original squad of fifteen giving R100 each per month out of their own pockets. That was it – and most of them could barely afford that.

'It was stressful for the athletes as they were expected to give all, pay their own way and simultaneously not being sure of a final Olympic spot.'

Despite that, we did win two silver medals: Elana Meyer in the 10 000 metres, and Wayne Ferreira and Piet Norval in the men's tennis doubles. That alone is outstanding when one considers our thirty-two years of isolation.

I have stressed that it was a unique experience being part of the first post-isolation Olympic team, and I have memories that I will treasure forever. But from a purely sporting perspective, the Games were a major disappointment. Most Olympians are proud purely to have taken part, but that's not who I am. I want to win, not just participate. I didn't get into the national team to get the blazer; I wanted to get the medal. The fact that I didn't is a failure.

What made this doubly disappointing was that some of the paddlers who did win medals in Barcelona were people I had beaten in other races. Many Olympians compete in the Sella Descent, and Herman and I triumphed over them all in 1986. Not only that, but I had won using my own training methods, without a fixation on bulking up and weight training.

Another medallist I had beaten before was Greg Barton, who raced against me in the 1989 Molokai. Greg had won two Olympic golds in Seoul in 1988, and was expected to win again in 1992. Instead he came third. He was beaten by twenty-year-old Clint Robinson, an Australian hailed as the new paddling phenomenon. For some reason, Clint reminded me of myself when I was his age – super-fit, super-confident and, some may say, a little cocky.

I didn't know it then, but twenty years later he and I would line up against each other in what many still consider to be one of the finest Molokais ever raced.

LESSONS LEARNT

PREPARE FOR THE UNEXPECTED. In this case, it was a lesson I learnt from Pierre Strydom. While everyone was saying we would never be allowed back into the Olympics, Pierre was busy training disadvantaged paddlers from the townships. As a result, kayaking was one of the first sports to get the green light for Barcelona.

NETWORK. NETWORK. NETWORK. I used the Olympics to network, if not win medals. I am still in contact with many of the athletes I met in Barcelona. In fact, Greg Barton and I later became business partners, forming one of the world's biggest kayak companies. If you don't build a network around you and continuously nurture those relationships, you are only paddling with one arm. There is no such thing as an individual athlete or businessperson. The great leaders and athletes of our time all have or had amazing networks of people surrounding them.

In other words, never miss an opportunity to foster relationships.

DECIDE WHAT MATTERS most to you, then do it. It was far more important to me to compete in the Olympics than continue earning lucrative commission cheques as an insurance consultant. As I said at the time, I could always make money later – but the Olympics for me was going to be a one-off event.

14

After the Olympics

From Barcelona, Mark Perrow and I drove to the far north of Spain to compete in the week-long paddling fiesta that started with the famous Sella Descent.

Unfortunately, a screw for my kayak seat broke during the race, which effectively meant I had to paddle using only my arms, as my core muscles had no grip with the yo-yoing base. This is not an excuse, as I should have checked our equipment more carefully. Still, we ended up third, beating several Olympians. The disappointment was somewhat compensated by winning every other race in the fiesta, again against some current and previous Olympic medallists. (Mark, who had a pilot's licence, died in a plane crash while monitoring the Umkomaas Canoe Marathon in 2020. He was only fifty-five – a tragic loss of one of our greatest kayakers.)

Back home, I needed to start making money right away, since Clare and I were living on a shoestring. I returned to selling insurance with a vengeance, using my diary and commission calculator to maximise my day. At any given time, I would know exactly how many phone calls to make, clients to see, referrals to bring in, and policies to sell. If I hadn't contacted the required number of clients by the time the office closed, I made appointments after work. If they were going for a sundowner afterwards, I would track them down. Often it was more about personal contact than sales, but I always hit target. Some said this was marginal obsessive-compulsive disorder, but it certainly worked. Even Clare was astonished at how accurate my calculations were. When I said I would soon be earning R40 000 ($10 000) a month, which was good money in those days, she initially didn't believe me.

Soon we were back in our plush Berea house and life returned to normal. Eventually it got to the stage where I had too many clients. As I was increasingly being consulted for financial advice, I could no longer provide a comprehensive range of options with only Sanlam's portfolios. I needed a wider spectrum of services to market, so it was time to start my own company.

In 1993, after six years with Sanlam, I formed Oscar Chalupsky & Associates. Business took off almost immediately, and soon I was employing five secretaries to handle the growing number of clients – and there was still a waiting list. I never changed my business strategy, always declaring how much commission I made on each policy, or in the case of PPS policies, charging no commission at all. I was, as far as I know, the first insurance salesman to do this.

The following year, 1994, was the most momentous in South Africa's chequered history. On 27 April, the first multiracial elections were held and twenty-two million people of all colours, creeds and ideologies voted. For most, it was the first time in their lives and emotions ran high. People were weeping as they patiently waited hours in queues that snaked up and down roads leading to polling stations. The African National Congress won with an overwhelming majority and Nelson Mandela became the first democratically elected president of the country.

This meant that finally South Africa was no longer blackballed in world sport. The dark days of isolation were banished to the trashcan of history. I was now thirty years old, and for the first time I didn't have to hide my origins or pretend to be from another country. I could compete as a South African.

After the Olympics and Sella Descent, I was in good shape and went on to win my eighth successive Port Elizabeth to East London race – previously called the Texan Challenge but now known simply as the PE2EL. I was up against some tough opposition, including my brother Herman, so it was time to return to the international arena.

However, I had to balance a gruelling training regime with a growing business. To me this was not an issue that I wasted any sleep over. I knew what I had to do. The reality was that even though I wanted to be a professional sportsman, there was not enough money in local fringe sports to sustain that dream. While many international kayaking and Ironman races were now paying decent prize money, particularly in Australia, travelling the global circuit was too expensive to be viable. In effect, I was a successful pro-am competitor, but financially I could not make the leap to become a full-time sportsman. I had to train outside office hours, and in that regard I am proud to say that I was as close to being a 'normal' person as any international contestant could hope to be. First and foremost, I needed to put food on the table, so everything had to work around my marriage, children and career. I never had the luxury of taking a rest day, or catching up on sleep after a big race, or taking time off for marathon training sessions. My time was rigidly structured and top priority was providing for my family.

But if 1994 was momentous for the country, it was even more so for the Chalupsky family. Almost a month to the day after Nelson Mandela was elected president, on 26 May our daughter Hannah was born. Like Luke, she was a big baby, a kilogram lighter than her brother, and we were blessed now to have a boy and a girl. Celebrations were huge. Everything seemed to be on track. My family was growing, my business was thriving, and at last I could take on the best in the world without boycotts or other political interferences.

To me, these essential activities are intertwined. I have the same dynamic drive that I apply to both business and sport. I was there to win, or else I was wasting my time. That meant long hours, commitment and a willingness to be a warrior both physically and corporately. Everything in life depends on how badly you want something and how many sacrifices you are willing to make to get it. That's an obvious observation, but it's surprisingly lost on a lot of people. The reality is that if you sit back and merely hope for the best ... well, good luck with that.

The days of Oscar Chalupsky & Associates were great fun and hugely productive. I look back on them with pride. But perhaps the best memories – warts and all – come from my stalwart personal assistant at the time, Glenda Rogers, who is also an amazing all-round achiever. These are her random recollections.

'I began working for Oscar in 1993 when he left Sanlam and started his own brokerage at his home. I remember him asking me at my interview if I knew who he was. I had no idea and had never heard of him before. Whoops! But I must have been qualified enough because then I got called in to meet with Clare as I would be working from their house and that was scary! She made me do typing and language tests and it was a proper interview.

'What was Oscar like to work for? First words that spring to my mind are stubborn, determined, and hyper-, hyperactive. It was difficult to set times for meetings as he was always on the go and often I couldn't get him to sit still long enough to give me a straight answer on something.

'As anyone who knows Oscar will attest, his handwriting is horrific! Illegible doesn't come close to describing it. Often all I could decipher on a contract was perhaps a client's name and some barely readable scribbles and I would have to figure out the rest. I'll never forget the one time Oscar came back from Johannesburg with a particularly unreadable application form in which some necessary medical information was missing. Data protection was not as strict in those days, so I had to phone the client and again read the questions to him. I swear I could hear Oscar laughing while I wrote down information about a sensitive operation on the client's nether regions!

'However, Oscar was an awesome boss. There was no stopping him from doing anything. If anybody challenged him to do something, he was up for it. And guess what? He always won. Even if he didn't win that day, he would continue until he succeeded. His perseverance and audacity and love for life always won.

'Sure, he was sometimes "uuurrgghhhhh" in the office, but it was never boring. He would call on his car phone from down the road to tell me he was on his way, and I would run out to collect the files from the morning meetings and hand him the ones for the afternoon meetings. He was always so busy! I even made up my own little song I used to sing to myself: "If I was an octopus in the middle of the sea, I would have eight hands to help Oscar Chalupsky."

'I definitely needed eight hands. Oscar seemed to be in eight different places at the same time. We had numerous "Where in the world is Oscar" challenges when he would be gone for months training and racing. But he always kept everything at the business afloat as well.

'He could be a slave driver to work for, but in a way it was for your own good. There was a lot of pressure, and when I got really angry I would grab his keys and – as I am not tall – would jump on a chair and hit him on the head with them just to get my frustrations out. He never got angry with me. In fact, he never lost his temper, unless you were a person that deserved it. No one who has worked for Oscar has anything against him.

'I resigned three times because I felt I couldn't handle the pressures (I was in my twenties and stupid, remember) and every time Oscar would wait quietly in the background until I reconsidered. When I needed help, he and Clare were there. I was a single mom when I started working for them, fighting an abusive relationship, and although I don't recall ever telling Oscar and Clare that, they seemed to have my back from day one. I can't express my gratitude at how they helped me in silent ways during those times.

'Oscar is an awesome man. And Clare is just amazing! An absolute queen. I remember thinking that she was definitely going to heaven because she must live a hell on earth dealing with Oscar, but she was happy, and her laugh was lovely to hear and contagious. Oscar adored her and still does and I felt comfortable working there. Clare would tell Nanny Jane, our office assistant, what to make me for lunch – just simple things – and I would be fed every day. I learnt to eat proper sardines on toast there, not the canned-in-tomato-sauce ones. I don't eat anything fishy but I loved Nanny Jane's sardines on toast. I have never tasted them like that again.

'Looking back, I've never met anyone with as much determination and inner strength as Oscar. I don't think I will ever again. And although he hates to admit it, Oscar always helped people. He still does! Even while battling with his own cancer treatment, he found the time to help my nephew from Zambia who was also suffering from cancer.'

* * *

Now that my new business was up and running, I could concentrate on serious paddling again. Which got me thinking – what were the key lessons I had learnt from the Olympics? What were the defining moments?

There were many, from networking with global icons to partying with the Cubans, but the most important issue for me was reassessing the coaching systems I had gone through in a fruitless quest for a medal. Throughout my life, every race from my first Iron Nipper victory at the age of twelve to the ocean marathons that I'd won, I had coached myself. Of course, I had huge outside support – from my mother, Mercia, and Clare driving me long distances to races and training sessions, to my father's uncompromising discipline, I was never on my own. There were many others: Bob Twogood opened his house to me in Hawaii, and Gavin Varejes flew out my racing kayak at a time when I was so destitute I couldn't afford a takeaway hamburger. It has not been a solo journey, and my debt to those who have been with me is infinite. No one succeeds in life on their own, and if there is one supreme snippet of advice I can impart, it is that. But even with all that support, I never had an official coach. Except once – at the Olympics. And now, after eighteen years of racing, one nagging question kept buzzing around in my head: Why was I beating Olympians in so many other races without coaching yet getting my butt kicked when I did have expert tuition?

Nandor, our Olympic coach, was great in the conventional sense and did the best he could for us in the short time available. But he was using the same old-school pumping-iron techniques as the Russians, Swedes and Eastern Europeans, and it didn't work for me.

So what did work? The short version is that I had always used technique rather than brawn. I was a natural surfskier; the ocean was my home. I also loved racing white-water rivers. I had never bothered before with gyms and indoor rowing machines, so treasured by sprint paddlers. Yet with my 'free-range' training background, I became – by Pierre Strydom's admission – the second-fastest flat-water sprint paddler in the country during the Olympic trials. So I had to be doing something right.

Yet whenever I brought this up, I got a strange look from the purists. The sport's gurus were adamant that surfski racing was vastly different from sprinting and needed vastly different techniques. I disagreed: correct paddling is correct paddling. Period.

Today I have been vindicated. Australian sports writers have found that an astonishing nineteen of the country's most successful Olympic sprint kayakers started out as surfski racers. It is now recognised that this is mainly due to the exceptionally high-quality strength development that surf paddling involves. Without even realising it, top surfski racers develop unparalleled balance skills and core strength as they train in supremely elemental environments with waves, rip currents and high winds. Compare that to sprint paddlers powering up and down demarcated flat-water lanes or mirror-smooth lakes.

I decided then and there that I was not going to listen to anyone else again. I was going to become a master technician using skills I had already mastered in oceans and rivers, rather than becoming a gym jockey or weightlifter. I was going to do what I did best, and no one was going to tell me differently. I would be my own coach.

I have done many online videos on coaching that are easily accessible. But the key winning techniques are to use non-feathered paddles, master the brace stroke, avoid a jerky 'punch and pull' rhythm, and ensure your back paddle stroke does not go beyond vertical. The most obvious illustration of this is tilting an outboard engine a few degrees off a boat's transom and seeing how much power is lost.

But having a good technique is one thing. The real challenge is maintaining it, no matter how agonisingly fatigued you are. Too many racers mindlessly try to slog ahead when exhausted or if a competitor is catching up, and their paddling becomes sloppy. I started training myself to keep as near perfect a technique as possible no matter how tired I was or how much pain I was in. Even in the most brutal conditions, I would talk – sometimes shout and swear – to myself to focus on technique. I modified lessons I had learnt from the Olympics into a supremely useful tool, returning to the world stage with a new, unshakeable belief in that what I was doing was right. And what better way to make a comeback than my favourite race?

So it was back to Hawaii, where the 1995 Molokai was being held in a couple of weeks' time. There was another Aussie who was starting to threaten my record, and some were claiming he was better downwind than me. His name was Dean Gardiner, and he had won three Molokais in a row. In Australia, he was being hailed as the new Grant Kenny.

That was enough for me. I packed my gear and caught the next plane out. This time, not only was I competing as a South African, I was part of a Springbok team.

LESSONS LEARNT

I AM A NORMAL PERSON. I never was a full-time professional sportsperson, as much as I would have liked to have been. My experiences are every person's. So if I can find the time to train hard and pursue a demanding career, anyone can.

WRITE DOWN EVERY GOAL. The diary I devised to perfect time management helped me to win in both sport and business. I cannot stress that strongly enough. I never deviate from it.

ALWAYS HAVE A PLAN. Most people think the most important aspect of building something is the foundation. It's not. It's the plan. Without a plan, you cannot build a foundation. After the Olympics, when I realised that I was beating champions with my own training techniques but losing when I used others, I returned to my original plan. It proved to be a winner.

15

Brothers-in-arms

Four of us were chosen for the Springbok team to race the 1995 Molokai: my brother Herman, fellow Durban surf lifesaver Brett Pengelly, Adriaan 'Stretch' Struwig from Richards Bay, and me as the captain.

We were the first to be awarded national colours for surfskiing in South Africa, so it was an honour – although, as I have stressed, I want to stand on the winner's podium rather than wear the blazer.

We arrived in Oahu and I had a minor upgrade from my usual 'home from home' – Bob Twogood's sofa – to sharing a room at the Diamond Beach Hotel. But even though we were Springboks, the South African rand was in free fall against the American dollar and once again we were travelling on a shoestring.

I was keen to meet Dean Gardiner, the triple winner, and it soon happened on the beach during a training session. I couldn't miss him as he had the unmistakable gravity of an athlete in his prime, even though he was nothing like Grant Kenny, the blond, clean-cut Australian poster boy of the 1980s. In fact, Dean was the polar opposite: wiry, dark-haired, with a mahogany-tanned, weather-beaten face. While Grant was a successful businessman who owned his own airline, Dean had been a rough-and-ready commercial fisherman. Marginally over 1.8 metres tall, it was obvious that he was as tough as a brumby, the legendary feral Aussie horse. Apart from trawling in the turbulent Gulf of Carpentaria between Australia and Indonesia, he had been a lifeguard and at one time had considered playing professional Australian rules football. Unlike the initial east coast Aussie invasion led by Grant, Tank Bennett and Guy Leech, Dean came from Perth on the blustery west coast, which meant he was a strong downwind paddler. In fact, the Aussies claimed he was the best downwind paddler in the world, something that would have been hotly disputed on the beaches of Durban and Cape Town. Whatever the claims, we would soon find out.

I liked Dean right away. I can't remember what I said when we met, but no doubt it was along the lines of reminding him that I had yet to lose a

Molokai. Not only that, I had won seven to his three. We continued with this hard-hitting, good-natured banter right up until the start of the race, and we are friends to this day. That's certainly saying something, as over the years we have had some fierce battles around the world, not only in Hawaii but also in South Africa, Hong Kong, Australia and French Polynesia.

In my first local press interview, I predicted that South Africans would be the first three paddlers across the finishing line. That sounded brash for someone who hadn't done the race in five years, but I was confident that Herman and I were in the form of our lives, and that Brett would be able to keep up with our blistering pace. Stretch was good, but I thought if the Aussies could beat any of us, it would be him.

The Hawaiian media had a field day, saying I talked the talk but querying whether I could walk the walk. That was how I liked it, and I hoped it would rattle Dean a little. In any event, our arrival generated a lot of interest and that is something the Molokai organisers always thanked me for. They had only reluctantly barred me in 1990 after unbearable international pressure, which I understood, and whenever I could I always repaid their loyalty.

We had two weeks to shake off jet lag, do some intense training, and familiarise Herman, Brett and Stretch with the turbulent vagaries of the Channel of Bones before the big day. I was happy with our training sessions and we were all close to one another in the warm-up races – hence my 'clean sweep' prediction to the press.

However, for the first time, I wasn't racing a Chalup-ski. In fact, all four of us would be competing in Hayden-skis, a craft designed by Hayden Kenny, Grant's father. This was a calculated decision as the last five Molokais had been won by paddlers in Hayden-skis, and we decided it would be far easier to buy surfskis in Hawaii than risk damaging our own ones in the eighteen-hour flight over. The Hayden is a traditional ski used by surf lifesaving clubs; it has more rocker – or curvature – to give stability in the wave zone, but it's not as fast as a longer, narrower boat. My preference is obviously the super-quick Chalup-ski, but as most of the top guys were racing Haydens, I was willing to take my chances.

As always, the *Maggie Joe* was my escort boat, but this time we bent the rules as the rest of the team didn't have a spare $1 000 to hire their own boats. Consequently, on the entry form, Stretch, Herman and Brett also listed the *Maggie Joe* as seconding them, which wasn't entirely legal but I figured we would get away with it as most of the official attention would be on me and Dean. The night before the race was, once again, spent cramped in a single hotel room with our squad catnapping on the floor. So despite racing in Springbok colours, nothing had changed since I first raced in 1983.

The starter's gun fired soon after sunrise, and from the word go, Herman and I pulled ahead of the pack. Within an hour, it was a two-horse race. We were neck and neck; one of us would surge ahead on a good wave, only to lose the lead when the other got a better ride. Brett was several minutes behind, followed by Dean in fourth place.

For three hours and almost fifty kilometres, Herman and I were within spitting distance of each other, straining to get an edge that seemed as elusive as a mirage. Just as I thought I had dropped him, he would catch an accelerating wave, spray flying like sparklers off his bow, and scream into the lead. His exhilaration was short-lived – sometimes only lasting a few seconds – as I would then catch an even bigger roller and furiously haul him in. My elation would be equally brief as he surged ahead on the next fast-running set. It was a non-stop, supremely strength-sapping yo-yo, but it was also possibly the most exciting duel many had witnessed. As someone on the escort boats yelled 'Oscar's in front!', Herman would rip past me.

It was blisteringly hot and I knew the final three kilometres when we turned into the twenty-five-knot headwind would be purgatory. However, I was confident I had the edge as I had won more races than him, ranging from the Surf Ironman to the Texan Challenge. This was my eighth Molokai compared to his first, but even so, I was more physically spent than I had ever been before. That alone didn't worry me, as I knew from countless contests fought to the absolute wire, that exhaustion is in the mind. No matter how bad you think your fatigue is, your body is capable of more. To reach that mystical, undefinable flame in the far depth of your soul takes training, and all endurance athletes have it. It is not a superhuman feat; we all can do it if we are willing to pay the price.

I knew Herman was willing to pay that price. I knew his pain threshold was above phenomenal. In fact, out of all competitors I have raced against, he is the toughest. But I also know him well, which gives me an added advantage. I grew up with him in the same house. We have laughed, fought, argued, competed against, mocked and ribbed each other all our lives. We are brothers not only in blood. We share the same will to win, the same attitude. It's hardwired into us. Neither of us knows how to surrender.

However, while I am gregarious, Herman is taciturn with a laconic sense of humour. His favourite quip is that he likes finishing first so no one is ahead of him at the pub afterwards. Outwardly he shows little, if any, emotion.

But don't be fooled. Much of that is a charade. Under that icy demeanour is a fiery temperament, and Herman hates losing as much as I do. Probably even more. When I lose, I move on as I realise that agonising over something that has already happened does nothing but corrode your gut. Also, I rationalise why I lost (even if it's just saying the other guy was lucky), but Herman broods over it. I knew if he lost this race it would rankle him forever. Maybe I could play on that.

The fact that we were still neck and neck after fifty kilometres, to have gone that fast for that long in such harsh conditions, dying from heat, fatigue and thirst, showed what great condition we were in. We were both at the peak of our game. But still, neither of us knew how strong the other was. I could only guess how much the past three torturous hours had drained him, and no doubt he was thinking the same about me. The only thing we both knew was that at China Walls, when we turned into a near gale, the sprint to the finish was going to be a metaphorical bloodbath.

As we reached the Walls, I shouted over to him: 'Herman. Do you want to come in as a tie or do you want to race?'

Herman kept paddling. For a while he didn't answer. Then, without looking at me, he said, 'How will you make sure that we will come in together?'

'We hold onto each other's skis and go across the line. Then they can't split us up.'

'How will I know you won't sneak ahead at the last second? And catch me for a sucker?'

Despite my screaming muscles, I almost smiled. I was his brother and he didn't trust me. That was Herman.

'I won't.'

He nodded, and just before the finishing line we grabbed each other's skis. Neither of us had held onto anything as tightly before. We drifted over together, our bows exactly equal.

Brett came in third, fulfilling my prediction of a South African clean sweep.

For the first time, the Molokai had resulted in a draw after almost three and a half hours of the most punishing conditions imaginable. I don't think it will happen again. Certainly not with two brothers.

The press loved it, hyping up the 'brotherly love' aspect as it was a great media angle. In fact, it almost got awkward as I knew without doubt that our sibling ties would be sorely tested in future races. This was no clairvoyant insight on my part. Instead it was the cold reality that, at the level on which Herman and I were competing, there was no room for sentimentality. We had won a great race together, but there would also be some not-so-great races. Not only that, it is a fact of life that contests are not always decided on the water. And while winning is not everything, which may sound surprising coming from me, it sure as hell is better than losing unfairly.

That's what happened four years later when Herman and I squared up against each other in the 1999 Heineken International Ocean Kayak race in French Polynesia.

This was a new event, attracting quality entrants from around the world, and the course was a tough fifty-two-kilometre crossing between the islands of Raiatea and Bora Bora. Also in the line-up was Tahitian paddler Lewis Laughlin, who was fast making a name for himself as a superlative surfskier and outrigger canoe racer. A big guy with shoulders as wide as an albatross's wingspan, the press dubbed him *le phénoménal* as he seemed unbeatable on the South Pacific islands.

French Polynesia has some of the strictest marine environment laws in the world, and rightly so. Any ocean race there has to avoid the pristine shallow reefs surrounding the islands. Even a kayak rudder can cause damage by scraping the fragile coral, and at the pre-race briefing we were specifically warned that we would have to go around clearly marked buoys to avoid eco-sensitive areas.

Lewis, Herman and I were closely grouped at the start, but after an hour or so I started pulling away. I was paddling fast, feeling relaxed and comfortable, and thought that unless there was some major mishap, I had this race in the bag. Then, as we approached one of the coral-reef markers near Bora Bora that we had to go around, I noticed Lewis cutting inside. Even more astonishingly, I saw Herman following him.

'Herman,' I yelled. 'Don't be a bloody idiot. Stick to the course.'

Clare, who was on the official boat next to the leaders, distinctly remembers hearing me shouting to Herman. So did others on the boat, including some marshals.

I carried on paddling the designated course, but in doing so I lost my lead to those taking the short cut. Herman, going beautifully, overtook Lewis and was first on the beach at Bora Bora. Next was Lewis, then me – furious, as I was the only one in the leading trio who had followed race rules. I asked

Herman what the hell was going on, and he said he had merely followed Lewis as he assumed the local paddler knew the route better than he did.

I then complained to the race committee. They were aware of the alleged infringement but said they could do nothing unless there was an official objection. Not only that, I would have to pay for the objection to be investigated.

This put me in a quandary. Should I launch an appeal against my own brother? Or should I shrug and let sleeping dogs lie, knowing that I had at least won a moral victory?

I have no problem losing, much as I hate it, but it has to be a fair fight. This was anything but that. The winners had taken a short cut, unwittingly or not. In other words, the most fundamental rule of a fair contest had been broken.

Also, there was the sensitive question of prize money. The winner pocketed $4000 – a fair chunk of change when converted into South African rands. Travelling around the world to race surfskis was expensive, and with a wife and two kids, I needed that money.

My objection was upheld. Herman and Lewis were given time penalties and I was declared the winner. There was a huge uproar, as even some who agreed that Herman and Lewis should be penalised were uneasy with brother lodging an objection against brother. I think the key difference was between the amateur paddlers, who thought it was 'unsporting' to take sibling rivalry to such extremes, and the professional paddlers, who know that at top level, sport is about winning. And winning fairly.

Herman was livid. He didn't speak to me for several weeks, and to make everything even more acrimonious, he, Clare and I were on the same plane back to England where we would spend a few days with friends before flying home. It was not a festive occasion.

Thankfully, we have all moved on from that. What might have helped a little was that a few months later we had another do-or-die dice, this time in Canada, which Herman won by out-paddling and outsmarting me.

The race, a one-off called the World Sea Kayak Championship, was in the St Lawrence Seaway finishing at Pointe-au-Père at the mouth of the St Lawrence River. It's the scene of Canada's worst maritime disaster, the sinking of the passenger ship *Empress of Ireland*, and has huge emotional significance for the people of Quebec. Dubbed 'Canada's *Titanic*', the *Empress* was rammed in thick fog by the *Storstad*, a Norwegian coal ship, in May 1914, and 1012 people died. So we would be racing in waters steeped in tragic history.

It turned out to be a brutal duel between us as the water was fractionally above freezing – maybe three or four degrees Celsius – and as flat as a sheet of paper. There wasn't a breath of wind, so the contest was little more than a grinding slog for close on fifty kilometres. It could not have been more different from our Molokai joint win, where we had strong winds, big waves and the sun hammering down like a furnace. But it was equally tense with Herman and I once again neck and neck, slipstreaming each other and trying every trick we knew to get whatever edge we could.

Unfortunately for me, in the final kilometre I misjudged the angle to the finishing line and Herman had enough juice to pip me by ten seconds. He took the better line, and all credit to him for winning an exceptional race.

Today, he and I seldom talk about those two races, but I still silently chuckle. The fact that there was such intense sibling rivalry made us both infinitely better paddlers, and my success was in no small measure thanks to him often breathing down my neck. When he wasn't in front of me, that is.

Ironically, the prize money in Canada was $10 000, more than twice the amount for the Raiatea to Bora Bora race. So for Herman, revenge was not only sweet but also profitable.

It was money I needed badly. That narrow loss was possibly the most expensive fistful of seconds in my life, as at the time we had suddenly been thrown into a turmoil of financial mayhem. It happened with astonishing swiftness. One moment I was on the brink of being able to retire comfortably at the age of thirty-five – the next I was on the bones of my butt.

LESSONS LEARNT

HAVE COURAGE IN YOUR CONVICTIONS. My decision to lodge an objection to what I considered an obvious infringement of the rules did not sit easily with some. I am confident that I made the right decision, but sometimes there are no right or wrong answers. In the end, you have to be the judge of your own actions, and also live with them.

DON'T BE SCARED TO MAKE DEALS, no matter how off the charts they may seem. Instead of going for a 'bloodbath' with Herman after an epic ocean duel lasting well over three hours, we crossed together. Some may consider that we both took the easy way out. Maybe. But even today, nearly three decades later, that race is considered to be one of the most memorable in the Molokai's magnificent history, and it always will be. It was worth it.
  Business deals can be the same.

The Chalupsky children on holiday on a Transkei beach in the early 1970s. From left: Walter, Herman, Alma and me.

The family just before my mother died in 1981. From left: Alma, Walter, Mercia, me, Paul and Herman.

My first win in the Port Elizabeth to East London race, 1981, pipping surfski legend Tony Scott by a mere seventy seconds. The race was marred by allegations of us slipstreaming each other, but Scotty and I are still friends to this day.

The South African national team that competed in Spain, Ireland and Scotland in 1981, pictured with our trophies. Matt Carlisle (back row, second left) and I (back row, third left) came second in the famous Sella Descent, but won almost every other race in which we competed together.

Photo: Graham Spence

Meeting Tom Selleck at the Outrigger Canoe Club on Waikiki beach in 1985. It was my third Molokai win in a row and 'Magnum', an avid surfskier, told me he had followed the race on his radio.

Lee McGregor about to throw a punch during the heats of the 1985 Iron Man championship. He said I swore at him in the surf – and thanks to that memorable fight, we both lost the race. Two years later he invited me to crew on his yacht during the Mauritius to Durban Beachcomber Crossing ocean race.

Lee McGregor's crew aboard his yacht *Hulett Aluminium* during the 1987 Beachcomber Crossing. I am at the back, fourth from left, while Lee is crouching on the far left. The youngster on the right is Lee's son Hank, whom I competed against in the 2006/7 World Surfski Cup championship series.

Rammed ... Herman (front) and I 'T-boning' the Spanish kayak that deliberately tipped us over as we were about to take the lead in the Villaviciosa race on the Spanish circuit in 1988. We were ordered to pay for repairs.

Marrying Clare on 9 July 1988 at the Holy Trinity Catholic Church on Durban's Musgrave Road. It was the same church where I had been christened.

Taking up golf in 1991. It was the only international sport in which South Africans could compete, albeit as individual sportsmen and not representing our country.

At the 1992 Barcelona Olympics with Aussie K4 bronze medallist Ian Rowling and South Africa's Zola Budd-Pieterse.

With the late great Mark Perrow at the 1992 Olympics.

CITADEL

A NEW NAME FOR AN ESTABLISHED INVESTMENT GROUP

In recent years personal investment planning on the highest level has always been associated with the name JMM. This group has now changed its name to Citadel Investment Services. A new name. The same top-level expertise. Innovative thinking, to let modern investors experience a powerful difference.

The group, JMM Investment Services, which has become well known for its unique approach to personal financial planning, has changed its name and will now be known as Citadel Investment Services.

The group specialises in financial planning and investment advice for professional people and individuals who are personally responsible for managing their own assets.

could be insuffic
had been paid at

Specific bene
• The service is
  different comp
  management.
• Only investm
  African finan

CITADEL TAKES THE LEAD IN INVESTMENT MANAGEMENT

Citadel's directors. Front, from left, Wikus Marais, Louis Fourie (Chairman), Chris Marais (Managing Director). Behind, from left, Hennie Fransen, Johan Marais, BM Griesel and Oscar Chalupsky.

Founders of Citadel, 1993. Front row: Wikus Marais, Louis Fourie and Chris Marias. Back row: Hennie Fransen, Johan Marais, R.M. Griesel and me.

The winning Springbok team at the 1995 Molokai, when Herman and I tied for first place. From left: Adriaan 'Stretch' Struwig, me, Herman, Brett Pengelly and Tim Guard.

The original founders of Epic Kayaks, 1999. From left: me, Greg Barton and Martin Deale.

Racing the Dusi Canoe Marathon with South African national soccer coach Clive Barker in 1998.

Paddling with soccer legend Doc Khumalo in the 1999 Dusi.

The Dusi with Miss South Africa, Peggy-Sue Khumalo, in 2000.

Boxer Baby Jake Matlala in the 2001 Dusi. Baby Jake couldn't swim a stroke.

Overtaking Dean Gardiner at the Portlock Cliffs for my tenth Molokai win in 2003.

At the 2003 Molokai. From left: Joe Glickman, me, actress Cameron Diaz, Herman and Greg Barton.

Catching Aussie speedster Nathan Baggaley and winning the 2005 Molokai.

Neck and neck with Herman while racing The Doctor in Australia, 2005. I won the race.

Photo: Anthony Grote

Winning the 2006/7 Surfski World Cup championship series against Hank McGregor in Durban. I overtook Hank in the final kilometre against all odds by using the winds and currents to my advantage.

Herman, Andy Leith and I won the K3 section in the 2011 Fish River Marathon.

Running a rapid in the 2013 Dusi with popular TV show *Idols* judge Unathi Msengana. She was my only celebrity who trained for the race.

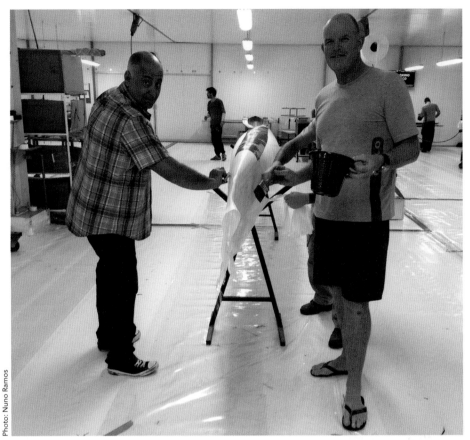

Nelo Kayaks owner and founder Manuel Ramos and I shaping the future of Nelo Surfski.

Above left: Paddling at my hometown of Vila do Conde in Portugal. *Above right*: Me at Nazaré, Portugal, 2015. The waves were peaking at more than twenty metres, but because the photo was taken at the lighthouse high above the beach, they look smaller. To give a true indication, my surfski was 5.6 metres long, which puts this particular wave at about twelve metres (almost forty feet).

At the 2016 Molokai with previous winners Herman (left) and Clint Robinson (right).

Me with good friend and arch-rival Dean Gardiner after winning the Hawaiian Coast Relay in 2017.

Racing with doubles partner Seth Koppes on my last Molokai, 2018.

With my family, Luke, Clare and Hannah, in 2016.

With top professional golfer Ernie Els at the Dimension Data Pro-Am, Fancourt, in 2020. Ernie sponsored me in the 2005 Molokai for my eleventh win.

My last race before being diagnosed with myeloma cancer – the Shaw and Partners Doctor in Perth, 23 November 2019. Following a slow start, I am on the left in a black Nelo surfski, wearing a green top.

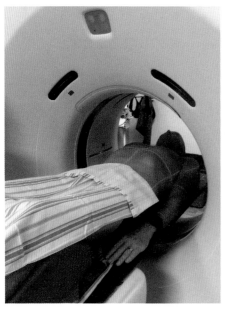

Receiving radiation therapy. The exact spot was mapped with three tattoos: one on my chest and two on either side of my ribs so that the radiation laser could accurately target the cancerous lump.

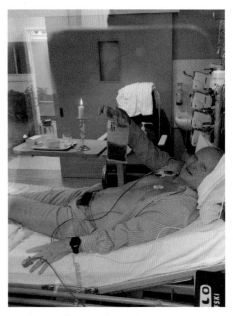

My stem cell transplant, 18 June 2020, where I received my life-saving bone marrow.

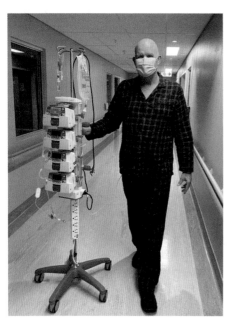

My daily exercise – shuffling down the narrow hospital corridor dragging my drip stand. I was on intravenous drips around the clock.

I was only permitted to walk for exercise from the day I was officially diagnosed in late November 2019 until December 2020.

16

Hard times

Oscar Chalupsky & Associates had several bumper years in succession. My business plan of targeting young professionals and being transparent about commission costs was reaping rewards.

So much so that in 1997 I won a best salesman award, which was a significant honour in the highly competitive insurance industry. It also marked a turning point in my life after a chance meeting with a television reporter whom I bumped into at the awards ceremony. We chatted for a while, then he said, 'I want to introduce you to Johan Marais. Come with me.'

I knew the name. Johan Marais was a Springbok rugby player and had been a member of the squad during the tumultuous tour of New Zealand in 1981. Continuous pitch invasions by protestors and flour bombs thrown from an overhead plane hammered the final nail in the coffin of international sport during the apartheid era. Johan went into business after that, forming a successful company called JMM – Johan Marais Makelaars (brokers).

Johan comes from an illustrious business family, as one brother is a Cambridge-educated economist, another a computer scientist and the third an actuary. Johan himself is a Bachelor of Commerce graduate, so I was introduced to some big hitters. He was interested in what I was doing and indicated that our two companies could be a mutually beneficial fit. While JMM, which was based in Pretoria, was looking after clients with large amounts of money, I was targeting a vibrant emerging market consisting mainly of young Durban professionals, particularly doctors, dentists, architects and lawyers. The synergy was self-evident.

That initial chat led to several others where I met the other Marais brothers, and where it was suggested that JMM and Oscar Chalupsky & Associates should join forces. I would run the Durban operation, and while JMM got the revenue stream from my brokerage, I had access to their advanced computer systems and the backing of a company with impressive financial clout. Our core business was planning and investment advice for people responsible for managing their own assets, and we became the first company offering a complete financial portfolio. In other words, we were a one-stop shop, handling everything from insurance, wills and estate planning to investment options, asset management and retirement advice. It was an effective package and we kept getting bigger and bigger.

Our success attracted one of the country's richest investors, accelerating our growth to even higher levels. The company was revamped and renamed Citadel, and as a founder member of the new venture, I was on the board that appointed the current CEO. We were catapulted into a different league, with full-time lawyers and accountants on our payroll.

Then we did a deal with Deloitte & Touche, where Citadel was chosen as the 'personal wealth preservation' section of the accounting company. This was the proverbial big time – on steroids. As a multibillion-rand corporation, Citadel was now a serious player in the economy, and as I had a 2 per cent shareholding, I was in a strong position.

Or so I thought. As it turned out, for me the 'big time' was not all it was cracked up to be. I was the only director without a university degree and I assume that some of the other head honchos were uncomfortable with that. Nobody ever said it to me directly, but the fact that I was not an academic 'fit' was hinted at more than once. Also, I was told the company was pulling back from some of the wealth-management portfolios that I had been involved in. So, to cut a long story short, my career with Citadel was over, and all that was left to do was pack my desk.

I was allowed to retain my 2 per cent of Citadel shares, but a restraint-of-trade clause stipulated that I could not start any company in competition, and, as I recall it, I could no longer remain in the insurance and investment industry.

To this day, neither Clare nor I are exactly sure what happened. To find out, I would have had to take legal action. This put me in a quandary as I had an impressive client base and had sold a lot of policies and investment portfolios on behalf of Citadel. If I suddenly decided to sue the board, it could adversely affect my clients.

I have been called many things – egocentric and arrogant, among others – some perhaps deservedly so. However, I am a subscriber to the Muhammad Ali school of thought that if you are good at something, you should not pretend otherwise. I make no apologies for that, and I'm happy to take such criticism on the chin. But one thing I have never been called is disloyal. To me, loyalty is not only an essential quality, it is the fundamental foundation of a successful life. So to suddenly tell my clients not to invest in Citadel or that I was leaving involuntarily would be intensely disloyal to them, as I had sold portfolios on the explicit premise that it was the best wealth-management company in the country. My clients were king.

I packed up my desk and left. Or, to be more accurate, the intensely loyal Clare packed for me.

I needed to sell my shares, not only to have money to live on but to invest in new projects now that I was unable to continue in the finance industry. I was about to sell the whole lot in one go when a Citadel investor, one of South Africa's most prominent businessmen, said I would be crazy to sell all my shares. He said that soon they would be worth ten times what they currently were and I should hold on.

This flew in the face of all the cautionary advice I routinely gave to my clients. It was like a mantra: never borrow excess money; always repay debts promptly; and if you are no longer directly involved in a business, get the hell out of it altogether. You have to have skin in the game.

The third caution was the most crucial. I did not want to be a mere shareholder/bystander in Citadel, as that meant I would not be in control of my destiny. But, hey – the guy giving me the advice not to sell all my shares was one of the wealthiest South Africans. Maybe I should listen to him.

So instead of selling all my shares, valued at about R8 million at the time, I sold enough for us to live on and invest in future ventures. As money was required at various subsequent stages, I sold further tranches of shares, bearing in mind that Citadel was not listed. After a couple of years, and contrary to my wealthy advisor's prediction, Citadel's shares plummeted. They went from huge to little more than a fire sale.

That was why it was vital at the time that I entered races with prize money, such as the Raiatea to Bora Bora in French Polynesia. I have never required an incentive to win, but being broke certainly gave competition a sharper edge.

I desperately needed to start earning money again and started Chalupsky Paddling & Adventure School with my old friend and kayaking partner Mat Carlisle. The name says it all; we wanted to bring back the adventure in kayaking and surfskiing, so we started sunrise and sunset paddles at Vetchie's Pier in Durban, as well as team-building events. It wasn't only surf adventures though, as we also set up a kayaking operation at Inanda Dam outside Hillcrest, which forms a major section of the Dusi Canoe Marathon. There we rigged a gut-swooping zipline, and Mat and I did everything we could to make it a fun paddling expedition, spiced with excitement and adrenaline. We also added 'extras' to the itinerary. As the Mahatma Gandhi Memorial was nearby in Phoenix township (where a settlement had been established by the anti-colonial activist in 1904), we took our clients to visit that unique bit of South African history as well. Although it had nothing to do with paddling, it was particularly popular with overseas clients.

However, despite plenty of rave reviews, it's hard to make much money from paddling adventure schools, and I needed to get involved in something more substantial.

It soon came my way – this time mixing business and sport. Even better, I would be linking up with former Molokai competitor and Olympic double-gold medallist Greg Barton.

It was called Epic Kayaks.

LESSON LEARNT

BELIEVE IN FOLLOWING your own advice. As an investment advisor, I was paid to give accurate advice. If the advice was wrong, people lost money. Investment advice is more measurable than anything else, so I made sure it was right.

And yet – I stupidly didn't follow my own advice. Instead, I listened to one of South Africa's wealthiest men in the star-struck belief that because he was massively richer than I was, he knew better.

The end result was that instead of retiring comfortably at the age of thirty-five and following my dream of being a full-time sportsman, I was looking for work. That is one of my biggest mistakes ever. I paid the price for many years, as did my family when we fell on hard times.

17

An Epic adventure

As mentioned, I first met Greg Barton in Hawaii during the 1989 Molokai race. He was hyped as the new threat, and as an Olympic double-gold medallist, I took that seriously.

Greg ended up several places behind me in that race and was the first to admit that being a flat-water specialist was vastly different from racing on the heaving ocean.

I met him again at the Barcelona Olympics, where he won a bronze in the K-1 1000-metre event, and we kept in contact. Despite his impressive sprint record, Greg is one of the humblest guys I know, almost to the point of shyness. But don't be fooled; he is a near genius. He graduated from the University of Michigan *cum laude* in mechanical engineering, and with all that arcane 'mad-scientist-gold-medallist' stuff in his head, you won't find anyone who understands the lore of paddling better than he does.

Our relationship was cemented when he invented the first adjustable split-shaft paddle. It was handcrafted, superlight and a masterpiece, the best in the world, so I asked him to sponsor me with free paddles. I expected him to jump at the chance, but Greg was not interested.

'Buy your own,' he said. Not only that, but he charged me full price. It was the first time in my life that I had bought a paddle as I'd always had sponsorships. In this case, I reached for my wallet and bought two on the spot, such was the quality of Greg's work. That's one lesson I have learnt: never skimp on equipment. However, I did ask if I could be his agent in South Africa, so I got something out of the deal.

Several years later, while running my outdoor adventure school, I designed and built a double kayak that I knew was far better than any other top-end plastic recreational craft. It was stable and fast, and I decided to test its saleability on the international market. The best way to do that was to exhibit it at the largest outdoor trade show in the world and see first-hand what the reception would be.

Outdoor Retailer is a summer and winter trade show held in Salt Lake

City, Utah, and no one of note in the international kayaking world misses it. I knew Greg would be there marketing his paddles, so I asked if I could stay with him. I was, after all, his South African agent. Greg replied that space was limited as he had rented a small room that he was sharing with his production manager, but I could sleep on the floor. So once again, nothing had changed for me.

I flew to Atlanta, hired a car, strapped my demo kayak onto the roof and drove 3 000 kilometres to Salt Lake City. I knew the show was big, but even so, I was staggered when I arrived. There were about 10 000 exhibitors, with some stalls such as Hobie Kayaks covering more than 1 000 square metres. Others were equally vast.

Unfortunately, Greg's stall was not one of them. In fact, I think it was the smallest at the show, barely a square metre, as he only had a handful of paddles on display. As all are handcrafted, it is the complete opposite of mass production.

He then introduced me to Mark, his manufacturing manager who would be my roommate. We shook hands, and to my surprise Mark promptly handed me a set of earplugs. 'I snore like a chainsaw,' he said.

That didn't worry me as I was asleep most nights before Mark – except once, when I decided to take advantage of the exhibitors' hospitality and turned in late after him. It was a fundamental mistake, for he wasn't kidding. Suffice it to say that even a chainsaw would have been embarrassed by that noise.

I showed Greg my kayak and floated the idea of us going into business, manufacturing it for the mass market. I could see he was interested in the design, but he said that plastic boats were a waste of time as the markup was so small. The only way to be profitable was to make composite crafts, even though they are labour intensive and expensive to build.

I shook my head. 'Greg, you're talking about America. Composite is not expensive in South Africa. There is no shortage of labour. We can build entire ranges of kayaks at knockdown prices. Plastic and composite.'

We looked at other kayaks at the show, comparing demand, quality and costing. My demo model was well received, so we decided we could do good business by combining high American buying power with low South African production costs.

However, Greg knew the American market well and stressed that we should initially only build sea kayaks rather than the tippy, ultrafast surfskis used by elite athletes. Sea kayaks are mainly for recreational use, and as America has lengthy Pacific and Atlantic coastlines, Greg said that even at full production we would never be able to supply all outlets.

We obviously needed start-up money and I was selected as the 'rainmaker' to find someone with deep pockets. As it happened, I knew of a South African living in Massachusetts whom I thought would be interested. Martin Deale had headed several start-up businesses back home and had pioneered the manufacture of plastic trolley carts in America, so this could be right up his street.

I was right. After stopping off at Boston on my way home and showing Martin detailed spreadsheets of what Greg and I planned to do, he agreed we were onto a winner. He was happy to invest, and with that we got the critical financial greenlight.

We formalised everything in December 1999, with Greg, Martin and me as the founder members of Epic Kayaks. I then set up a facility in Durban, which initially would only be making Epic paddles, as we planned to sub-contract our kayak building to other companies.

To run the paddle production, my youngest brother, Walter, joined us as a shareholder. Walter is a talented and experienced tool and die maker, and it was good to have him on board. Greg came out to South Africa to set up the production of his designer paddles, installing heated presses and also giving Walter a masterclass in production. He was happy with Walter's work and soon our Epic paddle-manufacturing section was going ahead at full steam.

Unfortunately, it was not the same story with our kayaks. Our first design combined my ocean-racing and Greg's flat-water expertise, resulting in a straight bow instead of the traditional banana-shaped sea kayaks, making it both stable and fast. However, a good design is worth little without manufac-turing excellence, and none of the factories we appointed as subcontractors could meet our stringent quality demands.

Consequently, I had to reject boat after boat. In fact, by the time the next Outdoor Retailer show in Salt Lake City came around, we didn't have a single completed boat to exhibit.

This was a potential disaster. Without exposure at such a prestigious show, retailers would not know who the heck we were. It was imperative that we had our product on display, otherwise we would have no foothold on the international market. But the only semi-decent boat we had was incomplete, as the hatch cover had not been moulded.

I decided we had no option but to get the boat to America as soon as possible and wing a sales pitch. We could field any inconvenient questions such as 'Hey, where's the hatch?' by thinking on our feet once we were there. Otherwise, sales for that year would fall off a cliff.

We flew the hatch-less boat, called a 16X Sea Kayak, to Utah and held our breath as we took it to the trade show's testing pool – a large man-made structure where potential clients can try out new craft on the water. This was not going to be a simple off-the-shelf sale; Outdoor Retailer buyers are some of the most astute of any in the world. They won't part with dollars unless they get a genuine feel of the craft's seaworthiness and test it in anger, so to speak.

At the test pool the first question, unsurprisingly, was 'Where's the hatch?' I was expecting this and answered, 'We deliberately kept the cover off so people can look inside and see for themselves the quality of craftsmanship.'

Soon Martin Deale and I were repeating that to anyone who asked, and it was not only willingly accepted but many even thought it was a good idea. They could see exactly what they were buying.

Orders started coming in like crazy. We grasped right away that there was a huge pent-up demand for this type of sea kayak, so we instructed the factory to make moulds for new 3.6- and 5.5-metre models. We now had a range of three boats on our books. Even though we had yet to produce a finished product, orders were pouring in.

Several months after the show, I hired a kombi and set off for a sales safari down the east coast of America. For three long months I drove 25 000 kilometres, from the Florida Keys to Bangor in Maine, close to the Canadian border, stopping off at every kayak retailer I could find.

It was a fascinating trip, not only from a sales point of view but also as a way to get to know that amazing country. Best of all, I experienced first-hand the incredible hospitality of ordinary Americans. In almost every city, town or village I visited, dealers would invite me home for a meal or to spend the night with their families. Not only that, but they referred me to retailers in the next town, who would also open up their homes. Even though I had a sleeping bag in my kombi, I seldom had to use it.

That roadshow was a massive success and I sold our entire production quota for the year. Every boat that we could build was now pre-ordered. For me, Martin and Greg, it was beyond our wildest dreams.

But reality soon hit home – and hard. We could sell our kayaks, but our subcontractors could not deliver on their end of the deal. This was not due to overestimating our production capacity but because of poor workmanship. Every boat rejected meant it had to be built again, and the backlog grew and grew until the molehill became a mountain. So while we were making a lot of money on paper, not much of it materialised as we could not invoice on undelivered goods. None of the directors drew a salary for most of that year.

It got worse for me and Clare. We had started renovating our house in Durban's Morningside suburb on the strength of Epic's record sales, but thanks to non-deliveries we were now so broke we had to rent the house out. Not only that, but the builder had done shoddy work, so we refused to pay the full amount. The case went to arbitration, which Clare handled as I was so busy at the time, and fortunately we won. However, the upshot was that we could no longer afford to live in our own home.

By now we had a new partner, Charles Brand, a Cape Town–based hotelier and avid windsurfer and surfskier, who had bought out Martin and my brother Walter. He saw that we urgently needed to make our own boats, so with Charles at the helm as our chair, we set up a factory in Umgeni Road, Durban.

Running parallel to this, I had the idea of developing and manufacturing a revolutionary plastic rotomoulded kayak we named the Getaway. I designed it with my godfather Gordon Rowe, a legend among the lifesaving and paddling community and one of the pioneers of the Dusi Canoe Marathon. Roto-moulded kayaks are traditionally heavy, but the Getaway set a new standard for lightweight plastic boats; it was extremely efficient, streamlined and easy to handle. Dealer interest was huge and sales generated from this kayak kept the company afloat, pun intended. To this day, I still smile whenever I pass distinctive yellow Getaways strapped to car roofs on South African roads.

Unfortunately, once again we couldn't keep up with demand and deliver on time. Manufacturing kayaks is scientific and precise, and working with costly materials and processes is difficult. Our biggest problem was that not all our factory staff were skilled kayak builders. For example, one supervisor who'd had much success in the clothing industry didn't know what a rudder was for. Even worse, as far as I was concerned, these managers ignored the fact that I had been constructing kayaks since I was fourteen and knew every twist and turn of the manufacturing process. Not only had I personally built them, but I had won many races in them. Yet because I was a sales direc-tor, no one took much notice of my technical input or feedback. As a result, quality problems persisted.

Consequently, it took a superhuman effort to keep the brand's reputation intact – so much so that I spent more time putting out fires than I did selling our products. Whenever I had to reject a subpar consignment from the factory, I spun white lies to the dealers about how excessive orders were hampering delivery. So while the overall quality of Epic Kayaks on the market didn't suffer – and no one disputed that our boats were top class – our reputation to distribute on time certainly did.

For me, quality was non-negotiable. On one occasion a dealer from Sweden phoned, seething with fury, claiming that the finish on every kayak he had ordered was substandard. I got on a plane and knocked on his door in Stockholm the next day. He was astonished to see me and I immediately started doing some serious damage control. I apologised profusely, took back the entire order and refunded him. I then flew to Denmark and sold the consignment to a dealer in Copenhagen, albeit at a substantial discount. This resulted in happy customers but still no money.

Despite this, Greg and I attended every summer Outdoor Retailer and without fail sold out our entire annual production quota. We became a familiar duo at the trade fair and created our own marketing vibe. On one occasion we staged a tug-of-war contest in the testing pool – the Olympian versus the ocean champion – and from a marketplace perspective, we were doing fantastically.

Sadly, the reality was different. Great designs from engineering maestro Greg Barton that incorporated our combined forty-odd years of racing, and huge interest from dealers and the general paddling public, were severely hampered by behind-the-scenes manufacturing and delivery issues. To compound matters, we were using a sophisticated composite process called INfusion, which was so advanced that it was not applied by any other kayak company at the time. Our factory struggled to get it right and our rejection rate was unsustainable.

The more I pointed this out, the more unpopular I became. The various factory managers believed that the problem was not the quality of the boats – it was my complaining. As a result, I was banned from going to the factory and was moved with my family to Epic Kayak's headquarters in Charleston, South Carolina, to concentrate on the American market. The factory remained in Durban, unhampered by my so-called meddling.

Despite this, quality problems persisted, and eventually I said there was a simple solution to the problem. The factory manager must come out to

Charleston with the next container of kayaks, and we would open it together. Each boat was boxed, and we would unpack them individually and grade them A, B or C. 'A' boats would be fit for market, 'B' would be sold at a discount, and 'C' rejected outright.

The first kayak we pulled out had a pair of rusty scissors in the hull, left behind by sloppy workers. The next had a hammer that had been discarded in the stern. I watched, mouth wide with shock. This was even worse than I thought. Surely these were fluke mistakes?

Sadly, they weren't. It soon became a joke. A significant number of the crafts we opened had rubbish inside them, ranging from dirty paintbrushes and old screwdrivers to used sheets of sandpaper and unattached nuts and bolts, all lying loose in the hulls as no one had bothered to check. It was tantamount to a surgeon leaving a scalpel in a patient's body, and for our reputation it was equally damning.

'You guys have smuggled out more tools in these kayaks than a pirate ship,' I said.

It wasn't only discarded tools. Some kayaks had such a rough finish that a paddler would cut his hands just getting in. Others had blisters in the resin that looked like bubble wrap. It was glaringly obvious that not one of the boats had been properly inspected, confirmed by the manager squirming with embarrassment next to me and saying, 'I don't know what happened here.'

My point was made. Production was slapdash, and that was being polite. But what was the production team going to do about it?

That question was taken out of our hands a few months later when a fire swept through the premises, gutting the entire factory. Thankfully we were covered by insurance, as Charles was fastidious about that, having experienced a hotel fire in the past. The manager left, and I was called back to South Africa to set up a replacement production plant.

So from being banned, I was now asked to come home and supervise the building of a new factory. This was a huge upheaval for my family since we had just started to settle into the South Carolinian way of life when we found ourselves packing a container, again, to relocate back to Durban.

No sooner had we arrived home than a senior staff member took the company to court, alleging unfair dismissal. This was another stressful issue, taking up much of my time while I was setting up the new production facility. Fortunately, we won. In fact, on hearing evidence of what I'd had to put up with, the judge openly wondered 'how on earth' I was still working for the company.

Epic's new premises were twice the size of our previous factory as we were about to bring out a new model, the V10, which would take surfski design to a new level. It was destined to be the first single footwell and fully adjustable production surfski, enhancing stability without sacrificing speed. Orders were skyrocketing and the factory was strategically situated close to Durban's harbour for bulk export shipments. We were definitely on to a winner.

A new factory manager was appointed, and for the first time there was someone in charge of production who understood that I knew what I was talking about. We were now honouring orders and delivery time frames. Quality problems declined rapidly. But in their place, new issues arose.

A key one was the AIDS epidemic sweeping the country. Within months, we were losing workers faster than we could train up new ones. It was a national tragedy and Clare regularly organised AIDS-awareness courses, which helped but could not stem the rocketing number of casualties.

Then the trade unions moved in, demanding exorbitant wage increases and going on strike when these were not met. Again, this was a national problem, and unrealistic expectations were crippling many South African industries.

After dealing with these escalating issues for close on two years, I knew that we needed a more stable operation. At the rate things were going, we would soon have to close down the factory.

As China was an emerging manufacturing giant, I searched for various businesses on the internet and found the names of three kayak manufacturers. I phoned the first, and thankfully the guy at the other end spoke perfect English – unusual in China. He said yes, they could easily do what I had in mind.

'Great,' I said. 'We're coming over.'

LESSONS LEARNT

DON'T SKIMP ON EQUIPMENT. From the moment I saw Greg's paddles, I knew I wanted one. He wouldn't sponsor me, so I paid – the first paddle I had ever bought. This was the forerunner of the high quality that we demanded of Epic products, despite major factory problems, and it was a quality we continued aspiring to throughout my tenure with the company. So whether you are a consumer or a producer, go for the best. It's cheaper in the long run.

THERE ARE NO SHORT CUTS. Despite the fact that we were making no money as so many kayaks had to be rejected, our strict quality controls were never compromised. Whenever there were problems, such as what happened with my Swedish client, I never quibbled, taking back entire consignments. As a result, Epic as a brand was not tarnished, even though our ability to deliver certainly was.

18

Smoke on the water

Despite being intricately involved in a new start-up company, I was still racing regularly. And, fortunately, I was still winning much of the time.

But, ironically, the year Epic was formed was the first time I lost a Molokai World Championship. It was in 1999, and it was to some extent due to a schoolboy error on my part.

Dean Gardiner was in the line-up looking for his seventh victory, and I knew the superb Aussie waterman was always a huge threat in howling downwind conditions. However, both Herman and I had beaten Dean in 1995, the last time I raced the Molokai, so I was confident I could do it again. But having said that, Dean had come back in 1996 to win the next three races in a row. If he won, he would be one behind my tally of eight victories.

There was a big wind as we set off, tailor-made for both me and Dean, and we took an early lead, although on different courses. I was in great shape and going strong in the gusting conditions, but with the mountainous swells it was difficult to see where the other paddlers were. There were some boats in front of me, but I was assured those were outrigger canoes that had started forty minutes ahead of us. In fact, Bob Twogood, who was in my escort boat, said I was going so well that I was bound to break the record.

I always keep something in reserve if I think I'm in front, because to go too hard when you don't have to can backfire near the finish. It's good to have something in the tank if someone catches up, and my tactics are primarily to make sure no one passes me. Conversely, if another paddler is ahead, I go flat out to either keep up or overtake.

'Are you sure I'm leading?' I asked as the escort boat came close. It was a question I repeated several times over the next hour or two. As a golden rule, my seconds have to know where the rest of the front-runners are. I know where I am – they need to know where everyone else is.

Both Bob and Clare, who was in Hawaii for the first time, assured me from the vantage point of the boat that I was in front.

'You're still on track for a record,' Bob said.

129

Suddenly, about ten kilometres from the finish, I noticed a boat ahead of me. It didn't look like an outrigger, so I called for confirmation.

I heard Bob whistle in surprise. It was Dean. For the past hour or so, we had thought he was an outrigger.

With only the final upwind section to go, I paddled furiously and started hauling him in. But it was too little, too late. I had plenty of energy left, but with a crafty racer like Dean, you cannot make the tiniest mistake. I was second across the line, bitterly disappointed but acknowledging that Dean had outthought and out-paddled me. I should have gone faster earlier on. The error was mine and mine alone. My seconds had unwittingly given me wrong information, but I still should have gone for broke earlier. It was a classic rookie blunder. But to lose to the great Dean Gardiner is no disgrace – far from it.

However, I had my revenge the following year when Dean and I squared up again. Herman was also there, and he and Dean were with me the entire way. Although the lead changed several times, it was not yo-yoing every few minutes as it had when Herman and I won jointly in 1995. But one thing was for certain: gone were the days when I led from start to finish. I was now older and the younger generation was extremely fast and just as motivated. I had to fight for every centimetre gained, and in Dean and Herman I was up against two of the best downwind ocean racers in the world.

We gave it everything we had, and I don't think any of us had a spare gasp of energy left when we crossed the finishing line at Hawaii Kai. I was first, followed by Herman, then Dean. It was my ninth win.

I didn't race the Molokai for the next two years owing to commitments with Epic Kayak roadshows, and Dean won them both. He now equalled my number of victories and the question was which one of us would reach the magical double figure first. I had to be at the next starting line or else Dean would beat me to it. There was no question about it.

However, it was just my luck that in 2003 I was up against what was said to be the most competitive field in the Molokai's history, dating back to 1977. Dean was there, of course, as well as Aussie superstar Clint Robinson, whom I first met at the Barcelona Olympics where he won a gold at the age of twenty. Since then he had won two more Olympic medals, four ICF Sprint World Championships, and been awarded the Order of Australia after winning thirty gold lifesaving medals. On top of that, I had to contend with Herman as well as Grant Kenny, and this would be the first time we had raced against each other in Hawaii since 1983. Grant's younger brother Martin, a perennial finisher in the top ten, was also there, as was *le phénoménal* Lewis Laughlin from Tahiti. Adding spice to the world-class mix was Dean's and my quest to be the first ten-times Molokai champion.

Dean and Clint set off at a blistering pace, rocketing ahead and dicing each other neck and neck across the entire channel with Herman and me chasing them. Behind us were Grant and Martin.

Then, some three hours later with surf ricocheting off the huge grey-brown rocks of Portlock Point, I put down the hammer.

First I caught Clint. Sidling up to him on the face of a fast swell, I asked, 'How're you going?'

'I'm cramping,' he said. His face was a mask of pain.

'Where's Dean, then?'

Clint pointed to an escort boat ahead. 'That's him up front.'

'Thanks. I'm going to chase him down. See you later.'

Six or seven minutes later, I pulled up level with Dean at Portlock Cliffs.

For the next few kilometres, we took turns passing each other in the swirling white water bouncing off the cliffs. Both of us had the magical figure of ten wins in our sights. I wanted it so badly I could taste it, and I'm sure Dean could as well. The question was, who would fall off the pace first?

Afterwards, Dean told journalist Joe Glickman, the finest surfski writer in the sport and a good paddler himself, what happened next. 'As I approached Oahu, my forearms started cramping. When Oscar came past, I gave it all I had for five minutes. But I didn't have enough left to respond.'[1]

I had done it. I had won ten races in eleven attempts. To make it even sweeter, I had done so exactly two decades after my first win in 1983. Dean and I embraced at the water's edge and, although extremely disappointed, he showed what a truly great sportsman he was.

On the Hawaii Kai beach, beer in hand, I gave a press conference. I said it had been difficult to prepare for this race, given my responsibilities at home, particularly with business. Paying tribute to Dean, I said I had to dig exceptionally deep to pull it off against such a truly great competitor.

But when asked what it felt like to win for the tenth time, I was at a loss for words, something few would say often happens to me. For a few moments I choked. Tears streamed down my face.

That had been the best Molokai of my life, although an even better one was in store nine years later. But the next race, 2004, was the worst.

I trained hard and was supremely fit, as I wanted to increase my tally of wins to ensure Dean could never catch up. However, as a company director, I now had to have a comprehensive medical assessment before the race to keep my life-insurance policy intact. No problem, I thought; it was just a formality.

The doctor did not agree, saying I had suffered a recent heart attack. It was a minor one, he said, but even so, he could not give me medical clearance.

I was shocked to the pit of my stomach. I had never had a heart attack – of that I was certain. In fact, I hadn't even suffered from the tiniest of chest pains. Still reeling from the damning diagnosis, which had come like a bolt out of the blue, I decided to get a second opinion and contacted Durban's top heart specialist. He told me to send over the electrocardiograms (ECGs) as soon as possible. I waited impatiently for him to come back to me, and when he did, it was great news. I hadn't had a heart attack after all. In fact, he said I was as healthy as an ox. However, I had an enlarged heart, which is what had confused the doctor doing the insurance assessment. Known as athlete's heart, it was a fairly new phenomenon at the time, as most athletes retired from competitive sport in their twenties or thirties. However, with the growing popularity of extreme sports and the introduction of veteran and master age categories, more endurance athletes were now racing throughout their lives. As a result, after decades of intense competition and exercise, their hearts sometimes became larger. Generally, this is not considered serious as a heart is a muscle and expands with exercise, just as a weightlifter bulks up in a gym. By itself, it's not a disease or medical condition and doesn't cause harm.

However, the specialist still wouldn't commit himself to saying I could now go flat out and push the pain barrier as I usually did. I suppose I should have expected that, since no doctor gives an unconditional guarantee in case it backfires. He merely said I 'should be fine'.

This was not the rock-solid reassurance I needed, but I still went ahead and raced. However, my mind wasn't right, and at that level one has to peak both mentally and physically. Instead, I let my imagination run riot and every twinge I felt, perceived or otherwise, I assumed to be a looming heart attack. It was the only time in my life that I started a race with a negative mindset.

Herman won that year, paddling magnificently to beat another Aussie hotshot, Dave Kissane. I came third, ten minutes behind my brother.

The following year I returned. I was now forty-two years old, and although I felt as strong as a racehorse, the clock was ticking. One more win was perhaps too big an ask, as some of the paddlers were half my age.

That year I was sponsored by the wine estate of world champion golfer Ernie Els. I had met Ernie during my golfing period when I thought I would never be able to race internationally again, and we'd become good friends. Known as the Big Easy because of his towering stature and fluid swing, his approach to golf is much the same as mine to surfski racing, so we got on famously. When he heard that travelling to Hawaii cost me six times more than the prize money on offer, he stepped in to help.

Dean was there, as was Nathan Baggaley, a new Aussie hotshot who had won a silver medal paddling with Clint Robinson at the 2004 Athens Olympics. Nathan was considered one of the world's fastest open-water paddlers and wasn't short on confidence. He said before the race that he was going to 'rip it apart' and set a course record. I smiled. It was almost like me talking when I was his age.

The 2005 Molokai started in dramatic fashion, with Dean and Nathan Baggaley breaking ahead early. They took off as though it was a 500-metre sprint rather than a strength-sapping marathon across a wild stretch of sea. In contrast, I went for an embarrassing swim, falling off my surfski for the first time in twelve starts. It happened when I turned around to get my juice bottle and my paddle snagged a rising wave, tossing me into the ocean like a coin. Fortunately, it didn't cost too much time clambering back on board, but I also lost my seat pad. Win or lose, I knew the next two hours would be hell on my butt.

Luckily for me, the leading bunch of Aussies went slightly too far north. I was on my own on what I was confident was the best route to Oahu, and after a few minutes I couldn't see anyone else.

Finding the right line is crucial because in big weather the swell usually thunders across the Hawaiian Pacific from right to left and is far too fast to catch on pure paddling power. The key instead is to catch the smaller wind-generated waves, pick up speed and then turn onto the face of the monster swells, which on this day were more than six metres. Consequently, reaching speeds of close to thirty kilometres an hour, I could ride the surging rollers and link up with a series of fast runs – sometimes as many as six waves – that could last a kilometre or so, all the while maintaining the correct general direction. This is second nature for downwind specialists such as me, Herman and Dean, whereas top flat-water racers usually stall out after a maximum of three runs.

After about two hours, Nathan realised he had made a mistake and corrected his course, coming over to where I was and dropping Dean in the process. He was still well in control of the race, and every time I pulled close, he sprinted clear again.

However, I kept on his tail, finally catching him at the pounding water off Portlock Cliffs. I cruised up, deliberately looking relaxed and controlling my breathing. He ignored me at first, but out of the corner of my eye, I caught him glancing furtively over. After several minutes I called out, 'Nathan, you are paddling really well. Keep it up.'

He looked at me, startled. I smiled back, hiding any suggestion of the fatigue I certainly felt. I hoped to rattle him with a little psychological warfare, and it worked beautifully. He fell to pieces after seeing how effortlessly I appeared to be gliding through the water. Then with another smile, I put on the gas and surged ahead.

I crossed the line two minutes in front of him, with Dean and Herman coming third and fourth, respectively. As a local beauty on the beach draped the victor's flower wreath – or *lei* – around my neck, I called for a beer. Seldom has any beverage tasted so good.

I had been celebrating for about an hour when another paddler, John Maclean, crossed the finishing line. According to journalist Joe Glickman, John asked people on the beach who had won.

'I was expecting everyone to say it was Nathan, given his record as an Olympian and World Champion,' John told Joe. 'But they pointed to an old big guy at the bar downing pints of beer. I thought they were having a joke. I wheeled over to him and asked if I could join him for a beer.'

It was the first time I had been called an old big guy, but I remember getting a beer for John. He is one of the gutsiest people I've met. As a paraplegic, John has completed the Ironman Triathlon and swum the English Channel, making the Molokai one of his 'short' races. He and his paddling partner Dave Wells came second that year in the double-surfski division with a time of 5:01:41 – a truly extraordinary achievement from a remarkable man.

Sadly, the same is not true for Nathan Baggaley. Voted the Australian Institute of Sport's Athlete of the Year in 2004, several years later he was convicted of drug manufacturing and dealing in steroids, Ecstasy and cocaine.

It is one of the most tragic downfalls of a massively talented athlete in any sport.

He is still in jail.

LESSONS LEARNT

AS AMERICAN baseball legend Yogi Berra often said, 'It ain't over till it's over.' In both the 2003 and 2005 Molokais, I only caught the leaders right at the end. Always believe that you have what it takes to win, no matter who is ahead. I cannot repeat that often enough. Telling Nathan Baggaley that he was doing well as I 'effortlessly' passed him won me that race in 2005. I believed I could do it; he no longer believed he could.

NEVER ENTER a race with a negative mindset. If you do so, you will be defeated and that is as true in life as it is in sport. Even though the diagnosis that I'd had a heart attack was incorrect, it threw me off balance mentally. I now have a full medical check-up every year.

I'm not saying I would have beaten Herman that day, but I am saying that by arriving at the starting line riddled with doubt meant that I had lost the race before the gun fired. This is one lesson I have learnt well. I have never let my mind get the better of me since, no matter how many curve balls have been thrown my way.

19

Riding the tiger

When doing business in China, two famous quotations spring to mind.

First is the Chinese backhanded curse, 'May you live in interesting times.' The second is an equally well-known Mandarin proverb, 'He who rides a tiger is afraid to dismount.' In other words, moving on from a bad situation is sometimes scarier than staying with it.

Epic Kayak's Chinese journey incorporated both sayings in equal measures.

I was racing in Tahiti when we decided on an exploratory trip to China in 2005, so Charles and Greg went ahead of me. I had given them the names of three manufacturers that built composite boats to check out, and the first on the list was Flying Eagle in Fuyang, a city in south-eastern China. A few days later I got a call from Greg saying they could not believe how good the factory was and as a result they were not bothering to look at the other two. A deal was struck, and we signed a contract with Flying Eagle to produce our sea kayaks and surfskis.

Fuyang is a city of over seven million people, about 250 kilometres inland of Shanghai, and when I arrived to help set up the factory, not many people there had seen a Westerner before – particularly not one almost two metres tall and with a mop of fiery red hair (in those days, anyway). They were so intrigued that random pedestrians would accost me in the street to rub my arms, which are moderately hairy and were a complete novelty to them. When Clare and our blonde-haired daughter Hannah arrived for a visit, they would stop and blatantly stare – on one occasion, two cars crashed into each other.

Nonetheless, Fuyang it is a thriving metropolis. Flying Eagle is an established family business owned by a father and two sons, and it didn't take long for me to agree with Charles and Greg that they were certainly capable of producing the high-end boats we had in mind. The father couldn't speak a word of English, but his sons were reasonably fluent, so communication was usually okay, if a little haphazard. The factory mainly made quality fibreglass rowing boats but had built a few kayaks before – although not on the scale that we were proposing. They were highly skilled in producing prepreg (that is, pre-impregnated) craft, but knew nothing about infusion moulding, so bringing the workforce up to speed on that was our initial priority. The main differences between the two methods are that with prepreg the fabric is pre-saturated with resin, moulded while wet, then cured in an oven. With fusion, dry composite material is placed into the mould and then resin is infused by vacuum-sucking it though the laminate.

The Flying Eagle deal was a joint-venture partnership as we would supply moulds and presses, oversee the manufacturing process, and supervise quality control. They would handle the day-to-day running of the factory, take care of the corporate intricacies of doing business in China, and manage the workforce. We jointly worked out the costs, and an agreed profit margin for the Chinese was incorporated in the overall package.

They then built an extra 10 000 square metres of factory space to house the assembly line, as they knew we were serious when we said an avalanche of orders would be coming in. It was a lot of work setting everything up, and either Greg or I had to be physically at the factory to keep the manufacturing process on track. We even slept on the premises. We also relocated two of our top staff from Durban, Tyrell Impson and Gean van Staden, to Fuyang to ensure a permanent Epic presence.

Once the moulds and ovens were ready, production took off. Flying Eagle made extremely good kayaks, and such was their efficiency that we were soon producing almost sixty a week. Our quality-control problems disappeared overnight, and one of the key reasons for this was that any mistake or shoddy work resulted in the employees responsible having their wages docked. This may sound harsh to Westerners – and in many countries would be illegal – but that is the Chinese way and is accepted by both management and staff.

We were doing everything right. Within a year, Epic had become an international yardstick for surfski excellence with lightweight, extremely strong, well-made craft. We were now one of the largest manufacturers in the world and could start concentrating on bringing out more advanced designs and models.

Indeed, things were going so well that the factory owner approached me and, with his son interpreting, said he would give me $100 000 if I could get him a contract to build 'big boats'. He meant top-of-the-range ocean yachts, and it seemed that was his dream project, rather than rowing boats and surfskis.

As it happened, I did have a contact in the sailing world, David Abromowitz, one of Africa's leading yacht brokers. I told him about Flying Eagle and he referred me to the country's biggest boat builder, Robertson and Caine (R&C). A couple of months later, the company director Ellian Perch arrived in China to have a look at the setup. Ellian was impressed – extremely so – and after much due diligence, R&C contracted out some of their projects to Flying Eagle. The owner of the factory was delighted as at last he had a 'big boat' order. R&C was equally happy, as they had substantially added to their global production capacity. The only loser was me: I am still waiting to be paid the $100 000 finder's fee. I think that boat has sailed – pun intended.

It's a crazy experience for any Westerner doing business in China as almost everything is about saving face. Take, for example, corporate drinking, which revolves around an ancient tradition called *ganbei*. The word itself means 'dry cup' and is the equivalent of the English toast 'cheers'. But that is where all similarity stops. Instead of clinking glasses once, Chinese propose a *ganbei* with every drink, and both proposer and the person accepting the toast have to down whatever fiery liquid they have in their glass in one gulp. This is usually a traditional Chinese spirit called *baijiu*, a vile, eye-watering concoction that is anything up to 60 per cent proof.

Sometimes you may find yourself drinking alone against a *ganbei* 'team' if more than one person proposes the toast and shares the same drink with others. So you have to be on your toes, a contradiction in terms when *baijiu* is involved.

The unbreakable *ganbei* rule is that there is no opting out once the first toast has been proposed. Unless you can persuade your host that you are a monk or pregnant, both difficult in my case, you have to match them glass for glass. The more you drink, the more respect you pay the person you are toasting. In fact, it's better to fall flat on your face in a drunken stupor than lose face by saying 'no more'. As a result, some Chinese businessmen hire hardened drinkers as their *ganbei* representatives, and having been at the receiving end of multiple toasts, I can understand why.

It was hard work at the factory – and I include *ganbei* sessions in that – but we also introduced an element of fun. I persuaded, or perhaps cajoled, many of the workers to take up paddling, not only for recreation but also as a way to intimately understand the product they were making. In doing so, I like to think I kick-started surfskiing as a sport in China. Fuyang is a landlocked city so all paddling is on flat water, but even so, we cobbled a team together that still competes in the annual Dragon Run off Hong Kong, now one of Asia's premier surfski races.

Although production problems, missed delivery deadlines and quality issues were now nothing more than a nightmare from the past, I was still putting out fires. In this case the problem was in South Africa, where we allowed a contractor to make Epic kayaks for the local market as it was too expensive to import the Chinese models. These were heavier and therefore much cheaper than the superb Chinese boats, and we expressly forbade any export deals.

Unfortunately, this was not honoured and the South Africans quietly let it be known internationally that they were selling Epic surfskis at knock-down prices. As a result, retailers in Australia cancelled Chinese orders and opted for the inferior brand. These surfskis were sneaked out of Durban in containers, and when we found out, I had to fly home and bang some heads, figuratively speaking.

In those days I was constantly on the move, doing quality control and teaching infusion manufacturing in China, then jetting off to America, Europe and Australia to sell surfskis that had come off a production line many thousands of kilometres away. I was also racing around the world, spending as much time at international airports as I did on the water. This was a highly effective Epic marketing strategy as there is no better way to get kayak buyers excited than by winning races. Clare and I worked out that I was on the road for at least two hundred days of the year on behalf of the company, either standing on a podium festooned with Epic Kayak logos or visiting retailers. I was also still doing it on a shoestring, as until Epic paid off the hefty capital expenditure for the China start-up, not much profit was coming the way of the directors. Our staff were paid well, but for me, the financial problems I had faced in South Africa continued. However, I wasn't too worried, as there was no doubt in my mind we would soon start making real money. I had also recently introduced a colleague of mine, who became the new distributor in Australia. Tony and Jacqui King came from corporate backgrounds and brought a new approach to the surfski business in Australia, and Epic sales were skyrocketing. There was gold at the end of the proverbial rainbow.

Or so I thought.

It came out of the blue. In November 2008, Flying Eagle management called us in and said our joint venture wasn't working. They weren't making any money. We would have to renegotiate the arrangement or else dissolve it.

We were stunned, pointing out that all costing had been calculated on the production figures that they had given us. Everything was above board, and generous profit margins had been assessed on wages, materials, rent and the general day-to-day running of a large factory. That information had not been concocted out of the ether by us.

They shook their heads. It was a bad deal for them, they said. There were three ways to resolve this: we could amend the joint-venture deal to make Flying Eagle an original equipment manufacturer (OEM), where we bought the kayaks directly from them; we could rent the building we were in from them; or we could move out and continue production elsewhere on our own.

The first option, an OEM, was out of the question as we would have no say over quality control. The second, leasing the factory from them, could possibly have been feasible if it wasn't for what I considered to be the extortionate rent of up to 30 per cent more than the going rate. Consequently, the only option was the third one – terminating the project. This was the last thing we wanted.

It was bizarre and we had no idea where this sudden hostility came from. It also was not based on fact – while considering our response, we visited a factory across the road and found we could get a significantly cheaper rental from them. So it seemed we were already paying above the market rate. In fact, we had also recently been approached by an opposition factory, as we discovered some months previously that Flying Eagle had been, in our opinion, charging excessive amounts for paddle shafts, but we certainly were not planning on moving the whole production process over. However, those tentative discussions provided a new option for us. Instead of our only choice being to find alternative premises, it became the best one. We decided to set up our own operation and lease a factory from Flying Eagle's opposition.

But, as mentioned, dismounting from a tiger is not easy. Although we had been doing business in China for three years, we still had little idea about how the country's ingrained corporate culture actually worked. It appeared that Flying Eagle had expected us to blink first and agree to the new terms, which would have been vastly in their favour. They were shocked when we refused. It was now a face-saving contest.

This time we were a little more prepared. Greg, Charles and I had a suspicion that Flying Eagle management would react badly to us terminating the partnership, so we quickly moved a batch of surfskis out of the factory. This meant that if everything went seriously south and all our equipment was seized, we could at least make moulds for new boats.

It's fortunate we did, as that's exactly what happened. Things started turning nasty. Flying Eagle initially agreed that we could take our moulds, presses, boats and materials, but when our truck pitched up at the factory gates, it was stopped by grim-faced security guards. The factory had been closed and no one was allowed in. Massive padlocks on the doors bore testimony to that, and we were told we would have to buy back equipment we already owned and raw materials we had already paid for at double the retail price.

We then called the police, telling them that we were trying to retrieve equipment that belonged to us. The police shook their heads, saying we could only collect our stuff once we paid Flying Eagle a whopping $1.2 million that the factory claimed 'we owed'.

It was, in effect, a ransom demand, as far as I was concerned.

It got worse. Flying Eagle then insisted that we sign a lopsided separation agreement stating that we would be fined $200 000 if we hired any of their employees, either present or former. We would also have to pay a $1-million penalty if we continued using the same resin systems that we always had, even though the systems did not belong to Flying Eagle and never had. In fact, the system they were referring to was not patented and was widely accessible on the open market. Apart from anything else, this was a bit rich seeing that we had taught them infusion-mould manufacturing.

We refused to sign. It was beyond absurd. There were absolutely no restrictions against Flying Eagle, while we were hamstrung by threats of spurious fines at every turn. In our opinion, this was nothing more than an opportunistic shakedown of a non-Chinese company. And it seemed clear from the police's reaction that we were not guaranteed of getting a fair hearing from a local court.

In the interim, we had containers of completed boats that could not be shipped, as well as hundreds of orders from around the world that we were legally obliged to honour. Yet all our equipment was under lock and key.

For us, it was a catastrophe. We were staring bankruptcy in the face. Even though we had new premises, to start again from scratch, making moulds, installing ovens and presses, importing materials, and recruiting a fresh labour force would be ruinously expensive.

But if we didn't do that, we would be walking away from a product that we knew was the best of its kind in the world at the time. If we closed down, we might never get another chance.

There was a lot at stake. The company was barely eight years old, and this, in essence, would be our third start-up. Could Epic Kayaks rise phoenix-style from the ashes? Could we pull it off?

I had my doubts.

All I knew was that we were certainly living in interesting times.

LESSON LEARNT

ONLY ONE FROM this chapter – but in my opinion it's a big one. NEVER be afraid of dismounting from the tiger. The literal meaning of this Chinese proverb is that those engaging in a risky endeavour may find it easier to continue with it rather than face the consequences of attempting to quit or abandon it.

If we had acceded to what in our opinion was little more than a ransom demand, we would have found it extremely difficult to continue doing business in the country. We could easily have been crippled by fines, penalties and possibly extortionate litigation. And we would have lost face, which in China is like virginity – never regained.

But even so, it was initially tempting to stay with Flying Eagle as all production systems were not only in place but working beautifully. It was almost a case of staying with the devil we knew rather than venturing into an uncertain future.

We decided against it. We 'dismounted' and started up from scratch for the third time, with new premises, new deals and new production ideas.

Today, fifteen years later, Epic is still in China producing kayaks. That speaks for itself.

20

Champion of the world

The fact that I kept racing kayaks throughout the turbulent years in China was, in retrospect, one thing that kept me sane.

Not only that, but my fifth decade was a personal golden era with several victories that many sports pundits thought impossible – something all ageing athletes could do well to take note of. They also provided me with some welcome prize money in financially stressed times and were great advertising for Epic Kayaks. One week I would be racing our kayaks or holding coaching clinics on the sun-drenched beaches of Hawaii and Polynesia, and the next I'd be shivering in the frigid waters of Germany or Scandinavia. I did a tour of England and Wales in freezing mid-winter. Even so, I loved every minute of it, promoting a great product, mixing with great people, and competing in some of the best races of my life.

Apart from winning my eleventh Molokai in 2005, I also raced another big hitter on the circuit, the Perth Doctor (now called the Shaw and Partners Doctor) – ironically one of Nathan Baggaley's most high-profile victories the year before. It was the first time I had entered this magnificent twenty-seven-kilometre dice from Rottnest Island to Perth. Apart from the local Aussie hotshots who are always a threat, this time it seemed my biggest challenge would come from home, from my brother Herman and brilliant Cape Town paddler Dawid Mocke, who was in devastatingly good form.

The Doctor almost always blows from the south-west, but if on a rare occasion the wind swings east, the race is switched around from Perth to Rottnest Island. So no matter what happens, it is a guaranteed downwind roller-coaster. In short, it's my type of race as gale-force gusts and surging waves are more often than not on the menu. The route is a back-to-front 'L' shape, with a shipping lane marked off by a buoy following a line of reef markers, before turning left and heading straight towards a small boat harbour called Hillarys.

As expected, the wind was pumping hard and Dawid took the lead right away. However, Herman and I caught him a couple of kilometres later at the reef markers, and from then on it was a straight downhill blast. Whoever found the best big-running swells would win, and luckily it was me, crossing the line fifteen seconds ahead of Dawid, who edged out Herman in the final kilometres. The judges later ruled that Dawid had missed going around the compulsory shipping buoy, so he was disqualified, putting Herman in second place.

I enjoyed The Doctor so much that I vowed to return and defend my title the following year. However, the 2006 contest turned out to be different as the race was now incorporated in a world championship series that was going to boost the surfski circuit beyond recognition. Up until now, some races I had entered were billed as 'world championships' but were not officially sanctioned as such. It didn't matter, as to top paddlers the premier ocean contest was still the Molokai, and it possibly always will be. Other so-called world championships only meant as much as we, the surfski community, chose to make them mean.

Consequently, in 2006/7 Surfski.info, the leading website for surfski news and a lively forum for offshore paddlers, decided to coordinate the circuit and create a world ranking system that would aggregate the results of what were then considered to be the top six international contests. The first race of this World Cup series would be the 2006 US Championships in San Francisco, followed by the Australian World Championships in Perth and the Dubai Shamaal a week later. After that we would fly out to New Zealand in March for the 2007 King of the Harbour, the Molokai in May, and finally Durban's ARB Surf Ski World Cup in July. The paddler with the most points at the end of the series would be crowned world champion.

This created intense interest among elite surfski racers, and it started with a record turnout in San Francisco where Dawid Mocke won the US Champs. I didn't enter owing to business commitments, but I was training hard for the next race, the Australian World Championships in Perth. This involved two races, one being The Doctor, and I planned to be the first person ever to win two in a row. I also needed the points from both races to stay in contention for the World Cup series. Having said that, I doubt any punter would have bet good money on me being crowned world champ, as I was now forty-three years old and would be forty-four before the series was over. To put that in perspective, the world's fastest marathon paddler, Hank McGregor, was twenty-nine. In fact, Hank's father Lee had been one of my main rivals when I first started competing. I still have that photo of him throwing a punch at me during the 1985 Ironman contest when I was twenty-two.

I was in China at the time, and despite the lack of waves in landlocked Fuyang, I was out twice a day doing sprints on the river that flows through the city. To spice things up, I often chased ships coasting up and down Fuyang's waterways to catch their wakes. The factory demanded much of my time, so to optimise training I put lead weights in the boat to make it as heavy as practically possible. This was nothing new to me – I always made training sessions as gruelling as I could, often sweating like a pig in thick wetsuits while preparing for races in the tropics.

That flat-water training turned out to be a blessing, as the first day of the Aussie World Champs, a twenty-five-kilometre dice from Fremantle Beach to Sorrento Beach, was on unusually calm seas. But what surprised people most was that I won against Daryl Bartho, a former Springbok from Durban considered to be a faster flat-water sprinter than me. It was a close call as I got out of the water fifteen seconds before Daryl, but the finishing line was 100 metres up the beach. I cranked my legs like crazy to hold off fleet-footed Daryl by eight nerve-racking seconds. Herman was third, two minutes later. The Aussie water-sport press, who labelled me 'too old, too fat' and only competitive in howling downwind blasts, had to eat their words. What made me happiest was that despite the tranquil conditions, my average speed for the wave-free course in little wind was a fast sixteen kilometres an hour.

The next week was The Doctor. For once, the famed wind did not blow and we started off in the lee of Rottnest Island on water that could have doubled as an ironing board. Daryl turbo-charged ahead, followed by New Zealand Olympic sprint paddler Mike Walker and Sydney Ironman star Dave Kissane, whom Herman had beaten in the 2004 Molokai.

It took me about a kilometre to work my way through the pack, and to my eternal relief, once out at sea the wind started picking up. At twelve knots it could hardly be called 'pumping', but even so I was able to thread some good runs together and took the lead. However, Daryl was barely a metre behind me and I was starting to get worried. He was young and strong and I was sure he still had a lot of gas in the reserve tank for the inevitable last-minute do-or-die dash.

Two kilometres from Hillarys Harbour, I slammed down the hammer hard, dropping a surprised Daryl by several boat lengths. I wanted that cushion, as the final half-kilometre would be in glassy harbour water tailor-made for Daryl's sprinting skills.

It was enough. I reached shore ten seconds before him, and this time there was thankfully only a short trot to the finishing poles. He stood no chance of catching me.

A great competitor on any day, Daryl was – by his own admission – dumbfounded. He said to journalists on the beach afterwards, 'Oscar hasn't beaten me all year and he comes here and does it twice in one week. Go figure.'

I actually had gone and figured. When training in Durban with Daryl and other top paddlers, I often either weighed down my boat to force me to work harder or sneaked off and did gruelling solo sessions beforehand. As a result, all the other paddlers would be far fresher than me and believe I was off the pace, little knowing that I had already put in an hour or so beforehand. I never mentioned these self-imposed handicaps as I considered them to be crucial psychological advantages. They were then completely taken by surprise at how fast I was on an actual race day.

A week later we flew to the United Arab Emirates for the inaugural Dubai Shamaal. 'Shamaal' is the Arabic word for the sandstorms that whistle across the Persian Gulf, but when we landed in the tiny country, there was barely a wheeze. It didn't take a genius to figure out that this was going to be a punishing twenty-kilometre flat-water grind in serious desert heat. However, with $10 000 in prize money, I had an added incentive and was prepared to sweat blood.

But if The Doctor had a quality line-up, this was as daunting, as Dawid Mocke and Hank McGregor, who had skipped the Aussie World Champs, now joined the party. There were twenty international paddlers in the field of fifty, including South African rising stars Barry Lewin and Clint Pretorius; top Australian marathoner Ash Nesbit; and Zsolt Szadovszki, the Hungarian-born American carving his way up the ranks.

Dawid, Hank and Daryl broke away as the starter's gun fired. In water that made a pancake look bumpy, they seemed unbeatable. Fortunately, in the last hour or so the Shamaal belatedly arrived but only half-heartedly managed to ruffle the water's surface. I somehow sniffed out a few rideable ripples and caught them.

It worked. I overtook first Hank, then Daryl, and was catching Dawid when the race finished.

Four months later, in March 2007, we flew to Auckland, the largest and most populous city in New Zealand, for the King of the Harbour contest. South Africans were in the majority among international paddlers as no Aussies were competing, while Kiwi Olympian Mike Walker provided the local interest. But still, it was a good race to win. The main event is a twenty-eight-kilometre dice around Rangitoto Island in Auckland's harbour, and Dawid Mocke took line honours convincingly. I came third.

By now with wins in every race he had entered, Dawid had a solid over-all lead in the series. But the next race was the Molokai, my speciality, and I needed to claw back some points.

Sadly, for the first time that I can remember, there wasn't a breath of wind in the Kaiwi Channel that day. The race was little more than a brutal paddling slugfest with no waves to catch and I came fourth – my worst-ever Molokai position. Tahitian Lewis Laughlin gave a masterclass in how to power through glassy seas to win, and an indication of the tough conditions was that his time of 5:20:06 was the slowest in twenty-seven years – and Lewis is one of the world's fastest long-distance ocean paddlers. Hank was second, followed by Dawid. I was disappointed, but even so, coming fourth in a qual-ity field in blistering heat with no surf or wind was still a decent result.

However, this meant that Dawid with three wins and a third place was now a clear four points ahead of me. It all hinged on the final race, the twenty-eight-kilometre ARB Surf Ski World Cup from Amanzimtoti to Durban. All thirty-year-old Dawid needed to do was to shadow 'the old man' and he would be crowned world champion.

This time the weather gods smiled as dawn broke on the first day of July. A downwind gale funnelled in from the south-west at thirty-five knots and waves crested at four metres, churning the ocean into a swirling mass of white-foam peaks. A record 196 paddlers lined up for the starting gun at Amanzimtoti Beach. Almost a quarter would fail in those harsh conditions, either smashing their boats or retiring exhausted. Several would have to be rescued by the National Sea Rescue Institute.

Hank and Dawid were first over the breaking backline surf and started thundering their way north to Durban. I, on the other hand, had a terrible start even though these were 'my' conditions, and I struggled to fight my way through the pack. Someone told me there were strong currents further offshore, so I headed out to sea.

By now Hank and Dawid were some distance ahead, and as I was so far

149

out, no one thought I was in contention. But the waves, wind and currents were working in cosmic harmony further offshore and I was catching long, fast, intensely exhilarating runs. I was in my absolute element.

Then a helicopter spotted me and alerted the press boat. Race photographer Greg Kitto came out to shoot some video, surprised at the deep-sea route I was taking.

'Who's ahead?' I yelled into the howling wind.

'Only Hank,' shouted Greg, cupping his hands over his mouth.

That news was like a sudden, sharp jolt of adrenaline. I knew I had been going fast, but even so I was stunned to hear I was now lying second after my lousy start. If Greg was surprised to see me, Hank also obviously didn't know where I was. And it seemed he had dropped Dawid. So it was just me and him.

I told myself I was going to win this or croak in the attempt. I increased my pace, surfing sets of waves for more than a kilometre in runs that had me yelling out loud in sheer exhilaration. Then suddenly, there he was, just in front of me.

Hank now knew he was being reeled in just as he thought he had the race in the bag and began to increase his already blistering pace. We arrived at Durban Harbour's breakwater barely a boat length apart. The large concrete jetty juts about 150 metres out to sea, and from there it was a 1.5-kilometre flat-out dice to the finish. However, a container ship at that crucial moment was about to steam into the harbour, and worried race officials temporarily stopped us. They said it was too dangerous to paddle in front of such a juggernaut.

'Guys, we'll easily get across in time,' I said. 'Let us through.'

They knew Hank and I had been going extremely fast and made a snap decision that we could continue. However, they gave Hank a boat-length start as he had arrived at the breakwater first. For someone of that calibre, that's more than enough to secure a win.

However, as we turned towards the beach finishing line, the wind was no longer our friend. Instead, it blasted straight into our faces. Everyone thought that in his current form Hank would demolish me in that head-on gale. No one considered that while Hank may be fifteen years younger, I had the edge in experience.

That was the key difference – I had done my homework. I had methodically trained for this race by regularly testing currents, winds and every conceivable condition across the breakwater mouth, and I'd found that the fastest route in headwinds was to hug the harbour wall. This defied all logic as it was nearly half a kilometre longer and in normal conditions would cost an extra two minutes.

These were not normal conditions. I set off at forty-five degrees to Hank, speeding across the wind-sheltered waters and milking waves that were bouncing off the wall while Hank headbutted straight into the teeth of the gale.

I reached the beach 200 metres and a minute before him but was penalised five seconds as he had been ahead of me when we were stopped at the harbour mouth.

Hank was understandably disappointed and claimed that if it hadn't been for the stoppage, he would have won. He didn't attend the prize-giving, which was unusual for such a great sportsman. However, few dispute that I took the better line, which probably would have beaten Hank's route in headwinds with or without the arrival of the ship.

Equally important for me was that Dawid came sixth, which meant that I moved into the top spot on the Surfski.info world rankings – winning the world championship by a single point. I also pocketed the R80 000 prize money for winning the ARB Durban World Cup, the biggest-ever payday in surfskiing. That settled a lot of our debts and the Chalupsky family was liquid again. It was an absolute lifesaver at the time.

Perhaps the last word should go to Rob Mousley, a founder member of Surfski.info, which was the brains behind the creation of the World Cup series. On the organisation's website, he wrote: 'Oscar's a big man in every way – physically, vocally, and he never holds back. In his mind, he is always right – no argument. His big match temperament is second to none.

'But love him or hate him, one thing is certain – Oscar's performance this year is worthy of the title of "World Champion".'[2]

The article also mentioned that at my age I should be past it. Next year I was turning forty-five. Could I do it again?

As far as I was concerned, there was only one way to find out.

LESSONS LEARNT

ALWAYS REMEMBER THE seven Ps: Proper Planning and Preparation Prevents Piss-Poor Performance. By all rights, Hank should have beaten me in the final race of the series. He was considered the fastest long-distance paddler in the world, he was ahead of me almost all the way, and he was fifteen years younger. Yet I had done my homework. I took the longer route, which was considered insane by people watching on the beach. But I held my nerve and won by a minute. I knew from years of experience that in ocean racing the shortest route is not necessarily the best. That is a good metaphor for life as well.

ALWAYS ENJOY YOURSELF. I never tire of taking pleasure in beating the odds. Every race except the ARB Durban was in flat or flattish conditions. People said that at my age I could only win if the weather was right. Despite that, I was among the first three positions for every race except the Molokai, and one of the main reasons is that I love competing. If I stopped enjoying myself, I would give up racing in a heartbeat. It hasn't happened yet despite cancer and encroaching age.

21

Too old and too fat?

The next World Cup, the 2007/8 series, would have a different format and include a wider choice of races.

But despite more events, not all races would be equal. Each would be awarded a star rating relevant to its importance, the type of course, the number of participants and the prize money. So the onus was now also on organisers to make their tournaments as appealing to top paddlers as possible. This was a bold move from Surfski.info to boost the sport internationally, and it worked beautifully.

Also, Surfski.info's quest to keep the rankings simple ensured a fair contest that was accepted by almost everyone. For example, in each race with a large number of entries, the top fifty paddlers earned points – fifty for a win, forty-nine for coming second, and so on. The points were then multiplied by the star rating so that winning a four-star (the highest-ranked) event would mean 200 points (four multiplied by fifty). Contestants could race as many of the ten events in the series as they liked, but only their top six results would count.

The first race I entered was one that I had skipped the year before: the 2007 US Championships in San Francisco. Despite its low rating – two stars – the line-up in the bay that day was star-studded by anyone's estimate. Current Molokai champion Lewis Laughlin was there, as was Daryl Bartho and Zsolt Szadovszki. Also raring to go was my Olympic double-gold-medallist business partner Greg Barton, which added the nice touch of having two of Epic Kayak's directors doing battle.

San Francisco's bay is one of the most beautiful in the world, as well as the most photographed, with the two-kilometre Golden Gate Bridge spanning the harbour like a colossus. It is also the only major sea-level gap in California's coastal mountain range, sucking cool Pacific Ocean air into a hot dry valley that detonates wind blasts of up to thirty knots. That's exactly what I was hoping for.

Unfortunately, it was not to be. This was the calmest US Championships in history with a slight ten-knot breeze barely rippling the bay's surface. The gun fired, and the lead pack consisting of me, Greg Barton, Bevan Manson, Daryl Bartho and Lewis Laughlin rounded the Point Bonita buoy almost touching one another. However, just past Bonita we turned right, heading out to sea into the current and I found some nice little runs bouncing off the cliffs. I surged into the lead, dropping everyone except Lewis. As we swivelled around the last buoy, eight kilometres to the finish, I was banking on some belated gusts coming off the ocean to blow me over the finish line. Combined with an incoming tide, it would have been a straight downhill race, which I was confident of winning. But the wind didn't arrive, and as a result it was a head-to-head slog with Lewis, one of the physically strongest paddlers on the planet.

I was still in front as we neared the iconic bridge. Lewis aimed for the centre spans towering above us while I took an angle into what looked like faster water. Wrong choice! I got sucked into a reverse current and within an eye blink Lewis was ahead. In fact, at one stage it looked as if I was going backwards.

It took me several seconds to break the current's iron grip, but by then Lewis was too far ahead and I had to be content with second place. Greg came in third, sixteen seconds behind me. It was an astonishing triumph for Epic Kayaks with both founder members on the podium after racing our own product.

The next month was the inaugural three-star Dragon Run in Hong Kong, which interested me intensely as we at Epic were instrumental in kick-starting Chinese surfskiing.

The Dragon Run is a spectacularly interesting course in many ways. Not only is the concrete panorama of skyscrapers stretching back to Kowloon unique in any kayak race, the maze of islands with steep cliffs, plunging waterfalls and crashing waves makes it arguably the most technical on the circuit. The direct downwind leg usually has a consistent two-metre swell, and speedsters can top twenty-eight kilometres an hour on some runs.

I would be up against Lewis again, as well as the supreme waterman Dean Gardiner. Equally dangerous, Dawid Mocke had recovered from a back injury and was also there.

We were in a loose bunch throughout the race, but nearing the end I made a stupid tactical error. Dean and I were neck and neck behind Dawid and Lewis when a passenger ship passed in front, blocking the course. Dean turned to go around the ship's aft, but I decided to slow down and wait for it to steam past. I even hoped to surf some runs off the wake – until I saw the size of the waves churned up by the giant propeller. They were massive, tantamount to a crashing two-metre shore break. Shocked, I managed to brace myself as the first wash dumped on top of me, miraculously not snapping my ski.

After that, I had to work hard to catch Dean and rode his wake for a while before dropping him to attack Lewis, who was now behind Dawid. The brawny Tahitian's stamina is legendary, but just as I was unable to catch him, he couldn't overtake Dawid. Even so, with a first and a second in two races, Lewis was now comfortably on top of the log.

Then it was off to Dubai for the four-star Shamaal. This was again a tough-fought race in flat water and Dawid managed to outsprint Hank McGregor to take line honours for the second time in a row. I came fifth, but as Lewis only managed an eighth place, negating his great win in San Francisco, I was now top of the leader board. Dawid, who had two wins but done one race fewer than us, was third. Of more concern to me was that we were now halfway through my designated six races and I still didn't have the win I desperately craved. But I aimed to change that in a few weeks' time with the four-star Doctor in Perth. If things went to plan, I would be the first person to win three Doctors in a row.

As with my previous Perth races, the main challenge came from the South African contingent. Dawid Mocke, fresh from his win in Dubai, was at the starting line with Daryl Bartho, whom I had just pipped the year before, and another young Durban hotshot, Clint Pretorius. But as Clint had recently recovered from a broken wrist, I was warier of Dawid and Daryl.

It was a perfect race day. The wind was blasting up to twenty knots with 1.5-metre swells running all the way from Rottnest Island to Perth. I could not have been happier.

Despite that, it was Clint who surged ahead, setting a scorching pace with Daryl, Dawid and me a boat's length behind. He held the lead for most of the race, but as we neared the finishing line we split, with Dawid edging further north, me in the middle, and Clint and Daryl on a slightly more easterly route. I pulled ahead and it was soon obvious that my line was the best one, so Clint and Daryl moved back to follow me. Dawid was now out of contention as he was too far north.

With the wind and waves pumping, Clint and Daryl couldn't catch me and I was about forty metres ahead approaching the final buoy to turn towards the beach. Barring being struck by lightning or grabbed by a shark, my triple Doctor victory now seemed a formality.

When I was almost at the buoy, race official Ash Nesbit in the escort boat shouted out to me. However, his words were incomprehensible, drowned out by the heaving waves and wind. All I could make out was 'buoy' and 'right', so I assumed he was telling me to go right of the buoy. I hit the beach and casually strolled to the finishing post twenty metres or so up the sand. This was no desperate sprint to the finish like last time. Clint arrived afterwards, followed by Daryl.

Then I got the bombshell news. I faced potential disqualification as I had gone to the right of the buoy.

'But Ash told me to go right,' I said.

Ash denied it, so the judges called up video footage from the escort boat. I had, in fact, misheard him. Instead of telling me to go right, what he actually said was, 'Oscar, there's a boat on the buoy. It's to the right of the groyne.'

But when he shouted that, the boat's engines were revving and I was twenty metres away with spray flying in a twenty-knot wind. Unfortunately, the only two words I heard clearly were the wrong ones. I could have gone left and would still have easily won. It had no effect on the outcome of the race whatsoever.

The judges decided that the error was a genuine misunderstanding and I'd gained no race-changing advantage, but even so I had broken a rule. I was given a thirty-second time penalty, which meant that both Clint and Daryl edged ahead – Daryl by a mere four seconds. Sporting as ever, Daryl told Surfski.info, 'Oscar would have won if he'd gone around the buoy.'

Even Ash agreed. 'Oscar deserved to win this race,' he said in an interview. However, he stressed that the judges had no option but to penalise me, and Clint had raced superbly as well.[3]

I accepted the decision philosophically. You cannot pick and choose which rules can or can't be broken. I knew that first-hand when appealing a decision against my own brother after Herman and Lewis cut inside a reef in the 1999 Heineken Championships in Bora Bora. I couldn't complain when a ruling didn't go my way. Having said that, the marker that caused all the confusion was never used in the race again.

Despite that, I was still top of the world rankings, increasing my lead over

Lewis, who had finished tenth. Dawid remained in third spot, eighty points behind.

From there we went to Hawaii to race the Molokai. For the second time in a row, the ocean was flatter than an airmail envelope. If my fourth place was disappointing in 2007, I was in for an even bigger shock this year coming seventh. Once again, Lewis excelled in the calm conditions but was chased all the way by Hank McGregor and Australia's Tim Jacobs, both of whom finished within a minute or so behind him. Dawid came fifth.

But even with Lewis's win, I was still ten points ahead in the world rankings thanks to my four top-five finishes. Dawid, despite wins in Hong Kong and Dubai, was now thirty-five points behind after finishing fourth in the one-star Cape Point Challenge, which had a relatively low turnout and only earned him twenty-seven points.

The final race was the high-scoring, four-star 2008 Durban World Cup, and once again it was down to the wire. Everything would be decided in a single no-holds-barred showdown. The course was changed to maximise the prevailing south-westerly conditions, and instead of starting at Amanzimtoti, it would be from Vetchie's Pier on Durban's Golden Mile to Westbrook Beach, thirty-three kilometres north. Two hundred paddlers would be at the surf's edge waiting for the starter's gun.

The buzz around the race this year was also different as the series was as wide open as a barn door, with three of us in nail-bitingly close contention for the world championship title. Consequently, the pundits were calling it a 'race within a race', as where Lewis, Dawid and I finished was of more interest than who actually won.

It was too close to call. Whichever way anyone looked at it, the statistical permutations were daunting. If Lewis won, I would have to come second or third to retain my world crown. If Dawid won, he would have to beat me by seven places and Lewis by four. If none of us won, to be safe I still needed to finish at least in the top ten, which I considered to be more than doable.

So for me it was a double-edged sword. I could take the safe – some would say sensible – option and just stay with the leaders or go for broke as I had the previous year. I wasn't sure what to do. All I knew was that I wanted to win both the race and the championship title equally badly.

That indecision nearly backfired. Conditions were great and I was going fast in three-metre swells when I noticed that among the leaders Hank was opting for a direct central route, while Dawid veered out to sea to catch even bigger waves and Clint Pretorius swung inshore.

After thirty-five years of racing, I am known for keeping my nerve in hard situations. It's what won me the previous World Cup in Durban, taking a longer route while Hank battled into the wind. Yet, for some reason that I am still not sure of, I suddenly started vacillating. What did Dawid know that I didn't? Why had he gone out to sea? And why had Clint headed inshore?

Consequently, instead of going straight with the superb conditions that were working well for me, I stupidly opted to head offshore and follow Dawid. That way I could at least closely shadow him, if not beat him, which would still give me the world title. However, I soon realised that this was not the best route and started worrying about where Lewis was. Had he now overtaken me?

Still dithering, I swung inshore following Clint. After a kilometre or so, I didn't see any sign of Lewis so figured he was on the direct route that I had initially taken. Once again, I changed course, now getting back into the centre. I then realised this was the right line all along, so I headed for the finish as fast as my arms could swing, hoping like hell that Dawid and Lewis hadn't capitalised on my mistakes.

As it happened, they hadn't. Hank's decision on a direct route, which had also initially been mine, paid off and he convincingly beat Clint and Dawid. I came fifth behind Herman, but while Dawid's third place was enough to leapfrog ahead of Lewis, who came eighteenth, it was not enough to oust me from the top spot in the series.

As I eased off my surfski, sucking in lungfuls of oxygen, it slowly dawned on me that once again I was the World Cup surfskiing champion. Not only that, but I had won the title back to back. This was even bigger than my Molokai victories. The World Cup series was the new acid test of offshore surfski racing, and thanks to Rob Mousley and the innovative team at Surfski.info, what had been a vague pipe dream for us was now a magnificent reality.

It felt good. In fact, I was on top of the world.

LESSONS LEARNT

CONSISTENCY MAY BE humdrum compared to winning, but it pays off just as much. In a series of races, the old axiom that winning is everything and second is nowhere is simply not true. Lewis and Dawid both won two World

Cup races, and I didn't win one. But my worst position was seventh, and Lewis's was eighteenth. While Dawid's lowest place was fifth, he also had a fourth in a one-star race that earned minimal points. So, you need to not only be consistent but also choose your battlegrounds well.

FLEXIBILITY IS VASTLY different from indecisiveness. It's good to think on your feet but terrible to vacillate. I had a solid game plan for the Durban World Cup, but I didn't follow it through and that could have cost me the overall trophy. Luckily for me, I realised reasonably early that I had made a wrong choice and turned indecisiveness into flexibility by finishing in the top five. I have always loved the saying that 'he who hesitates is lost'. Make a decision and stick by it.

22

Enter the Dragon

Once Epic Kayak's divorce from Flying Eagle was finalised, we had to move lightning fast to resume operations in China. With a backlog of orders longer than a dragon's tail, we had no other option if we wanted to survive.

However, things looked bleak as no machinery had yet been installed in the new premises, which had originally been leased three months earlier to produce paddles. We didn't even have moulds to make new boats, while those that had been finished and paid for were locked up in the Flying Eagle factory. But we still held a single trump card: the kayaks that we had sneaked out before the factory doors were bolted. We would make moulds from those.

That was without question crucial to our future plans. We had shipped those surfskis to a fictitious address in Hong Kong when everything started going south, then rerouted them back to our new factory under the noses of our former partners. Our new Chinese company was called Hangzhou Epic Boat Co. Ltd., and was a wholly owned subsidiary of Epic Kayaks Inc., giving us complete control of the manufacturing process. We now deliberately shied away from any local partnerships, and the new premises were soon transformed into a beehive of activity as we worked feverishly to fit temperature-controlled laminating rooms, high-capacity vacuum pumps and a large oven for post-curing. The round-the-clock work paid off, and in January 2009 we were ready to start production again.

However, the problem wasn't only eliminating the enormous backlog of orders; our reputation was at stake if we could not honour our deals. We had just recovered from supply and quality-control problems stemming from our previous South African factory, and now we were in another crisis. Fortunately, the kayaking world was well aware of our hassles in China and we had some sympathy. But even so, I spent most of that year putting out fires. If I wasn't a seasoned troubleshooter beforehand, I certainly was now through sheer force of necessity. As the public face of Epic Kayaks, either through racing or marketing, I was the go-to guy whenever something went pear-shaped. Believe me, in those tumultuous times, a lot was going wrong and I did plenty of arm-twisting to keep our clients happy and the orders rolling in.

Greg, Charles and I also decided this was an ideal opportunity to launch a new range to show we were back and that we were still the prime mover and shaker in the surfski world. That year we brought out the V-12 and V-14 models as well as an updated version of the V-10, which stimulated further orders, albeit putting our production team under even more pressure. 'V' in Epic-speak is the stability factor of a surfski, so the V-12 is designed for advanced paddlers, while the V-14 is for the elite. We also launched a new V-10 double-surfski, which again sent our assembly lines soaring into overdrive.

With these new products, most of our stock still being held by Flying Eagle was now obsolete. Consequently, when they did return our moulds and materials – up to three years later – they were useless to us. Hangzhou Epic was a start-up from scratch in every conceivable sense: new machinery, new staff, new moulds and new products. Although Tyrell Impson and Greg project-managed this transition, it was still a major team effort. However, I think that by being the most gregarious member of the team as well as a co-founder, I was the natural person to handle flack when the smelly stuff hit the fan.

Then, to my surprise, I was approached by the management of Flying Eagle with what they called a 'top secret' offer. They wanted me to leave Epic and start my own brand of kayaks that they would build, and they would also sponsor me in races around the world. Tempting as that sounded, I considered it for about a nanosecond. My loyalty was to Epic, and there was no way I would jump ship at such a critical stage for the company.

In fact, the exact opposite happened. Instead of me jumping ship and joining Flying Eagle, some of their senior staff joined us, making our shift to full-scale production much easier. Talk about rubbing salt into wounds! We openly called their bluff to 'fine' us if we recruited their staff, as one thing there is no shortage of in China is labour. Even the most partisan court would hesitate in penalising a company for providing large-scale employment.

Our new landlord was great, and as he had no interest in the manufacturing side of the business, he was the perfect partner. When he saw we were rapidly outgrowing the original premises, he leased us another 10 000-square-metre factory about three kilometres away. After a few less-than-effective supervisors, I eventually persuaded Charles and Greg to appoint Tyrell as factory manager. Tyrell had worked closely with me since our Durban days and was a huge success.

The launch of the latest models kept me busier than usual, as I entered as many races as possible to show how good the new boats were. Everything started falling into place – except that I was still not earning much money. However, that was because we were still paying off the exorbitant start-up costs of the new factory, so the situation would soon improve dramatically. Or so I thought.

Then, in 2009, I was thrown a curve ball that was totally unexpected. Charles informed me that the company was in financial difficulties and that it had been agreed that my salary was going to be suspended for the foreseeable future. Reeling from shock, Clare and I had to leave our home in Mount Edgecombe and move to a compact three-bedroom apartment at the Point Waterfront, a renovated quarter next to Durban's dockyards that had once been the city's red-light district. As always, our friends rather than our business associates came to our assistance. Dr Len Nel, my dermatologist for more than thirty years; Richard Downey, owner of the outdoor and transportation company Thule South Africa; and Richard Barrow, a long-standing family friend and co-owner of Barrows Design and Manufacturing, stepped in and offered to pay our monthly rental so that at least we could stay in our own home. We declined, as we needed to fight this on our own, but the magnificence of Len and the two Richards' gesture will never be forgotten.

We could no longer afford two cars, so we had to get rid of one. I felt that my family and I had been hung out to dry. In my opinion, there is no other term for it. The only money I would now earn from Epic was a per diem rate while travelling. This forced me to be continuously on the move, away from home as much as possible, just to pay the bills. To supplement my shrinking income, I started coaching clinics in whatever town I was in at the time. These began with small gatherings at various kayak clubs but rapidly spread through word of mouth. Within a year, I was holding Coach Chalupsky sessions around the world – Europe, Hong Kong, Australia, New Zealand, you name it. Whenever I found I had a couple of spare days, groups of paddlers would gather on beaches or lakes for what I promised would be masterclasses. These were also a good marketing tool for Epic as I knew first-hand that getting bums in boats was a sure-fire sales technique.

Epic management didn't seem to see it that way. Instead, they deducted the money I earned from coaching from my per diem rate. Even so, I persisted and continued with clinics that spread from Amsterdam to Auckland, and we also started a paddling school in Tarifa on the southern tip of Spain. It's an ideal spot as the wind funnels down the narrow Strait of Gibraltar, providing some of the best adrenaline paddling in the world.

However, I needed alternative income badly, and Herman gave me a part-time job selling property at his real-estate company, Chalupsky Properties. Herman was the challenger I feared more than any other on the water, but to friends and family his loyalty is unsurpassed. In fact, when I was travelling and Clare was tied up doing other stuff, he would drive Luke and Hannah to school. He is a true blood brother.

The most embarrassing episode of all was when I was unable to pay Hannah's school fees. I told the principal I never defaulted on debts and would settle the account in a couple of days, as I feverishly scrambled around to find funds. Thanks to loans from my dear mother-in-law Norma, brother-in-law Sean, and Herman, Hannah was soon back in class. Our family and friends always stepped up to offer assistance, but disappointingly the same wasn't always true of my business partners.

Then, as often happens in the midst of financial adversity, out of the blue a stroke of luck came my way. Dean Gardiner, the downwind flyer and nine-times Molokai champion, offered me a top-dollar job coaching in Australia. Dean, who is also a veteran boat skipper, had chartered a luxury catamaran and come up with the great idea of charging people five-star rates to hone their surfski skills along the Kimberley coast of north-western Australia. It's without doubt one of the most spectacular stretches of coral reefs and beaches in the world, and I would do most of the coaching while Dean handled the overall organisation. It was billed as the Trip of a Lifetime, and for once the advertising hype was spot on. The beautiful coastline consists of more than 12 000 kilometres of untouched wilderness with more than 2 500 castaway islands and archipelagos. The area is unique, not only in marine life but also in the red sand cliffs that glow like fires in the sunset. With winds blowing constantly from the south, it is also a surfskier's paradise.

Dean is an immensely likeable guy, and with our combined reputations the charters were fully booked almost a year in advance. People raved about them: the scenery, the gourmet food, the crystal waters, the unsurpassed reef diving and – I'm happy to say – the coaching. However, because of the volatile hurricane season in that part of the world, we could only do two a year, taking ten passengers per trip. I coached on these charters for three consecutive years, which significantly boosted our income in a time when we needed it most.

After that came a welcome blast from the past. Johan Marais, a co-founding member of Citadel, asked me to be marketer and sales representative of a new company he and his brothers were starting. It was called Spice Mobile, and with the explosion of the cellphone industry in South Africa, we planned to get in on the ground by marketing lease-cost routing. It has now morphed into a company called NuMobile, and today we are one of the country's leading smartphone providers to low-income employees. Clare was my assistant, and NuMobile salaries also helped keep us afloat in some of the darker days. I am still actively involved with the company.

However, even with the other jobs, Epic still took up most of my time and I was doing a lot of travelling. The company's books in South Africa were in disarray, mainly owing to a lack of dedicated staff and my constant travelling, but still, when I got a call demanding a full professional audit, it was a bitter blow. Until the audit was completed, even my travel allowance was suspended.

I was overseas selling kayaks, visiting our Chinese factory, racing and attending kayak shows, so Clare had to wade through a morass of receipts and invoices, and Sean McCarthy of the SMG Group, who was also a great friend and sponsor, instructed his company's accountant at the time, Ken Burt, to assist and provide a spreadsheet of my income and expenditure. This information was then further checked and correlated with Epic's financial documentation by accountant Mark Bradley of BVDM Accountants in Port Elizabeth.

Even that didn't stop Epic Kayaks from calling on me to troubleshoot when there were difficulties. I remember on two occasions when containers of surfskis arrived from China with no one from the South African side of the business to receive them, so they could not be offloaded. As usual, I was overseas on Epic business, so Clare and Luke stepped in, employing casual workers to unpack the containers and warehouse them. The second time Herman again came to our rescue, letting us use his underground garage as we simply didn't have storage space.

Unfortunately, Epic appeared to take all this for granted. If there was a problem, 'the Chalupskys will sort it out' seemed to be the prevailing attitude. My suspicions were to some extent confirmed when a new employee in the accounts department inadvertently sent me a spreadsheet listing the salaries of staff in our US office. As I wasn't on the administrative mailing list, I had little idea of what anyone else was paid.

I scanned the list with absolute amazement. While I was not earning a regular salary, all other managers were being paid top rates in the industry. I immediately confronted Charles, who said that as I lived in South Africa, my expenses were lower than those of staff in America. Consequently, I didn't 'merit' the same payment. I pointed out that I was paid for the job, not where I lived, but that didn't make any difference.

I was now seriously considering quitting, but I decided to make a final decision after racing the Molokai of 2012, which was a couple of months away.

It was a good choice. That race was destined to be one of the biggest and most memorable milestones of my life.

LESSON LEARNT

LOYALTY HAS TO BE EARNED, as the saying goes. But what happens when loyalty is unrewarded?

That was the dilemma facing me at Epic Kayaks. I worked my butt off marketing our products around the world; I gave 100 per cent even when my salary was suspended. But, as far as I was concerned, that was not being reciprocated. Consequently, I had two choices: stay or go.

It was not a new situation for me, in either sport or business. In endurance racing, you have to know when to go for it. You can break too early, which is forgivable, or you can break too late, which is not.

In business, you also have to know when to make a strategic break. Timing is crucial. That's why I decided to play my cards with Epic close to my chest – despite the fact that in my opinion they took my loyalty for granted.

But was I too late?

I still had a trick up my sleeve: the Molokai.

23

Race of a lifetime

As the 2012 Molokai approached, I was the fattest I had been in my life. I tipped the scales at 122 kilograms, or in old currency, 268 pounds.

To put that in perspective, when I raced in the Barcelona Olympics almost twenty years earlier, I was ninety-six kilograms. Joe Glickman joked that my weight fluctuated more than the national debt of a banana republic.

So once again the press was writing that I was way too ancient and, even worse, too corpulent.

As I was holding down four jobs, unlike professional athletes I couldn't dedicate 100 per cent of my time to preparing for the race – so much so that I had to time-manage my training down to the last minute. I also gave up alcohol for a month and started a ketogenic low-carb, high-fat diet. The main benefit of a keto diet as far as athletes are concerned is that energy-wise, fat is the equivalent of avgas and carbohydrates are kerosene. I also gave up sugar-saturated energy drinks and now drank only water while training.

It was an exceptionally busy year. I was attending dealer conferences and boat shows, while also coaching around the world – even in Mumbai, where Proteas captain Shaun Pollock, who was playing in the IPL Twenty20, joined a clinic. To squeeze in some competitive paddling, I raced in Hong Kong, Spain and Sweden, and won the K-3 section of the Fish River Marathon with Herman and Andy Leith. As most paddling pundits say that at least a year of dedicated training is needed to win the Molokai, my demanding travel schedule took up far more of my time than I would have liked.

Clare and I arrived in Oahu twelve days before the race, following my iron-clad rule that you need a day in Hawaii for every time zone crossed to shake off jet lag. But gone were the days when I arrived broke, having to sleep on Bob Twogood's sofa and hoping like hell my surfski would arrive in one piece from the flight over. Instead, Clare and I were feted at our good friend Kate Rose's magnificent beachfront home overlooking Hawaii Kai, while everything from my hired car to my escort boat was sponsored. This is no mean consideration as the Molokai is now one of the most expensive surfski races in the world, mainly due to its global prestige. Entrants are either professional paddlers out to win at all costs or enthusiastic amateurs who have this great race on their bucket list, regardless of cost.

On the island I trained hard with Greg Barton, his double-ski partner Zsolt Szadovszki, and Patrick Dolan, an exceptionally fast Hawaiian paddler. By now I had lost about twenty kilograms, so I was in good – if not great – shape. I also spent some time installing a new bailer on my V-12 surfski, as the standard one is an automatic venturi suction system that operates through a hole in the hull. It has a short pipe that creates a slight drag, so I fitted a drag-free bailer that I could open manually to drain when necessary.

Greg queried why I was going to so much trouble for a minor issue.

'This will give me an extra ten seconds,' I said.

He laughed. Ten seconds in a three-and-a-half-hour race? Neither he nor I realised how prophetic that would be, but that's the type of detail I insist on. The same applies to my training regimen, and as sea temperatures in Hawaii are seven degrees Celsius hotter than Durban, at home I had been paddling in full winter gear on a weighted surfski.

This year the race favourite was Matt Bouman, a fellow South African, and he certainly cut an imposing figure; lean, ripped and standing well over two metres tall. Thirteen years younger than me, he's a health fanatic, obsessively fit and doesn't touch a drop of alcohol, so most thought he would be the one to watch. But the rest of the line-up was equally impressive, particularly among the Aussies with Olympic gold medallist and last year's winner Clint Robinson, course record-holder Dean Gardiner, Bruce Taylor and Martin Kenny all raring to go. Herman, who was not competing that year, told Joe Glickman in a pre-race interview that he would eat his underpants if I won. Except Herman calls them 'underrods'.

On Sunday 20 May, sixty-five paddlers lined up at Molokai's Kaluakoi Beach, comprising the bulk of the world's elite surfskiing brother- and sister-hood. At forty-nine, I was the oldest by some distance. It was also twenty-nine years, almost to the day, since my maiden win in 1983.

As the starting gun fired, Greg and Zsolt shot into the lead with a batch of singles in hot pursuit. I saw Matt, Dean and Clint in the group, but I didn't try to keep up with them as we were still in the lee of the island. I had to remind myself that needed to bide my time until we were further offshore where I could start riding swells.

The wind was strong, gusting up to twenty-five knots, and once we were in the open sea I began getting good runs and concentrating on technique. For me, this was the cat-and-mouse stage of the race. It only really starts once you can clearly see Portlock Point on the southern tip of Oahu. So much can – and does – happen in the final few kilometres.

At about the halfway stage I called out to Chris Laird, skipper of my escort boat, asking where I was lying. In the Molokai you can never tell with complete certainty where you are as the field is so spread out, and in big winds the waves are too steep to keep track of other racers. However, it's essential to keep within striking distance of the leaders, and that is where information from escort boats is vital.

Chris had his young son and daughter on board with him, and they were the best fan club I could wish for, shouting shrill encouragement at the top of their voices. They said I was in about eighth position, which wasn't too bad.

I then started upping the pace, reeling the field in. The first person I over-took was Martin Kenny, who was nearly always in the top five, then Bruce Taylor. That put two of the Aussie stars out of the way.

As I crested a giant swell, I saw Greg and Zsolt about 700 metres ahead, marginally in front of Matt, Dean and Clint, which was good news. Those three are superfast downwind, but then so am I. The main thing was that they weren't flying away from me, and I was happy at that stage to keep it like that. I would put the hammer down as soon as Portlock loomed clearly into view.

Then, about five kilometres from the Point, I saw Dean – but neither Matt nor Clint.

I shouted across to Chris Laird on the boat. 'Where's Robinson?'

'Out of sight,' came the discouraging reply.

That news nagged. How could Matt and Clint have suddenly disappeared? But first things first. I needed to speed up and catch Dean. Even though I knew I could pass him, I could not fall into the old sloppy trap of just paddling furiously because the top slot was in sight.

However, it's not that simple, as after close on three hours of unrelenting pace, a fatigue-fogged brain tends to wander and you miss a run. To win at my age, I had to catch every wave – but it had to be perfect, surging not only in the direction I wanted to go but maintaining enough speed to accelerate onto another run. In the Channel of Bones, the swells sweep across the ocean rather than straight downwind and riding these runs correctly can be highly technical. Mistakes are extremely costly.

I forced myself to concentrate on good technique, screaming over the wind and swearing, 'Stop using your f**king arms! You have the strongest body … drive with your legs … nobody has as much power as you, NOBODY!'

I tried to surf up to Dean and use my old trick of psyching opponents out. There is nothing worse than someone coming up close and saying, 'Hey, keep it up mate, you're going well' – then effortlessly shooting past. This worked magnificently on Nathan Baggaley in 2005, and I thought it would also work on Dean, even though he is a genuine hardman of the sea. But my angle was too sharp and I couldn't get close enough to convey some choice words of 'encouragement'.

For the next few kilometres, my long-time friend and arch-rival sped downwind with grim determination. Dean was going for his tenth win, and before I arrived that must have seemed tantalisingly close. He was pushing himself to the absolute limit, but even so I reached the edge of the striated cliffs of Portlock first, five boat-lengths ahead.

The saying is that if you still have the balance and the balls, after Portlock you head close to China Walls and catch the heart-stopping runs over the shallow reef at the end. That's exactly what I did, and it was what I had been practising since I had arrived in Hawaii twelve days earlier. I knew it was cutting it fine, as the wind and currents are always surging, not to mention the absolute exhaustion at this stage of the race.

Suddenly, to my horror, I felt a thud. I had touched the reef. Disaster! The race is over when that happens as the coral snaps a rudder like a toothpick. Without a rudder, your race is history.

I pushed tentatively on the pedal and whistled a huge sigh of relief. The rudder was intact, but wow, that had been close.

At the same time, I heard spectators lining China Walls shouting and pointing. I also saw Chris and his kids from the escort boat frantically waving their arms, trying to attract my attention.

Wondering what all the commotion was about, I violated one of my golden rules and glanced behind me. Sure enough, there was a paddler coming up fast, but it didn't look like Dean. If it had been, I wouldn't have worried as I knew I could beat him on that horrible final stretch of flat-water grind.

It was definitely someone else. And he was gaining on me. I then recognised the black boat. An Epic. It was Clint Robinson, one of the quickest paddlers on the planet.

What I didn't know was that Clint had cramped more than an hour earlier and taken a line into calmer conditions further south to make it easier for him to recover. That was why I didn't see him at Portlock Cliffs, and he was now making up for lost time.

There were only two kilometres to go, but this is the worst part of the race. It is slap into the wind and properly hideous. Most paddlers are beyond shattered after running along the Walls, and turning head-first into the wind for the finish at Hawaii Kai is unadulterated torture. It's made even worse by little waves that seem to be there only to tease you. You're so drained that catching them is idiotically hard. Anyone who thinks that once they've rounded Portlock they're going to sprint to the end is delusional.

Clint was flying under these horrendous conditions, but I had another trick up my sleeve. There were about five minutes of the race left and I had already shortened my paddle to 210 centimetres, which meant that I was in top gear. Paddle length is like gears on a racing bicycle, and a shorter paddle is a higher gear. In other words, while your cadence – how quickly you are paddling – is the same, the speed-to-power ratio is increased. So just as a cyclist changes gear when going uphill, a kayaker shortens their paddle as they get more tired or go into the wind. I had started with my paddle at 219 centimetres, then shortened it by two centimetres every hour, so I was in top gear during that final exhausting stretch. Greg Barton invented the adjustable paddle, but very few – if any – surfskiers initially linked length adjustment to gear ratio. In fact, as far as I know, for several years I was the only one doing so. Now most top paddlers do.

I crossed the line twenty seconds ahead of Clint. Perhaps it would have been only ten if I hadn't put on a manual bailer, as Clint was using a venturi. Who knows? But it proved my point that attention to detail is vital.

People say I was subdued at the end of the race. But there was a good reason. I was so wrecked that I was hyperventilating. I could barely muster a smile, let alone raise an arm in victory. I could not have paddled another metre. I had given it everything I had and judged the race to absolute perfection. It was the finest performance of my life.

The press seemed to think so as well, and the story gripped journalists, athletes and sports scientists around the world, all trying to rationalise how I had beaten elite athletes who were half my age. Some said it was the paddling equivalent of Jack Nicklaus winning the 1986 Masters at the age of forty-six, still the oldest-ever winner of that golfing classic.

The answer to why I was still winning was best articulated by top sports scientist and nutritionist Professor Tim Noakes. He said that while I didn't have the same flexibility, power and strength that I once had, I made up for it in two key ways: technically and mentally. I agree with that and would add that it's also because I still love doing it.

Whatever the reason, at that moment I was riding on a high like never before. To add to the celebrations, it was the first time Clare had watched me take the Molokai trophy. She had been out to the islands a number of times before, but she'd never seen me win. In fact, she thought she jinxed me!

The best compliment was from Australian Mike Booth, who finished eleventh. 'For someone who is basically my father's age to win is mind-blowing,' he said. 'It's one of the best sporting performances I have ever been part of.'[4]

Mike, who today is a world champion stand-up paddleboarder, was twenty-one at the time.

Matt Bouman, who finished by his standards a disappointing eighth, was equally magnanimous, showing what a great sportsman he is. He said to Rob Mousley of Surfski.info afterwards that my win was 'without doubt the single most impressive human performance in a sporting arena, that I have witnessed. I salute Oscar for it.'[5]

Meanwhile, back home, Herman faced a bit of a dilemma. What pair of underrods was he going to eat?

LESSONS LEARNT

AGE IS NOT EVERYTHING. I have regularly been asked if I felt any different racing the Molokai at forty-nine than I had when I'd last won it at forty-four. The answer is simple: not one bit. I have the same brain, the same confidence, the same skills. I've always maintained that age is more about motivation than anything else. My times on many runs that I've done for the past twenty years are still much the same. In fact, the stopwatch worries me far more than Father Time.

SET YOUR GOALS HIGH. Unfortunately, many of us have too many doubts. Too many 'cant's'. We don't set goals that are ambitious enough, and if we do, we often don't have a plan on how to achieve them. I can't stress that strongly enough; first know what you want, then have a plan on how you aim to do it.

For this race, I had a plan that I stuck to. I spent most of a day modifying my bailer to give me an extra ten seconds over a fifty-three-kilometre course. I adjusted my paddle length at crucial times, so when Clint made his break at the end, I was ready for him.

No one, least of all Herman, thought I could win that race.

BALANCE OF LIFE IS CRUCIAL. I would not be racing today if I didn't love it. Enjoyment is everything, and to enjoy life you have to have the right balance. I train hard, race hard and have fun at the same time.

The story is still told about one Molokai when Herman and I split a case of beer the night before the race. He came first; I came third. While I don't necessarily recommend that everyone does that, the point is never to lose your sense of fun. That's why I think so many people burn out at a young age.

Even now fighting cancer, I am still out there on the ocean, having fun and racing – and loving it!

24

An Epic farewell

Although my first Molokai against Grant Kenny was probably my most exciting, this was the best race of my life. Not only winning it but defying all prevailing logic made the victory even sweeter.

The Molokai is not known among surfskiers as the world championship for nothing. Most consider it to be the toughest race on the circuit, as it's a titanic contest not solely against top competitors but also against unyielding forces of nature. The fact that it's not directly downwind also makes it one of the more technically demanding. No other ocean-paddling race involves such a high threshold of pain and skill, and there is no other contest that requires competitors to struggle for so long in sheer bloody-minded survival mode. Whoever survives the longest will win. In contrast, Ze Caribbean Race in Guadeloupe that I won in 2018 is roughly the same distance, but it's a perfect downwind run and comes nowhere near the Molokai in terms of mind-numbing, muscle-grinding exhaustion.

I had now won the Molokai in three different age categories: seven times in my twenties, twice in my thirties, and three times in my forties. Could I now do so in my fifties as well? That seemed insane, but the way I felt at the time, anything was possible.

However, one of the most noticeable changes for me was that the race fundamentally changed the dynamics of my relationship with Epic Kayaks. I was no longer just a co-founder and shareholder: I was a highly visible asset. Not least was the symbolism of the number twelve – the 2012 Molokai was held on 12 May, I had now won twelve times, and Epic had been in existence for twelve years. And, of course, I was racing an Epic V-12. That gave the marketing department a field day for great, if hyperbolic, advertising copy.

To add a cherry on the top, the doubles section was won by the other co-founder, Greg Barton, giving Epic surfskis a clean sweep. In fact, no one was more surprised at my victory than Greg – barring Herman, of course. Even when he and Zsolt turned into the wind at China Walls and saw me catching Dean, he still thought there was no way that 'the old guy' could prevail against such a strong field. When he told me that, I pointed out I was actually catching him and Zsolt at the end. Despite their combined muscle power, they only finished a couple of minutes ahead of me.

I don't think it's happened before that an ageing director goes out and beats the top athletes their company is sponsoring, but winning that race was undoubtedly a corporate turning point. Disputes over my basic earnings were settled, my salary was increased, and I was paid a retainer as well as a daily rate while travelling on behalf of the company.

We also sold a shedload of boats, as nothing breeds success like success. Both Clint and I were racing Epic V-12s, a fact not lost on the kayak industry, and orders soared.

With everything progressing well on the business front, Charles decided to open another factory. The problems in China, where we had so nearly lost everything, had scarred us deeply and Charles was determined that we never again had all our eggs in one basket. It was true that our current Chinese operation was running smoothly, but we needed to find another base just in case.

The most promising venue seemed to be the Philippines, an industrious although poor nation that was going out of its way to attract foreign investors. Consequently, in 2013 Charles went on an LSD (look, see, decide) mission and visited Mactan in the Cebu province. Although densely populated, Mactan is a beautiful coral island with some of the finest diving, snorkelling, sailing and surfskiing activities of any island in the Philippines. It's also close to the commercial hub of Cebu City and he decided it was ideal for our purposes.

The cost of starting up a factory in the Philippines was marginally cheaper than our Fuyang operation, but the biggest attraction was that everyone spoke English. This was in stark contrast to China, where negotiations were hampered by torturous, time-consuming translations. At times we were never sure whether we were being misled or misunderstood. Or both.

This would be Epic's fourth start-up operation in our relatively short history. Once again, it was a team effort and I was tasked with making contacts, finding the right people to approach, playing golf with decision makers, and feeling our way around the different business and cultural environments.

The first thing we did differently from our China operation was that we bought the factory outright. It belonged to us, and we decided to use it for building our most expensive prepreg boats and any other models that we suspected would be knocked off in China, where copyright laws are not exactly sacrosanct.

Our staff were mainly women, and they were honest and hardworking. Theft problems were almost unheard of. The work environment was terrific, and once again I made sure every staff member learnt how to kayak. This was much easier than in China as the weather was superb, the waters less polluted, and the Philippines is an island nation already familiar with paddling. We didn't have to start from scratch, as we had in Fuyang. Also, the expats were among the friendliest foreign communities I've ever come across.

At roughly the same time, I came up with an idea for another model that would be our most successful boat to date. We called it the V-7, and it would be a major game changer for Epic.

The 'lightbulb incident' happened at a kayak expo in Nuremberg, Germany, where among the hundreds of new products I came across a lightweight polyethylene sea kayak on display. In paddling, weight is crucial as the average sea kayak is a fairly cumbersome thirty-five to forty kilograms. Every manufacturer is constantly trying to juggle that downwards without sacrificing strength, and my goal was to bring out a virtually unbreakable model that weighed at the most twenty kilograms.

I studied the lightweight boat carefully, spoke to the manufacturers, and then had a brainwave. This was breakthrough technology we could adapt, as the Italians were already making 'rock-and-roll' rotomoulding machines that produced cost-effective linear polyethylene that was much lighter and stiffer than any comparable product on the market. Using that, we could make an almost indestructible surfski that everyone could afford. The total cost would be $999, half the price of a standard model.

I told Greg about it and he was equally excited. My skill is dreaming up new concepts and his is designing them to my specifications, so we got to work right away. Once we had a blueprint, we started negotiations with a South African kayak manufacturer, Celliers Kruger, who operated out of a factory in Parys on the Vaal River. Celliers said he could build the ideal rock-and-roll oven to make the V-7. We told him to go ahead, then had an aluminium mould built in China, which we would install in Parys as soon as we could.

I had no doubt that sales of the V-7 would go through the roof. There was no way that a shatterproof surfski that could also be used on rivers and was half the price of anything else on the market would not take off like a skyrocket. In fact, I was so confident that I started telling dealers about it before we had even built our first one. As a result, we sold many boats on pre-order, sight unseen. As far as I know, nothing like that had happened before, not only at Epic but in the entire kayak-manufacturing industry. The first boat I co-designed that had turned Epic's fortunes around was the hugely popular Getaway, and now just over a decade later, history was repeating itself with the V-7. One of Epic's American managers later told me that the V-7 was fundamental for the company's continued success in an era of snowballing costs and fierce competition.

Once the aluminium mould arrived from China, production started in earnest. But with such large orders, we had to work around the clock and soon started encountering staff problems. Morale was low from the long hours of each shift, and unfortunately there were some blemishes on the boats. Consequently, a lot of supervision was needed in those early stages.

I had been through this before, so when not travelling I spent whatever time I could in Parys. As I have said, my whole approach to working with colleagues, staff and factory workers is to earn respect and loyalty. My boisterous enthusiasm for the V-7 project in Parys was tempered by my efforts to build relationships with the staff and workers.

Consequently, to keep morale buoyant, I made sure I was present at all shift changes, brought in buckets of Kentucky Fried Chicken on weekends, ran an in-house WhatsApp group with daily progress updates, organised fun paddling days on the river during time off, and generally did whatever it took to boost team spirit. This was not always easy as the assembly-line staff, including the two very capable shift managers, were working like slaves without getting any credit for their hard work. I sensed that more than anything else we needed to foster good staff relationships, otherwise there would be the predictable domino effect of shoddy workmanship and order backlogs. In short, I wanted to correct all problems at their source rather than put out fires later.

The fact that I deliberately promoted one-on-one relationships with staff – providing food, fun and encouragement – didn't seem to sit well with Celliers. I accept that I may have unwittingly demonstrated a sharp contrast to how I perceived Celliers treating staff, which could have created resentment on his part, but at the time I believed that the positive gains I thought I was making with staff and workers, and the resulting increases in production quality, could only make me be seen as a welcome asset to the business partnership. Whatever the reason, he wrote a letter to Charles listing a host of grievances about me and ending with an ultimatum: either I go or he does.

Incredibly, I was banned from visiting Epic factories unless I was personally invited by managers, and worse, I had to apologise to Celliers. So I found myself grappling with this bewildering reaction from Charles after creating another successful product line for Epic that became a major cash cow for the company. I had been at the coalface in Parys from the beginning, worked extremely hard to achieve a winning team ethos among staff who were being asked to work punishingly long hours, and delivered in volumes on my original vision.

Charles had only visited the Parys factory once or twice, but he was aware that Celliers was often not on the premises. As far as I was concerned, Charles had caved in to a commercially foolish ultimatum by a seemingly disgruntled factory owner we had been working with for less than twelve months, and then delivered what I believed was an even more foolish ultimatum to an Epic co-founder and shareholder.

I pointed this out to Charles, along with the irrationality of the situation. We had experienced far more serious situations over the years and had mostly worked through them together. It was my opinion that Celliers was merely wanting to have his ego restored, which could be achieved with a united front and a professional problem-solving approach. Rather than Charles listening to what I thought was reasonable, however, during the course of my discussion with him he pointed out that a subordinate staff member had now also made a complaint about me, and to my utter disbelief he asked me to apologise to her as well. I had endured the indignity of having my salary cut, earning less than other senior staff members, continuously having to travel and be away from my family, and devoting a large part of my life and energy to building and promoting the Epic brand. This was the final straw. There was nothing more to say.

I handed in my notice and left with immediate effect.

Seven months later, the Parys factory closed down.

LESSON LEARNT

ALWAYS FOLLOW YOUR CONSCIENCE.

Even though I felt I had resolved problems with Epic after my twelfth Molokai win, sadly it was short-lived. Their willingness – in my opinion – to jeopardise a fifteen-year partnership on a whim was bad enough, but the notion that I was no more valued than the next employee was too much to contemplate. The timing was now right for me to leave Epic Kayaks. I did so with regret but secure in the knowledge that I had always loyally done my best for the company.

And remember, if one door closes, another will open – as we shall see.

25

Cool canoeing

The most celebrated river race in South Africa is the Dusi Canoe Marathon.

It's a three-day, 120-kilometre dice down two rivers that come together in a jagged valley of a thousand hills and ends in an Indian Ocean lagoon. It's easily the biggest river race on the African continent, and one of the largest marathons of its kind in the world.

Unfortunately for my family, it is the only major kayak race in the country that no Chalupsky has won. That hasn't been from lack of trying. Indeed, my father and all three of his sons have given it a full-throttled go. My best is a third-place finish, although I held the record for the fastest final day with Springbok Les Keay for more than a decade.

The race, starting on the Umsindusi River in Pietermaritzburg and finishing at the mouth of the Umgeni River in Durban, was founded by world-renowned conservationist Ian Player, elder brother of the even more famous golfer Gary. The idea, almost a vision, first came to him as a homesick soldier huddling miserably around the campfire on the battle-ravaged Italian front. Tired to his bones of bloodshed and bullets, his only escape from the horrors of the Second World War was dreaming about the absolute freedom of roaming the pristine bush in his native land – specifically the rivers spanning Natal's two major cities. He vowed that if he survived the war, he would paddle those wild waterways to celebrate being back home.

In the first race, Player was the only paddler to finish. It took him six days and eight hours, having survived two days of low rivers, then a flash flood, and finally a night adder snakebite. That was in 1950, and the magnificent legend of the Dusi was born.

Paul Chalupsky, my father, was one of the earliest contestants. But as mentioned, the Chalupskys are not fleet of foot and the Dusi is more of a biathlon than a pure paddling race. What my dad gained in the water, he lost on land.

But to live in South Africa and not race the Dusi is missing out on one of the country's great sporting highlights, so the Chalupskys kept entering.

I eventually accepted that the river would have to be at Everest levels with no portages for me to stand a chance of winning.

But there were other ways I could contribute. In the early 1990s, marketing guru Ray de Vries and I came up with the idea of enticing celebrities to take part as a publicity tactic to boost race entries. However, as few – if any – celebrities knew how to paddle, this was a problem.

'We'll need someone to hold their hands,' said Ray.

'I'll do it,' I replied.

I didn't say this lightly. The Dusi is a hard race. It has a number of hazardous rapids and at least two paddlers have lost their lives. If the water is low, you risk holing your boat on the gazillion jutting rocks strewn like primed grenades along the riverbed. If the water is high, the rapids rage and flip boats with explosive abandon. The slick portages up steep hill slopes are gruelling. Many contestants don't finish, and each day sees scores of splintered kayaks littering the banks as paddlers feverishly try to patch them up. I would have to be super-vigilant ensuring any celebrity's safety. The fallout of such a potentially high-profile failure would be frightening.

We decided to take it even further. Not only would I be escorting them down the river, but most would also stay with me and Clare at our home for the duration of the race. So it would be an intense, all-consuming kayaking experience for them, being with me almost around the clock.

The first person we approached was Springbok rugby legend Naas Botha, one of the finest fly-halves in the world. Botha, who was in great shape and still playing at top level, eagerly accepted. However, apart from his sports commitments, he was also making a name for himself as an astute rugby commentator and was extremely busy. Consequently, we had no time to train together – just a brief paddle in a rain-filled quarry on the side of the N2 highway.

He had to do a TV broadcast in Johannesburg the night before the race, so he caught a red-eye flight to Durban, where I picked him up and then sped to Pietermaritzburg. The Dusi start is a gut-swooping drop down the wall of the Ernie Pearce Weir, thick with flailing paddles and crashing boats, providing a terrifying baptism of fire for a novice.

Not only did Naas survive that, but we shot every other rapid in sight, only getting out when the water was too low. As expected, Naas was intensely competitive and whenever we got caught in a logjam of paddlers on the portages, I just shouted, 'Naas Botha would like to come through!' Such was his status that the crowd in front of us opened like Moses parting the Red Sea.

At the end of each stage, Ray's organisational flair had the media thronging the overnight stops, where Naas, often clutching a paddle, gave interviews. The publicity was so widespread that more people knew Naas was in the race than who was actually winning. Most major newspapers gave daily blow-by-blow accounts, with Naas in the headline.

On the third day we shot the Grade 4 rapid called Tops Needle, a major feat for a beginner, and had our first case of capsizing. I think we even broke a paddle, and I remember Naas's blond head popping up out of the foaming water with that famous toothy grin. He was having the time of his life. We ended up in the top 10 per cent of the field, a phenomenal achievement even for a fit, world-class sportsman like Naas. The Dusi is extremely unforgiving for inexperienced paddlers.

Naas was a great advocate for the race and for weeks afterwards would mention it even when commentating on rugby games for SuperSport, the country's premier TV sports channel. He was also at pains to point out how tough it could be.

The publicity we got from Naas's 'guest appearance' was so phenomenal that the following year the Dusi attracted more than 1500 entrants. Consequently, Ray and I decided to stick with our winning formula and invite another celebrity. This time we approached Clive Barker, the South African football coach who steered the national team to victory in the 1996 Africa Cup of Nations.

Unlike Naas, Clive was not in peak condition. In his fifties and nursing a knee injury from his professional football-playing days, he had trouble getting in and out of the kayak. But Clive was not one to complain, although perhaps it is fortunate that we didn't have a single swim in the entire race – again, remarkable for a novice.

Taking Clive down the river was an incredible eye-opener for me. Although rural, the Umgeni valley is not by any stretch of the imagination sparsely populated. The days of Ian Player dreaming of 'pristine bushveld' while fighting in war-torn Italy are long gone. Today, it's home to many thousands of people, and it seemed that every one of them had come to see Clive. I had no idea how revered he was among black South Africans. Huge crowds lined the riverbanks, cheering like crazy when we appeared and mobbing us on the portages. Knowing that Clive had a crook knee, I told him to ask the kids to carry our kayak. The response was simply staggering. At one portage I think we had thirty youngsters vying to get a hold on the boat as we clambered up a hill. It was superb to see how much they loved him, and he reciprocated magnificently, signing autographs, chatting, joking and enjoying himself immensely.

The unbelievable reception in the valley spurred us on the following year to invite another football star, and through Clive we reached out to Doctor Khumalo, the country's most famous midfielder. This was quite a feat as Doc was not only one of the busiest people I know and forever on his cellphone, he had never seen a kayak before – let alone watched a river race. Indeed, when we arrived at the start, he asked where our 'team' was. He had expected the equivalent of an entire football squad to accompany us.

'It's just you and me, Doctor,' I replied.

As we were about to glide down the fast-flowing Ernie Pearce Weir wall, barely 100 metres from the start, he shouted, 'WHAT? Are we going down there?'

I nodded. 'That's where we're going.'

We were soon through, and as with Naas, I shot every rapid we could. But the roar of the raging water was nothing compared to the ecstatic cheering along the river. The crowds went even more ballistic than they had with Clive, and the chant 'V16' – Doc's nickname – thundered throughout the valley. Once again, neither Doc nor I had to carry our kayak anywhere on the portages. He was not that concerned about where we came and didn't push as hard as either Naas or Clive had, but he was still competitive. In fact, he blamed me for the one and only time we fell out. I had to stop myself from laughing out loud. But it was a great race and we finished in the top third of the field.

Then the organisers noticed an amazing side effect of the celebrity factor. The crime problems that had plagued the race for the past few years largely disappeared. There had always been petty theft at the overnight camps, but more worrying were the increasing instances of stones thrown at kayakers, and even fishhooks dangled on string over bridges to snag hats off paddlers below. With Clive and now Doctor Khumalo participating, this ceased almost overnight. It seemed that the locals now felt they were part of the race in their backyard. In retrospect, that – as much as the publicity generated – was our biggest achievement.

The next celebrity was one of the nicest people I have met. Jacob 'Baby

Jake' Matlala was a former welterweight boxing champion and, standing a mere 1.47 metres barefoot, is to this day the shortest boxer ever to win a world title. I was half a metre taller and we must have been a sight for sore eyes coming down the river, as he also only weighed about 48 kilograms compared to my 118 kilograms.

For the first time, all entrants that year were required to pass a river-proficiency test and Baby Jake, like most of my celebrities, couldn't swim a stroke. In fact, he sank like a stone, even with his life jacket on. Somehow we got him through the test, but as fate would have it, a boat crashed into us at the Ernie Pearce Weir and we capsized. The water was shallow, but I couldn't see Jake anywhere. I had stressed to him that if we overturned, he must rip his splash cover off, lie on his back and go downstream with the current, making sure his feet were in front to fend off rocks. But I couldn't see his head bobbing anywhere among all the other debris in the swirling water. I started to right the kayak, and there was Jake, upside down and hanging on for dear life with his splash cover and even his hat still in place. I pulled him ashore, but he refused to get back into the boat unless I brought it to the riverbank. He didn't want to set foot in the torrent again.

Fortunately, that was the only swim we had. But Jake had genuine rock-star status in the valley, with schoolkids and adults ecstatically chanting 'Baby Jake! Baby Jake!' whenever we appeared. There was also no shortage of people wanting to carry our boat, so once again portages were a pleasure.

Despite the adulation, Baby Jake was extremely humble and truly appreciative of his fans, responding to their cheers with lively banter, victory salutes and being really interactive. He may have been tiny, but he had a giant heart. I was shocked and saddened to hear of his death from pneumonia complications in 2013. He was only fifty-one.

Once again, the publicity for the race was astonishing. We even got coverage from newspapers such as *The Sowetan*, which would never have previously covered a kayak race as it was considered too white and too elite.

The next celebrity was Miss South Africa 1996, Peggy-Sue Khumalo. She was not only beautiful but tough, and she never complained, even when stung by a wasp on the third day. She was also a great ambassador, raving about the race, and again the message of the Dusi was spread far and wide. By now I was used to valley kids carrying our boat and asked Peggy-Sue to make sure we had no shortage of porters. Like Clive Barker, she was the only other celebrity not to take a swim, and I don't think many novices in any fast-flowing river race can claim that. Also, watching Peggy-Sue chatting gaily with hordes of people of all colours following us, I was struck by how far South Africans had come in reaching out to each other. Here was a black beauty queen taking part in an overwhelmingly white (at that time) event, cheered to the rafters by spectators from all walks of life. Obviously we have further to go, but during those celebrity Dusi events I experienced nothing but genuine optimism.

What also helped, although I only found out later, was that some years back I had started the Chalupsky Paddling & Adventure School at the Inanda Dam, which is in the heart of the Umgeni valley. There were often barefoot rural kids on the banks watching us, and every now and again Mat Carlisle and I would put them in a kayak and show them how to paddle. I thought nothing of it at the time, but many people in the valley remembered me for that.

After Peggy-Sue came Sibusiso Vilane, the first black person to climb Mount Everest from both the south and the technically far more difficult north ridges. The north summit he did with the world's most famous explorer, Sir Ranulph Fiennes. Sibusiso is a great guy, very strong and competitive, and was one of my few celebrities who could swim. So it is perhaps fortunate that my worst 'celeb swim' was with him at a rapid called Taxi (so named for the simple reason that a minibus taxi had tried to ford the low-level river during a drought and got swept downstream). The rusting wreck is still lodged among the rocks, but Sibusiso and I managed to retrieve our boat without further mishap.

Almost all Dusi rapids, like Taxi, have practical names. Another one is called Sewage as it's below a sewage farm that sometimes overflows into the river. Many paddlers suffer from diarrhoea – dubbed 'Dusi guts' – during the race, and I was very proud that none of my celebrities did.

Another big-name athlete I took down was Bruce Fordyce, the ultra-distance maestro who won the Comrades Marathon a record nine times. This time we were sponsored by the retail and design fashion company Platinum Group, whose CEO Marcel Joubert accompanied us in a K-3. Marcel does everything with flair and panache, and we raced in a style to which I was certainly unaccustomed with gourmet food and champagne at overnight stops. Bruce is one of the country's most respected runners, and our progress down the river was followed with intense interest.

My final celebrity was Unathi Msengana, a judge on the hit TV show *Idols* and also a radio presenter. She's extremely popular and the only celebrity who actually trained for the race, so she was not only in good shape but also had the basic skills. As a result, she was an avid convert to the sport, saying that for her it had been life-changing.

'This has been one of the greatest experiences of my life and Oscar has been incredible in bringing his wealth of experience to the game,' she told reporters afterwards.

That seemed to be the sentiment of most of the celebrities. However, we did get a couple of rejections: one from firebrand politician Julius Malema, who turned us down flat, and another from the Zulu king Goodwill Zwelithini. I had met His Majesty before, and when I phoned the palace I was put through with minimum fuss. When I said that I wanted to take him down the Dusi, he roared with laughter.

'Oscar, I am far too old,' he said. But he said he appreciated the invite.

Sadly, King Goodwill died in 2021. I am sure he would have loved the race and probably would have been our greatest publicity coup, but I still shudder thinking of the security needed if he had accepted.

But my biggest disappointment was that my good friend golfer Ernie Els couldn't come down with me owing to hectic commitments on the world circuit. Ernie would have loved it as he has the same outlook on adventure and adrenaline sports as I do. However, we later made up for it with a memorable paddle, catching a big swell at the Knysna Heads. This is a legendary spot, as when waves break over the shallow bar, they surge like tsunamis all the way into the Knysna lagoon. It was an exhilarating ride, and I like to think it was as exciting for Ernie as breaking par in a World Masters event – although a little less profitable.

As far as Ray de Vries and I were concerned, our Dusi marketing exercise exceeded the remotest of optimistic expectations. When Ray was appointed media, marketing and sponsorship consultant in 1995, he faced formidable problems. The race had lost its main sponsor, violence and criminality in the valley were skyrocketing, entries were spiralling, and there was no sign of any of the social transformation sweeping through the rest of the country. At most, there were six black paddlers out of a field of 1500. The future of the event looked bleak, and he had little time to turn it around.

'Oscar taking Clive Barker down the river in 1998 was the turning point of the Dusi,' said Ray. 'Suddenly it was cool for the locals to participate and black participation grew exponentially. The race grew in numbers, media attention grew enormously from a handful of journalists in 1995 to over a hundred accredited media in 2000 and the result was that sponsorship grew 100-fold to that of 1995.

'Whilst I was credited with the success of the growth of the Dusi over the nineteen years that I marketed it, a lot of that success was due to media attention as a result of the celebrities that Oscar took down the river. The last year that I marketed the Dusi was 2013. It had grown massively in every area of the race and was rightly one of the big five events in South Africa. Charities received record amounts, there were more black paddlers than ever before, overall numbers of paddlers had exploded, and sponsorship increased from thousands to tens of thousands, to hundreds of thousands and into the millions.

'It could not have been easy for Oscar as the celebrities had little or no paddling experience. Yet each and every one of them told me that Oscar was amazing and it was a highlight of their lives to have done the Dusi with him.'

As Ray says, one thing that cannot be denied is that taking black South African celebrities down the river was a major catalyst in converting kayaking into a truly multiracial sport. Black paddlers now dominate the first ten places in the Dusi Marathon, which says it all.

As for me? To this day, when I am introduced to black South African business clients, many still say, 'I remember you. You won the Dusi.'

If only it was true.

LESSON LEARNT

THE MORE WE THINK we are different, the more we are the same. The best way to discover this self-evident truth is to reach out and make contact with others.

What started out purely as a public-relations exercise for a kayak marathon ended up not only easing crime problems in the Umgeni valley, but also generating significant goodwill among athletes and the people in whose backyard they were racing. We didn't plan that, but by reaching out and making personal contact, it happened by magnificent osmosis.

Life is like that. If you make the effort to get to know people, in the vast majority of cases they will reciprocate.

26

Mellow Nelo

It was one thing to close the door on Epic Kayaks. But it was another thing altogether to decide what to do next.

I initially wasn't that worried as I am a serial entrepreneur and wanted to start my own surfski brand. I probably had more experience in the combination of racing, marketing and production than anyone else on the scene and reckoned I could make a good go of it.

Clare was not keen. She said we had started so many companies, from finance to adventure paddling, which took ages to make profits. Start-up processes are expensive and require a lot of capital and energy to make them work. Even after fifteen years with Epic, we were still having setbacks, despite being the world's largest surfski-manufacturing company. On top of that, I was fifty-three years old.

She had another suggestion. Why don't I speak to Nelo Kayaks?

I stopped dead in my tracks. What a great idea. The Portuguese company is the world's leading top-end sprint kayak manufacturer, winning more global championships than any other. Since the Athens Olympics of 2004, Nelo Kayaks has won a staggering ninety-three Olympic medals. They scooped twenty-seven out of the thirty-six kayaking medals on offer in the 2016 Rio de Janeiro Games alone.

But although their sprint boats were the choice of champions, Nelo Kayaks was not a major force in the surfski market. Perhaps they would be interested in talking to me about expanding that side of the business.

They were, and a third party set up a meeting. I had a good feeling about this, not least because the owner, Manuel Ramos, like me, comes from Africa.

Manuel – whom everyone calls Nelo – was born in Angola. At the time, the West African country was a Portuguese colony, but when the colonialists hurriedly left in 1974, a bitter civil war erupted between three guerrilla armies: the People's Movement for the Liberation of Angola (MPLA), the National Front for the Liberation of Angola (FNLA) and UNITA. The Ramos family returned to Portugal amid the raging battles. Nelo was fourteen years old.

A keen paddler, Nelo had polio as a child, which would have severely hampered most aspiring athletes. Not him. If he didn't walk with a limp, you would not know he'd had polio, as Nelo never mentions it. He does not consider it a handicap. It is what it is, something to overcome, not to discuss. His powerful chunky shoulders are a result of his dedication to his chosen sport, and the fact that he is a former Portuguese K-1 champion speaks volumes of his grit, determination and uncompromising will to win. He started Nelo Kayaks in 1977, and through the same persistence shown in kayak racing, built up the company into what it is today.

Elite paddlers move in relatively small circles, and Nelo and I knew each other but not well. He says he met me in 1979, but I think he means the 1981 Sella Descent in Spain where Mat Carlisle and I came second. We spoke a bit after the race, and what I remember most was that he told me he owned a Chalup-ski, the surfski I had co-designed in South Africa. I have a soft spot for Chalup-skis as I won the bulk of the early Molokais and Texan Challenges in those boats.

At Clare's suggestion, I was keen to renew this old acquaintance and see what followed. However, my first contact with the company after leaving Epic was not with Nelo himself but with André Santos, the CEO, who handles the day-to-day running of the business. This was no surprise as Nelo is a backroom genius, concocting groundbreaking designs among clouds of fibreglass dust and resin in the factory workshop rather than an air-conditioned office.

I had also met André before at various kayak regattas, and during the 2013 World Surfski Championships in Vila do Conde, Portugal, I ran a coaching clinic hosted by Nelo Kayaks. André and I had chatted for a while afterwards, but as I was representing Epic in direct opposition, it was more of an exchange of pleasantries than anything else. He also took me on a tour of the Nelo Kayaks factory.

That all changed in May 2015 when a third party phoned on my behalf saying I had left Epic Kayaks and was looking for new opportunities.

'Let's talk,' said André.

Clare and I flew out to Portugal for preliminary discussions. However, Nelo excused himself saying his English wasn't good enough for such high-level talks, so André and I started thrashing out a deal. It took us ten days to reach an agreement, and the short version is that I would be CEO of the Nelo Surfski division with the specific brief of making the Nelo brand as prized in surfskis as it is in kayaks. It was a big task, with both Epic and Fenn surfskis dominating the global market by some margin.

When André and I told Nelo we had reached a deal, he was delighted. André, who is also hands-on in the factory, said in kayaking terms it was the equivalent of Sporting Football Club poaching the top coach from Benfica. I suppose you might have to be Portuguese to grasp the significance of that, but these are the biggest clubs in the football-mad country and the rivalry, dating back more than a century, is unimaginably huge. Their grounds are also situated across the road from one another in Lisbon.

It seems André was right about that. When I announced my resignation from Epic on Facebook and that I was joining Nelo Kayaks, comments among the surfski community went viral. Apparently one of my followers had 'Epic' tattooed on his back and was desolate – hopefully because he would need a new one.

The big question was whether the dealers would follow me. I had spent the past fifteen years building up retail bases around the globe and a reputation as Epic's most accessible point of contact. I was known as 'Mr Epic' and had also been intimately involved in developing the company's prototype models, although Greg was the chief designer. Consequently, many dealers had placed large orders on the strength of my being part of the Epic team. Now suddenly I was on the other side of the fence. Would they come with me? Would my credibility remain intact?

We would soon find out.

Two months later, Clare and I moved lock, stock and barrel to Vila do Conde outside Porto, Portugal's second-largest city. It was an easy and quick move as the kids were no longer dependent on us. Luke was working for Chalupsky Properties and Hannah was studying at the IMM Graduate School in Stellenbosch.

During my talks with André, he stressed that, considering my history with Epic, there must be no 'copying' of other designs. Epic's management also warned that they would be scrutinising our new models to check for any copyright infringements. I replied that I had never copied anything in my life, and in any event I didn't have to as I had been designing surfskis for the past forty years. My sole aim was to produce the best boat on the market.

At the time, Nelo Kayaks was only making about thirty to sixty surfskis a year, which I planned to increase radically. However, André said they did not want to change the essential DNA of Nelo products and wished to retain their most popular surfski model, the 560 (which is 5.6 metres in length). Would I be happy working with that?

It was music to my ears. The prototype Chalup-ski was 5.6 metres, which I thought was the ideal size, even though most designers claimed the optimum length was 6.5 metres. With that in mind, I immediately started implementing some new concepts that I believed would put Nelo Kayaks firmly on the surfski map.

The reason I was happy to have the 560 model as my starting point is that shorter surfskis with less wetted surface area accelerate quicker – which is absolutely essential when catching waves. While longer boats are theoretically faster, that is significantly sacrificed by the power needed to increase their speed. In downwind conditions, a sleek, shorter, manoeuvrable surfski gets on a wave quicker – and once you are surfing downwind, it doesn't matter if you are on a 5.6- or even a 7.5-metre boat as it will go at the same speed as the wave.

So length was no problem in the Nelo 560, but the design of the boat's paddling seat was. For some reason, these were devised for short people and were about forty millimetres too high, affecting stability. Marathon surfski racing is one of the most gruelling sports and an essential requirement is to have a good seat. It's difficult to race at 100 per cent capacity if you are uncomfortable, and even a few millimetres make a difference. We started fixing the problem and I discovered that one of the joys of working in the Nelo Kayaks factory is that it's only a couple of hundred steps from the beach. Any design tweaks or shaping adjustments can be tested vigorously on the water right away. Within a few weeks of my arrival, we had built the first prototype of a revamped 560 surfski, a light, low-volume, sleek craft with wave deflectors making it exceptionally easy to handle and turn. Nelo and I were very happy with it, although it took a little longer for all the new models to have optimal seats.

However, the shorter length stirred up a far bigger hornet's nest of con-troversy than the seats. The opposition said our boats were only suitable for small people in small waves, with their length being short solely to comply with European Union transportation laws rather than to be competitive. I pointed out that I had won seven Molokais in a 5.6-metre boat compared to five on a 6.5-metre, and even weighing well over 100 kilograms, I had paddled the fastest times of my life in the shorter models. To shut them up further, two years later at the age of fifty-five I won Guadeloupe's fifty-two-kilometre Ze Caribbean international surfski race in a Nelo 560.

It was true that EU laws favoured smaller boats, as most shipping containers are six metres long, while the average size of a house garage is 5.8 metres. So not only were the 6.5-metre surfskis cumbersome to transport, you couldn't store them in your garage. But for us that was merely a happy coincidence. Believe me, if I thought longer surfskis were faster, I would use them. More than anything else, I am results-driven.

But would the market like it?

I spent the next year travelling the world, visiting every major retailer, holding clinics, re-educating people on our new designs, and explaining why I had switched to Nelo Kayaks. It wasn't difficult as most dealers, many of them old friends, were well aware that Nelo kayaks were hoovering up medals at both the Olympics and world championships. Basically, what dealers wanted most from me was an ironclad assurance that this excellence would be perpetuated with Nelo surfskis. That I could categorically guarantee.

Whenever asked why I was promoting another boat when I had been with Epic Kayaks for so long, I replied that Epic was a phenomenal product. However, so was the iPhone 6. But now I was promoting and co-designing the kayaking equivalent of the iPhone 13. We were moving with the times.

And so it proved. Not only did every European dealer except one start stocking our surfskis, it became the accepted norm that the championed length of 5.6 metres by Nelo Kayaks became the preferred-sized craft for downwind ocean racing.

In fact, the bigger surfskis were now being outclassed in most conditions. A key indication was that our shorter boats were consistently finishing in the top spots in both the men's and women's categories of the Nelo Summer Challenge – one of the largest surfski races in the world. The race attracts about 450 entrants, and my highest position was fifth in a Nelo 560, which I achieved at the age of fifty-four.

From the original handful of surfskis in 2015, we are now selling more than 1100 a year. Nelo wants us to expand at 10 per cent annually. I believe we can do that even faster as we are currently at the forefront of an incredible surfskiing boom in South America, particularly Brazil, which has some of the best downwind ocean paddling in the world.

My greatest pleasure is now working with a highly skilled, loyal and motivated workforce in a state-of-the-art factory. Quality-control and salary issues are something from my past life.

But equally important is my friendship with Nelo. When I first joined the company, he was overweight, smoking too much, and enjoying the good life after many years of hard work. He still paddled but no longer pushed himself. He lives on one side of the Ave River and I on the other, and the best way to visit is to kayak across, which he would do leisurely in his K-1. However, with our new surfskis, I persuaded him to start paddling a 560, saying it was far more fun than a flat-water boat. He could surf downwind and sit on motorboat wakes and ocean waves that would flip a K-1 like a pancake.

Today he is a total convert. In fact, I don't think he has any K-1s left in his garage. I also encouraged him to quit cigarettes, cycle uphill to work, and eat healthily following at least the basics of a keto diet. Now in his sixties, he's in good shape and comes on vigorous long-distance paddling safaris with me.

I believe my joining Nelo Kayaks has been great for both of us, business- and health-wise.

Then came the fateful day when I had the MRI scan on my upper back, which had given me such pain for the past two years.

It was Nelo who, on behalf of the distraught doctor, broke the news to me and Clare that I had advanced secondary cancer, with perhaps six months to live.

LESSON LEARNT

IT'S NEVER TOO late to reinvent yourself. I put my heart and soul into Epic Kayaks, and many were shocked when I left. But times change, and I had to as well.

In doing so, I was completely honest with dealers who had supported me, stressing that although Epic was a great product, I was now putting my reputation on the line for Nelo Kayaks. I guaranteed Nelo surfskis were top-notch by personally racing in them, holding coaching clinics, and letting people decide for themselves. To further show I was all in for Nelo Kayaks, I sold every share I had in my former company, even though the terms were not favourable to me.

I don't believe in half measures.

27

Cancer

There is no good day to get the news that you have terminal cancer, but mine was especially bad. It was the day before Clare's sixtieth birthday.

I had planned to make it a memorable event, booking a room in the magnificent Six Senses Douro Valley Hotel, nestled in Portugal's famously beautiful port-producing district, and we were going to have a five-star meal with Nelo, his wife Helena, and Tiago and Raquel Campos. It was also going to be a surprise party. I knew she would love it.

Instead we were told that I had six months to live.

Clare was in tears and said she was cancelling all birthday festivities. I said no, I was still alive and we would honour that fact on her big day. She was not interested, saying this was no time to celebrate, so I had no option but to ruin the surprise by telling her I had already booked a room at the luxury hotel in the Douro Valley. We would be with friends, so there was no way we were cancelling.

'Listen,' I said. 'I'm still alive. I've got some pain in my back, but we are going to live every day as it comes. If I have only six months left, let's enjoy them.'

It's a good thing we went ahead. There were lots of tears, hugs and emotion, but also a lot of positive vibes. I had made up my mind to treat this as a world championship race: if I pitched up not believing I was going to win, I sure as hell wouldn't. But rather than saying I was going to beat the Big C by 'mind over matter', as many have tried before, I decided I was going to cherish every minute of life left to me. If I did that, cancer would not defeat me. Clare, although devastated, sensed that was the best way to help both me and the rest of the family. She was magnificent.

Luke and Hannah flew to Portugal after Clare's birthday, as they couldn't make the actual day owing to prior commitments. We were dreading breaking the news to them. How do you tell your children that their dad is knocking on death's door? Clare did so as gently as she could, but the shock and anguish on their faces was heartbreaking. At first they couldn't believe it. To them I was indestructible. I had spent almost all my life in peak condition. I had won more Surf Ironman awards than anyone else – how could I now be laid low by some disease? How could my strength and endurance, the code by which I lived, be crippled by a voracious internal monster for which there was no remedy?

'This is how we handle it,' I said. 'Believe it or not, there is still a positive side. I'm not dying suddenly without saying goodbye, as happens to so many people. We still have time together. I've lived a great life and done more than most people have in three lifetimes. Six months is better than six days, and we are not going to waste a single day.'

There were nods among the tears. There would be no what-ifs, no anger, no resentment, no pettiness, no tantrums. There would be no wasted seconds of what time we had left. No retreat. No surrender.

Dr Erik Borgnes, whom I had sent the MRI scans to in America, was an absolute stalwart and advised me to go back to South Africa for treatment. With this type of rampant cancer, he said I would need plenty of family support, and as Clare's family lived in Cape Town and mine in Durban, it made sense to go home. I thought that was a good idea and said we would probably leave in about three weeks.

'No,' said Erik. 'Go right away.'

I had faith in the Portuguese doctors, but the main problem was communication as neither Clare nor I are fluent in Portuguese, although I have a good grasp of it. South African doctors are among the best in the world and we arranged an appointment with two top specialists in Cape Town, Professor Robert Dunn and Dr Greg Symons. They wanted to take a sliver off the top of the tumour to see where the primary cancer was. About two hours before I was about to be wheeled into surgery, Greg noticed something odd about my blood-test results. He delved deeper, and using superb forensic diagnosis skills he found the primary cause: multiple myeloma, among the most lethal of bone marrow cancers. The reason this was not discovered earlier was because my blood tests did not 'present' typical myeloma indicators, which normally show cancer spikes. Instead of the spinal operation, I had a bone marrow biopsy where they drilled into my hip to get the actual marrow out.

The doctors were not only shocked at how advanced the cancer was but that I had been racing successfully at top level while riddled with it. Had I not noticed any symptoms?

I hadn't. Typical bone marrow cancer symptoms are weakness and fatigue, bruising, infections, thirst and loss of appetite, none of which affected me. In fact, during our first consultation, Professor Dunn remarked that I looked the picture of health. The intense pain in my back was from the tumour pressing on the spinal column, not from the actual cancer.

Greg and Professor Dunn then asked how long I had been suffering from tumour pain and were astonished when I said at least two years. The first indication had been a persistent ache in my shoulder, which a specialist had diagnosed as bone-spur calcification. This made sense after decades of intense physical competition, so he put me under the scalpel and cleaned up the rotator cuff. It initially seemed to work and I raced the Molokai forty-five days later, a feat unheard of after an operation of that magnitude. I did it for the first time in a double-ski with Seth Koppes, who was a great partner and treated me and Clare like royalty on the islands.

However, some months afterwards in France for the world champion-ships, a nagging pain similar to a broken rib spread to my back, hindering my training. A specialist had a look and said it was nothing serious. All I needed was rest. After that I raced the Fish River Marathon in the Eastern Cape with Herman and Andy Leith, and although my back was sore, I still had a lot of power. In fact, we won the K-3 section. Ominously, the Sunday after the race, I suddenly got the knifing pain again in my back. It never went away.

Consequently, on returning to Portugal, I had an MRI but only on my lower back, a mistake possibly due to the language barrier and miscommu-nication. Looking at the scans, which showed nothing wrong, the specialist was as mystified as I was. He said it seemed as though the pain was from wear and tear, as experienced by many athletes. I then asked whether I should race the Shaw and Partners Doctor later that month in Perth. He said it boiled down to how much pain I could endure.

'I am used to beating up my body,' I said. He nodded, as he knew that was certainly true, and said if I thought I could handle the hurt, there was probably no harm in doing it.

As we were scheduled to go to Australia anyway for my brother Walter's daughter Rebecca's wedding, I decided I would do the race.

From then on, the pain started worsening dramatically. I could barely get into a car, and sitting at a table for meals was excruciating. Lying down to sleep was impossible and I had to rest standing, a contradiction in terms. I went to see an Australian sports physiotherapist who performed deep-muscle back massages, really digging his fingers into my spine, which seemed to help a little so I got Clare to continue doing that. In retrospect, this was one of the worst treatments as it directly pummelled the tumour.

As described earlier, the race was pure, unrelenting agony, and on returning to Portugal, I finally decided I'd had enough and had my upper back scanned. It was then that the MRI clearly showed the malignant tumour. It was far advanced, Stage 3 or 4, and as they could not determine the cancer's origin, I was given six months to live.

Now that South African specialists had found multiple myeloma, I was handed over to haematologist Dr Mike du Toit. As luck would have it, Mike had gone to school with my good friend Tim Noakes, who assured me that Mike was one of the best in the world. I knew I was in good hands.

My first question was how soon I could start paddling again. I wanted to fight the killer disease the best way I knew how. On the water.

Mike hesitated, so I persisted. 'What about next week?' I asked.

He shook his head. 'It'll be a little longer than that.'

Initially, the only exercise I would be allowed to do was walking. Absolutely no running, kayaking or golf. In fact, any form of rotation could snap my spine, which had been weakened by the bone-destroying myeloma and tumour. If that happened, I could be paralysed. Mike said I was fortunate it hadn't already happened, seeing as I had been competing in championship events for two years. He said that most myeloma sufferers live for about three to five years. But as mine was a particularly aggressive type, which I'd already had for a couple of years, all bets were off.

I knew this was a fight I had to win. I also had to be realistic. Barring miracles, it's extremely unlikely for anyone to survive an incurable disease. I am a firm believer of mind over matter, but that concerns issues that I have some control over. When I line up at the start of a race, it's up to me whether I win or lose. If I don't believe with every fibre of my body that I can do it, I am wasting my time. But self-belief has to be rooted in reality – obviously no amount of positive thinking would result in me outsprinting Usain Bolt, for example. Similarly, in a kayak race, he could never even dream of beating me.

That I could control. In fact, some describe my self-belief as borderline insanity. Be that as it may, it's well documented that I have won races against younger, fitter and stronger paddlers that no one except me thought possible.

But for the first time in my life, I was no longer in control of my destiny. I had no control over the rogue multiple myeloma cells stalking like a horseman of the apocalypse. All I could do was put myself in the hands of specialists and hope for the best.

And yet ... the more I thought about it, the more I decided that wasn't strictly true. I *did* have control. In fact, far more than I imagined. Control is about how you *choose* to react to circumstances. It's not the situation confronting you; it's how you handle it. I could beat this killer in the same way I had won multiple ocean marathons, often against far more fancied opponents. I simply had to outlast it.

It suddenly became crystal clear. After more than forty years of racing, many of my victories were in essence a case of outlasting everyone else at a pace that I set. Sure, I have good technique and unfailing confidence in myself. Sure, I train hard, often much harder than anyone else, and sure, I love beating the odds. But in the closing do-or-die dashes, particularly in my later races, it had boiled down to judging my own strength and endurance to the last tiny ounce of energy.

This marathon for my life would be no different. I would outlast the Big C. At the end, I would still be standing.

Three decades ago, any cancer diagnosis was invariably considered a death sentence. That is no longer the case. Doctors are successfully treating more and more types of the disease. For example, the five-year survival rate for breast, prostate and thyroid cancer is now 99 per cent. In the not-too-distant future, myeloma will be the same. One day there will be an equally successful treatment and I was going to make damn sure I would be around to get it.

My goal was clear. I would hang in there until a remedy was found. I would live life to the full, go to parties, play golf, cherish my family and friends, and continue working. I would be as active as I always had been, entering races and competing, not as a cancer sufferer but as a world-class kayaker in my age group.

I would beat the devil. Or, at the very least, spit in his eye.

LESSON LEARNT

THERE IS ALWAYS a choice in life, even in the direst situations. In this case, my choice was how I handled cancer – how I played the cards handed to me, even if they were dealt from a stacked deck.

I chose to treat it like I have everything else in life: as a challenge. This was not wishful thinking. I had a plan, and that is vital. As I have said before, without a plan you don't even have a foundation.

I knew I could not beat something incurable just by hope and luck. Instead, my plan was to outlast the deadly disease until a cure was found. That was realistic as cancer treatments are becoming increasingly successful. I had to hang in there, and the best way to do so was to continue living life to the full.

28

Come hell or high water

Doctors decided that the immediate priority was to shrink the spinal tumour to relieve the crippling pain.

I could not have agreed more. It was unbearable. I still could not sit still for any length of time, and while driving I had to regularly stop and get out of the car just to stand for a few minutes.

Dr Mike du Toit then outlined my treatment and recovery regimen for the rest of the year, giving a clear breakdown of each of the various stages. It would start off with ten days of intense radiation therapy beamed directly on the tumour, alongside weekly chemotherapy sessions continuing for at least seven months, and then a stem-cell transplant. Recovery from the transplant would be frustratingly slow and debilitating, involving powerful medication, but I geared myself up for what I knew had to be done.

Precise pre-preparation for radiation was vital, and to ease the spinal pain beforehand I dosed myself with twenty millilitres of morphine syrup three times a day. I then had four CAT scans to pinpoint the tumour. The exact spot was mapped with three tattoos: one on my chest and two on either side of my ribs so that the radiation laser could target the cancerous lump with sniper accuracy. These tattoos, the size of match heads, are the only ones I've had in my life. I wouldn't be competing with David Beckham in body art.

On Christmas Day 2019, I came off morphine completely. The radiation therapy had worked, significantly shrinking the tumour and substantially easing my back pain. However, I was still not pain-free as the process damaged my oesophagus and I could barely eat or drink anything, even water. The least painful liquids to swallow, amazingly, were Guinness and very expensive red wine. As I told a slightly incredulous Clare, I had to drink something.

Each chemo session lasted three and a half hours, and all I had to do was lie down with a drip in my arm while the drugs were applied intravenously. Bone-hardening medication was mixed into the drip on every sixth session.

Clare always came with me, and we met a lot of interesting people in the ward also having chemo treatment. As there was not much else to do, we all talked a lot. Most other patients enthused about cannabis oil, saying it was the new wonder medication, so I decided to speak to Dr du Toit and see what he thought. He said it was still unproven, so I didn't go down that route.

I also started sharing my experiences on social media and soon had quite a following among cancer sufferers and their families. It was great to offer and receive support and advice from such a caring network. I was very lucky as the chemo barely affected me – I wasn't even taking anti-nausea pills – but that certainly was not the norm. One woman told me her husband Andrew was having the same chemo as I was and it knocked him so badly that he had to stay in hospital, whereas I went home after each session. While in hospital, he tripped over his platform of drips and fractured his spine in six places. The cliché that it's a small world is remarkably true, and some months later I met the man himself on my golfing partner Dave Abromowitz's yacht. Thankfully Andrew has made good progress, but he told me that in the fall his wife described he had actually fractured his spine in *twelve* places, not six – graphically showing how severely myelomas weaken the bone.

Another woman contacted us to share her journey, then asked if we had upgraded our medical aid to the top level of cancer-treatment support. Clare and I looked at each other, surprised. We had no idea that this could be done. Thanks to her advice, we upgraded three days before the option expired, saving us thousands of rands.

I found the stories of some of my fellow cancer warriors so awe-inspiring that all I could do was shake my head at such courage. Stuart Lowe, a former publisher of *CAR Magazine*, was also diagnosed with myeloma, but got the terrible news while his daughter Jenna was fighting for her life after being stricken with pulmonary arterial hypertension. It's an extremely rare disease and Jenna needed a double lung transplant. As the family were so focused on her illness, Stuart didn't want to burden his loved ones further and never told them about his own cancer. He was secretly taken to chemotherapy treatment by close friends sworn to silence. Sadly, his daughter died four months before her twenty-first birthday, prompting her mother, Gabi, to write a magnificent book on Jenna's supremely inspirational struggle for life. It's called *Get Me to 21* and has done more to raise awareness of organ donation than anything else I know of. Stuart and I are currently working on a fundraising programme for myeloma sufferers in South Africa, the majority of whom are not wealthy. It's a sad fact that without expensive treatment, life expectancy for myeloma victims is short, sharp and painful.

I got some idea of how powerful the drugs pumped into me were when I noticed that the chemo drip had 'mustard gas' on its label. This was one of the deadliest chemical weapons used in the trenches of the First World War and was banned by the Geneva Convention. However, mustard gas, or nitrogen mustard, is what later provided the breakthrough in cancer treatment and today has saved and extended countless lives, despite some brutal side effects. After every chemo session, Clare and I would celebrate ticking it off the 'done' list by sitting down to lunch with a bottle of good wine. It was also a way of refusing to let the treatment get us down.

In March 2020, while I was still undergoing chemo, Clare and I flew to Portugal for the launch of Nelo Kayaks' new surfski range. It was a huge success and great to see my Portuguese friends again. On our way back home, we met Herman at Dubai airport, where he was returning from a skiing trip in the Italian Alps. Covid had just surfaced in Europe and Herman advised us to stay one and a half metres away from him. None of us knew much about the disease at the time, but we took his advice. It was extremely fortuitous that we did. Italy was initially the worst-hit European country, and Herman's group of skiers were among the first South Africans to catch Covid. They voluntarily spent two weeks' isolation in a remote residence in the KwaZulu-Natal Midlands, so as far as we know they didn't infect anyone else. Clare and I definitely dodged a bullet.

A couple of days later, Luke flew in from Asia and Hannah arrived from the UK on one of the last planes allowed into the country. We didn't know it at the time, but it would be several months before they would be allowed to fly out again.

We had rented an apartment in Camps Bay, but because Luke and Hannah had been overseas, they had to isolate. Thankfully, Pierre Strydom, who had been with me at the Barcelona Olympics, generously lent Clare and me his Cape Town apartment where we could stay during the isolation period without being too far from the hospital.

Then full lockdown came into force and the entire country was confined to virtual house arrest in one of the strictest clampdowns in the world. Only limited driving was allowed, such as for medicine and food shopping, so I had to get a special permit to go to hospital. On most occasions I was the only civilian vehicle on the road, and there were police roadblocks everywhere checking travel credentials.

Fortunately, the day before the total lockdown was imposed, I bought several cases of wine from a friend who owns a liquor store. When I arrived home, Clare was aghast at the quantity. But after the alcohol ban was announced along with the lockdown, I was suddenly a hero among the rest of the family.

To this day, I am still stunned by the generosity of family, friends and strangers who came to our assistance in this supreme hour of need. For example, Craig McKenzie, a loyal school friend and former provincial water polo player, lent us his beachfront home in the beautiful Murdoch Valley. There was no better place in the world to recuperate from chemo, and we moved there with Luke and Hannah when the lockdown eased. During those dark days, battling a killer disease in the midst of a global pandemic, being with my family was an incalculable blessing. Craig knew that, and it was these acts of exceptional kindness that kept our spirits up.

I was determined to keep as fit as possible under the circumstances, but it was difficult to walk distances as we weren't allowed to go anywhere. In Pierre's apartment building, Clare and I would walk up and down a park-ade ramp, while on Craig's large property, we did laps around the garden. Sometimes I would extend this by sneaking along the boundary of the property. When lockdown conditions were eased and we could exercise from 6 to 9 a.m., we would walk up to sixteen kilometres most mornings.

After six months of chemo, I was ready to start the stem-cell transplant process that would hopefully replace bone marrow cells destroyed by cancer and increase the number of healthy red and white blood corpuscles. This is vital for fighting cancer – or any infection, for that matter.

Whenever possible, doctors prefer to harvest a patient's own cells, either from bone marrow or blood, but if these are not of high enough quality, a donor is needed. Fortunately, mine were good and I was scheduled to have what the medicos call an autologous stem-cell transplant.

Two days before cell harvesting, I suddenly came down with a high temperature, uncontrollable shakes and nausea. In those heightened times, the first thought that crossed our minds was Covid, so I was rushed late at night to hospital. The test was negative. I had done a fifteen-kilometre walk earlier that day and Clare said it was probably due to overextending myself with all the chemo in my system. No one was sure, so I was given a powerful anti-biotic and kept in hospital for a few days of observation.

I then called the doctor and suggested that seeing as I had been admitted, why not start the procedure to harvest stem cells right away? As per instructions, I had already injected myself with the drugs prescribed to boost healthy blood cells, so I was as prepared as I would ever be. He agreed, and over the next twenty-four hours, ten litres of chemo were pumped into my system through a port in my jugular vein to wipe out cancerous cells. Inserting the port was a big deal and had been done some days earlier under anaesthetic as the tube goes straight into the aorta. It's the most effective way of 'mainlining' massive doses of chemo.

I was then ready for the harvesting procedure but stupidly didn't bother to ask questions about how it worked. I thought it was a quick operation, so I didn't even go to the toilet beforehand.

I only began to realise how complex it was when a nurse inserted three drips – one in my left arm and two in my right – and I was told that under no circumstances could I move during the harvesting. I couldn't even twitch an arm or leg – nothing – as my blood was about to be circulated eight times through a centrifugal machine to separate the cells. I had to remain dead still for the next six and a half hours.

It seemed a lifetime. The agony of being unable to do anything except blink is indescribable. Even worse, after about three hours I desperately needed to pee. The nurse had to help me with a bottle, and I apologetically told her that if I had known how long this would take, I would have gone to the toilet beforehand.

Eventually it was over. At long last I could move. I fervently hoped I would never have to go through such torture again, and to my eternal relief the doctors told me the procedure had gone well. They had harvested 450 millilitres of healthy stem cells, enough for two transplants. The surplus cells would be stored.

I was given a two-week break from chemotherapy to get my strength back before the healthy stem cells would be reinjected into my body. It's a dangerous procedure owing to the impact on the immune system at the best of times, but doubly so with Covid running rampant.

And so it proved. As Clare and I were driving to the hospital for the transplant, I got a phone call from the hospital.

'Sorry, Oscar,' said the nurse. 'We're going to have to postpone. Some of the operating team have caught Covid.'

'What?'

'Go back home. We'll call you when we're ready.'

I turned the car around. To say Clare and I were dejected doesn't begin to describe how deflated we felt.

A week later I was called back to hospital. The first stage of the transplant was to bombard my system with chemo for three days, involving four separate drips. These were placed on a stand with wheels, and I had to do everything from ablutions to washing while dragging them along.

For the rest of the week I felt as though I was on my deathbed. The medical staff cautioned that I had a tough six days ahead, mentally as well as physically, but even that wasn't enough forewarning. As an endurance athlete, I have a high pain threshold – but a transplant isn't just about pain. It's about everything you can imagine coming at you. There is no getting away from the fact that fighting cancer is all-consuming. My vision became blurred from the high doses of chemo, and my mouth was riddled with ulcers. Swallowing anything was pure hell. Compounding that was the terrible food provided. I was on a low-carb keto diet, but as the hospital tried to get me to eat what I considered to be mainly starch and sugar, I refused everything except eggs. The well-meaning dietician got a bit irritated, wanting me to drink a high-energy powder shake that she said was a 'lifesaver'. I declined as it was straight carbo-loading, which as an athlete I knew had been disproved. I lost fifteen kilograms in less than three weeks.

Despite that, I religiously exercised every day, which consisted of walking around my small isolated room. Patients also took turns walking in the corridor, which was about thirty metres long, dragging their drip stands, but to maintain social distancing we could only do this one at a time. Exercise has always been a mainstay of my life, but this time I was walking to kill time as much as anything else. There was nothing else to do. I couldn't read as my vision was blurred from the drugs, and even boring TV programmes were too fuzzy to watch. Worst of all, my cellphone wasn't working.

In the room next door was Anthony Hitchcock, whom I had met in the army forty years beforehand. Fortunately, we could chat through an open door while exercising, making sure we were social distancing. He was four days ahead of me in his treatment and provided valuable information about what was coming next.

As my family were not allowed to visit, Anthony was the only person apart from medical staff who I spoke to in those dark times. The entire block was a sterile area, so human contact was rare. And precious. I could not have asked for a better next-door neighbour.

I discovered that he had been a botanist at the famous Kirstenbosch National Botanical Garden and had done pioneering work restoring critically endangered fynbos areas in the Cape. He was an extremely interesting guy, and those chats made the relentlessly boring days bearable.

Then one morning I stepped out for our usual exercise routine and he was not there. I asked a doctor, 'Where's Anthony?'

'Not doing too well, I'm afraid. That's why he's not coming out of the room.'

The death toll among cancer patients waiting for treatment is depressingly high and I feared the worst when Anthony's doctor later came into my room.

'I just want you to know that your neighbour has Covid,' he said. 'He's been moved to a Covid ward.'

At least he was alive. But as he had been in the next room, I had to have yet another Covid test. It was negative, but without Anthony I felt lonely as he and I were in the same boat. Cancer sufferers have a tight kinship and in those few days we had formed a close bond.

Finally, I was ready to have my healthy stem cells transplanted back. This is a big deal – an intricate operation with high stakes and as precarious as a lung or liver transplant. If unsuccessful, my treatment would be severely set back, perhaps irrevocably. Obviously my immediate family wanted to be there, but the closest Clare, Hannah and Luke could get to me was to come around the back of the hospital, look through the window of my ward, and say a prayer as a candle was lit. I felt as though I was getting last rites, although I was determined that even in my weakened state I was going to whip cancer's butt.

The operation takes two hours to reinject the mass of healthy stem cells. I felt terrible afterwards, debilitated to my soul, but the good news was that the operation had been a success. The cells had not been rejected, and everything was looking as positive as possible under the circumstances.

All I wanted now was to go home. I hate hospitals and this was further aggravated by Covid isolation. I can honestly say that was the worst time of my life, even though the staff were fantastic.

After three weeks I was discharged, and we moved from Murdoch Valley back to Camps Bay. The relief to be out of my sickbed was overwhelming. I had now passed the most critical stage of the treatment. We still had a long way to go as a stem-cell transplant can block myeloma progression but doesn't cure it. However, the healing could now begin. The shrinking of the tumour and the injection of healthy cells signalled that my fightback had started in earnest.

Not long after being discharged, I was scrolling through Facebook and read that Anthony Hitchcock had died. I was shocked rigid, saddened beyond belief. No one in the hospital had told me. Tributes poured in from around the world for the highly talented, groundbreaking botanist who had been such a passionate protector of South Africa's rich biodiversity. It was an honour and a privilege to have spent a few days with him, even in such dire circumstances.

Although Anthony had major underlying issues with myeloma, his cause of death was listed as Covid. I suddenly realised that this was my second near miss during the deadly pandemic. Anthony had been in the room next to mine and caught it, while I hadn't. Herman had been with me and Clare at Dubai airport. He got it, we didn't.

All I can be is thankful for what blessings I had during these sad and difficult times.

LESSONS LEARNT

CONTACT IS CRITICAL. When stricken with cancer, it was humbling in the extreme to discover how strong my network was. The beneficial effects of people rooting for you and being on your side are incalculable. You have to have an unbelievably positive frame of mind to deal with adversity, and a strong network is fundamental to that.

SHARE YOUR EXPERIENCES. I made invaluable contacts by posting on social media and just talking to people. I received advice and assistance I would never have got without personally reaching out, and in some cases I was also able to help people. I met astonishing, courageous individuals, such as Stuart Lowe and Anthony Hitchcock.

At the end of the day, if you don't share your experiences, some people might not know they have cancer. By talking about it, you could save a life.

29

The Joe Glickman Award

I have met a lot of free-spirited paddlers. In fact, I was once one myself, sleeping where I could and surviving on ninety-nine-cent tacos in Hawaii as any money I had was blown on travel costs.

The time spent in Australia competing on the Ironman circuit in the mid-1980s, cadging lifts from one beach to the next, was also a University of Life degree in my carefree days as a surf bum, and I wouldn't trade it for the world.

That's probably why I got on so well with Joe Glickman, a kindred paddle bum who loved the sport with an intensity unmatched by almost anyone else I know. What made his passion even more remarkable was that he came from New York, where he said surfskiing was marginally more popular than bull-fighting. But despite that, Joe was as tough as any ocean warrior, once having kayaked the 3190-kilometre Yukon River, which is big, cold and miserable, not to mention dangerous with gnarly rapids and gnarlier grizzly bears on the banks. You have to be truly radical to do something like that. Joe certainly was.

Although he competed hard and often at surfski races, he was seldom on the winner's podium. Instead, it was his skill with words that had such a profound impact on the global surfskiing movement, making him one of the most recognisable names in ocean paddling. His eye for offbeat detail and rich imagery is unequalled. In my opinion, his writing is right up there with the best sports journalism in the world. A Joe Glickman race report was so vividly penned that you could have sworn you were there, even if you weren't. His humour and wry observations were unsurpassed and I was sometimes the brunt of his beautifully barbed wit. After a memorable party in Mauritius, he advised his readers, 'Don't drink anything with a Chalupsky; if one of the brothers hands you a piece of a garden hose, hail a cab.'[6]

Joe's articles soon became required reading. He was also great fun, an entertaining and resourceful travel companion, larger than life, and loyal to a fault. He was always joking and talking rubbish, and paddlers around the world loved him.

As far as I can remember, we first met at the 2000 World Sea Kayak Championship in Canada and soon became firm friends. He travelled with me to many of my big races, financing his trips with his superb journalism, books and videos that he posted online. We kept in constant phone contact and he joked that the more inconvenient the time zone, the more often I would call.

Then, in 2014, Joe was diagnosed with pancreatic cancer, ironically by the same doctor who later advised me I had secondary cancer, Dr Erik Borgnes. Erik, also a surfskier and known as the 'paddling doctor', picked up the severity of Joe's illness even before top oncologists had. American surgeons said it was terminal, declining to operate, and the surfskiing brother- and sisterhood went into shock. Boats in races around the world had stickers with the acronym OMMFG (One More Mile for Glicker) plastered on the hulls. As Joe could no longer paddle regularly, the surfski community decided to take up the slack for him and go an extra mile.

Joe fought the disease with uplifting courage and indomitable grit. He was always joking with the nurses at the oncology hospital, and they adored him. As did we all.

While he was undergoing chemo, he and I entered the double-ski Blackburn Challenge in 2014. Joe's strength and endurance may have been sapped by brutal cancer treatment, but that unconquerable spark still burned bright and I could feel the force of his willpower solid as steel behind me. We won that race, setting a course record. Little did I know at the time that although I was literally with him in the same boat, four years later I would be metaphorically so, waging my own fight against cancer. That makes memories of the Blackburn Challenge with Joe, his last race, doubly poignant.

Joe died the following year. I was travelling much of the time and luckily often stopped over in New York, so I saw a lot of him and his fabulous wife Beth in those last months. Sad as they were, Joe was always upbeat. He never let it get him down, which I admired more than anything else. Clare and I attended his memorial service as the global surfskiing family grieved.

A few years later, I got a call from Bruce Seymour, race director of the Hong Kong Dragon Run. I know Bruce well, and when working at Epic's factory in China, I assisted him in setting up the inaugural Dragon Run from Clearwater Bay Beach to Stanley. I also always tried to make sure we had a team of our Chinese staffers competing.

Bruce had come up with a great idea. We needed to honour Joe's work and suggested we establish a trophy in his name. It would be called the Joe Glickman Award and presented annually for outstanding achievement and commitment to the sport of surfski paddling.

'I was thinking that this sport of ours, of which so many of us are so passionate about, has no recognition besides winning races,' Bruce said. 'Cricket has cricketer of the year; rugby has rugby player of the year ... but we have nothing. Yet there are so many people who have put so much into the sport and contributed in so many different ways. Consequently, I thought it would be nice to recognise those contributions that have made surfski paddling what it is today.

'Joe was a big part of surfski paddling. He was at all of the races and he'd take part and do well, but he also interviewed everyone and wrote a lot and really moved the sport forward.'

Bruce stressed that to make the award 'quintessentially Joe' it should represent the same qualities that made him so endeared around the world.

'It's a combination of commitment, dedication, respect and so many other things that are the cornerstones of our community,' he explained.

I could not have agreed more.

Bruce then set up a committee to pick worthy recipients. I was honoured to be part of the selection panel, along with the great Dean Gardiner; paddling legend Dawid Mocke; 2013 Women's Surfski World Champion Michele Eray; and Jim Hoffman, an influential paddler as well as executive vice president of NBC.

The inaugural presentation was scheduled for July 2020, and I suppose I should have got suspicious when I suddenly stopped receiving updates. The next missed clue was when I was about to join an online coaching session hosted by Dawid Mocke and Clare told me to 'wear a nice shirt'. I mean, who dresses up for a video call about surfski paddling, the least sartorial sport in the world?

I logged on and the first person I saw was Beth Glickman, Joe's widow. 'I don't believe it,' I thought. 'Beth is learning how to paddle with Dawid?'

Then the rest of the award panel popped onto the screen, all grinning at me. It suddenly dawned. I was getting the inaugural Joe Glickman Award!

I was stunned. For a moment I couldn't speak – possibly because I was choking with emotion. Despite recovering from a transplant and annihilated by chronic fatigue, despite the ceremony being conducted on a long-distance conference call, despite being in isolation with the entire world crippled by a pandemic, this was a highlight of my life. It was right up there with my finest victories on the water. And being awarded in honour of one of my greatest friends was uniquely special.

I had to wipe my eyes when I read the award panel's summary of their verdict: 'The decision to name "The Big O" as the inaugural Joe Glickman Award winner needs no explanation, as while he's one of surfski's greatest-ever athletes, he's also its most prominent advocate.'

Each panel member then gave their reasons for selecting me.

Dawid Mocke: 'The thing that always stands out for me watching you at events, it doesn't matter who the person is that comes across your path, you're always so willing to help, to coach and to give advice.'

Michele Eray: 'It's incredible, your reach. People that you've never met always come up to me and want to talk about you. They don't personally know you ... but somehow you've had contact. It's just incredible.'

Dean Gardiner: 'You have done so much for paddling and been such a good ambassador over so many years, you're certainly a fitting winner. Your relationship with Joe makes it even more special as well.'

Jim Hoffman: 'I don't think there's anyone in this community that has taught more people than you. Probably tenfold. You're so far-reaching in your influence and effects on people, and for that I'm forever grateful of you.'

Bruce Seymour: 'Besides the obvious record of the twelve Molokai wins, for me, your relentless travel schedule to spread the surfski stoke and enthusiasm, coaching people from all walks of life from all over the world, is a showing of amazing commitment.'

The final word was from Beth Glickman: 'You have always been willing to share your love of surfski, your experience and your help no matter how much of a rank beginner – and who was more of a rank beginner than my husband, Joe Glickman. I have thought many times that Joe would want to be there for you now in the same way you were there for him. Now he can be. You've got his award.'

Fortunately, I was sitting at the time. My shock and gratitude were over-whelming. There is no doubt that such an incredible morale-lifting boost did as much to help my determination to get better as anything else.

I was about to start the next critical stage of my cancer treatment. I like to believe I helped Joe six years before, and now, with the award that carries his name, I know with absolute certainty that he is in my corner.

LESSON LEARNT

I CAN DO no better than recite the words engraved on the Joe Glickman Award trophy. It was written by Joe and selected by his wife, Beth, and daughter Willa.

> Remember that feeling as a kid when you got close to the beach and the solid ground of every day turned into soft sand?
>
> Your heart would quicken and you would pull your parents' hand like a restrained dog desperate to break free.
>
> I still feel that pull.
>
> When I paddle off and leave the land behind, heading out to an island or lighthouse or with no destination in mind, I feel instant peace and constant challenge.

If you can live your life with the same passion, humour, enjoyment and determination as Joe did, you will have succeeded.

30

Fighting the good fight

It wasn't just the Joe Glickman Award that boosted me in my darkest hours. The overwhelming global support from people wishing me well, some of whom I had never met before, was beyond humbling.

Emails, texts, and Facebook and social media messages poured in daily and I responded to them all. It's impossible to measure how important they were. Suffice it to say that it's so much easier to remain upbeat when you are being bombarded with positive vibes from around the world.

This, from a guy in New Zealand, is a good example of what was in my mailbox every day:

Oscar.

I don't expect you to recall meeting, but be assured I'll never forget meeting you. Today I paddled solo way out to sea here in Tutukaka, NZ, and somehow your *wairua* … your spirit … was there with me. Not in a morbid sense, more in the form of your voice chiding, encouraging, coaching, laughing, hollering.

To say I'm gutted at your news is a massive understatement. But I'm always been up for fight so I'll send some of my *mana*, my *wairua* your way mate and hope it adds something tangible at your end. *Kia Kaha* (stand strong) Oscar. You're a f***ing awesome character dude and I enjoy the ocean all the more since you put me on the right path with my paddling. My gratitude is endless.

Tim

On leaving hospital, I had no idea how valuable such support from people like Tim would be. But I soon had an inkling when one of my fellow cancer warriors advised me to get a Zimmer frame. He said the utter debilitation after stem-cell surgery was incomparable to most other diseases. Even walking was a mission.

I shook my head. Zimmer frames? Those were for old people. They would have to put me in a coffin first. But I soon discovered what he meant.

For most of my life I have been supremely fit. It's what I do, and not only for a living; it's also the lifestyle I love. But now I could not walk for any distance without at times having to lean on Clare. For the first dire few days, she was my Zimmer frame.

In fact, life was equally bad for her as it was for me. She and I had to live in total isolation. Any Covid compromise could be a death sentence for me, and every day she had to sterilise much of what I came in contact with, from what I ate to the clothes I wore. All food had to be thoroughly washed and cooked, so my favourite raw snacks of sushi and biltong went out of the window. I was not allowed any fruit, unless it had been completely cooked or had a thick skin such as an avocado pear. Boiling water was poured over all knives, forks and spoons, and Clare could only use plastic or glass cutting boards. No wooden utensils were allowed. Clothes had to be ironed moments before I dressed to kill lurking bugs. Also, because we were not allowed even socially distanced contact with others, Clare's mother Norma and sister Tessa did our shopping, leaving bags of groceries outside our front door.

For me, exercise was key to my recovery. We found an isolated nature reserve below a school cricket field and Clare drove me there for a walk each morning, making sure no one was in sight. Despite the supreme effort it took to hobble a mere 200 metres, I persevered, going a little bit further every day.

After the walk, I was fatigued to my bones, sweating like a sumo wrestler on even the coldest Cape winter day. Also my heartbeat was galloping, which was of concern as I had suffered an atrial fibrillation attack several years ago and doctors had done a cardiac restart. The procedure worked perfectly and I've had no more problems, but it was still in the back of my mind.

It took me twenty-four hours to recover from even that pitifully small walk. To stop the sweating and bring my racing heart under control, Clare would drive along the beautiful Cape coast to Hout Bay and Llandudno with the windows wide open to cool me down.

Ten days after the transplant I was put on lenalidomide, an oral immuno-modulatory agent that uses the immune system to attack cancer cells. It was a disaster. Within two weeks my skin went haywire, blistering with ugly reddish-purple craters that looked like third-degree burns. It was also as itchy as a thousand mosquito bites, and no matter what creams or ointments I slathered on, it got worse. Doctors were worried that it could be latent rejection of the new stem cells, and when nothing worked I was put on a high dose of cortisone. That eventually cleared it up.

Despite this setback, I kept on struggling with my walks and they started paying off. It was in tiny increments at first, but those half-staggers, half-walks at the speed of a lame tortoise started getting longer. Eventually, after about three months, I was walking between ten and twelve kilometres a day. If ever I needed proof that persistence is life's supreme quality, this was it.

Then I got skin cancer. At first doctors thought it was a melanoma due to the inescapable fact that I am red-haired and fair-skinned and have spent most of my life in the sun. However, that seemed unlikely as far as I was concerned as I have always liberally used sunblock and worn a hat. Like most beach bums, I suffered from occasional sunspots but had them burnt off with liquid nitrogen by top Durban dermatologist Dr Len Nel. I immediately contacted Len, who said I was probably suffering from a squamous cell carcinoma, not a melanoma, but still needed to get it cut out quickly. He said it was probably due to my run-down immune system and a reaction to the lenalidomide drug.

Len then booked an appointment with plastic surgeon Dr Greg Ash, who agreed that the growths on my shoulder and back, as well as one on my ear, were squamous cell carcinomas and told me to make another appointment for surgery.

'Can't we do it right away?' I asked. 'I'm already here.'

That's what I love about South Africa. No one stands on ceremony. Greg shrugged, checked his appointment book, saw he had some time available and ushered me onto the operating table. The surgery was done under local anaesthetic and I could smell burning flesh as he removed the growths and cauterised the wounds.

Two days later I got another call from Greg. He said that unfortunately there was no margin around the carcinoma on my ear, so he would have to cut part of it off. Today one ear is shorter than the other, but the growth is gone.

During a follow-up appointment with Len in Durban, he noticed a cancerous growth on the top of my head. That was removed by heating a surgical spoon and 'scooping' it out.

At the time I was getting a little despondent, as the curve balls thrown at me – from blistering skin 'fungus' to squamous cell carcinomas – seemed endless. Every two steps forward resulted in one backward, so I had to make a conscious effort to ruthlessly snuff out negativity. In any fight against cancer, you can never let the bastard get you down. Never.

Clare and I then returned to Portugal as I needed to get back to work. We had new models of surfskis to bring out, and I was raring to go.

However, once back in Vila do Conde, I noticed that the carcinoma on my head that had previously been scooped out appeared to be resurfacing. I went to the IPO (Portuguese Institute of Oncology), where doctors decided that they needed to scrape deeper to root out remaining cancerous cells. It was more ingrained than the South African doctors had initially thought, so much so that the IPO surgeons started preparing me for a skin graft. However, that was a major procedure as they would have to graft skin from other parts of my body, so they decided to go with one more scrape and see if it took. I now have an 'axe mark' on my head, which is not as pretty as a skin graft, but it was successful.

Then fate tossed another curve ball. After this operation, my eyes swelled up to the size of plums and my forehead jutted out like a Neanderthal. I couldn't see much and was worried that my vision had been permanently impaired. I phoned Len in Durban, who advised me to have an urgent consultation at the IPO in case it was a blood vessel that had burst in my head. I rushed back to the cancer ward and my doctor, Dr José Mariz, said it was the result of the trauma and shock to my body. I was given a crash course of anti-inflammatory drugs, which thankfully brought down the swelling.

After that, Dr Mariz took me aside. 'Oscar, it's no good us trying to control your myeloma if you die of skin cancer instead. We are going to put you on another regimen altogether.'

He immediately took me off lenalidomide and prescribed Velcade chemo injections alongside dexamethasone, a corticosteroid. These are not the same as anabolic steroids but a copy of a hormone the body makes naturally. Today they're also widely used as a first defence for Covid patients. My skin conditions improved dramatically, as did my eyes, and I will be on Velcade and dexamethasone for the next two years.

That's where I am at this stage. And I can honestly say that despite everything, despite the seemingly continuous obstacles, I am in a good place.

Taking a deep breath and looking back over the past year and a half, Clare and I started wondering what had caused my myeloma. Cancer does run in the family as my mother died from it, but I have lived a supremely fit and healthy life. I have never smoked or taken recreational drugs, and although I like beer and a glass of robust red wine, that never interferes with my fitness regime. So what was it?

It's difficult to say, as not much is known about myeloma, which is why it is incurable. But the three key causes are thought to be stress, radiation and contact with toxins.

Taking the first cause, stress, it is true that I live on the edge and have had business issues that perhaps could have caused anxiety. To me, this is an unlikely reason as I have always 'sweated' out any problems on the water and confronted difficulties rather than stewed over them. I am also known to be optimistic – some say to the point of lunacy – so nothing really gets me down in the long run. My fight against cancer is proof of this.

The second is radiation. That could be interesting, as I have spent much of my life travelling the world, either to market surfskis or race them. My air miles would fill a telephone directory. Obviously, this involves going through numerous airport X-ray machines, and it's known that the rate of myeloma among airline pilots is abnormally high. Perhaps that is a possibility.

Thirdly, toxins. I have been building kayaks for as long as I can remember, which involves extensive use of resins and other chemicals. As a kid, my nickname was 'fibreglass'. Could that also be a reason?

We don't know.

By November 2021, doctors had done all they could, and they have been magnificent. I have had superb treatment, lifesaving surgery, state-of-the-art medication, a stem-cell transplant – even intricate skull scoops and a shortened ear – and the ball is now in my court. I have to fight the disease the most effective way I can, so I have decided to live the best way possible. This involves plenty of exercise, following the healthy keto way of eating, fasting, getting sunshine and revelling in the ocean, alongside healthy dollops of cheerfulness and optimism.

Myeloma is just another hurdle in my way, and it's up to me how I leap over it. That is my choice. I will not squander it.

LESSONS LEARNT

CANCER IS A DISEASE, not a shame. Don't hide behind the perceived stigma, because it isn't that at all. There are many millions of people suffering from it and in a similar position to the one I'm in. It's only through discussion, acceptance and interaction that you discover how many hidden gems of advice and wisdom are out there, and that everyone wants to help. If you don't open up, it's like paddling in a bubble and not learning the secrets of riding downwind.

REMAIN CHEERFUL. Okay, that's a cliché, but once you accept reality, the battle is so much easier. There is nothing I can do to alter the fact that I have incurable cancer, but there is plenty I can do to make life as upbeat and positive as possible. Everyone has done good things in their lives – relentlessly reflect on that instead of moping about cancer. Even in bad times you can always think of good things to lift you up.

31

Living with the Big C

Whenever I'm asked how I am doing, I respond honestly. I am doing as well as I can, but would rate myself as operating at perhaps 75 per cent of full capacity.

I still experience back pain and an overall feeling of stiffness. Knowing I have an incurable disease, I'm obviously concerned that the multiple myeloma is in check and if the pills are working. But I don't dwell on it. Life is for living, not worrying.

Despite not being able to operate at full throttle, I'm still living at 100 per cent capacity beyond cancer. Often I don't even think that I have it. The key thing is to keep active, both physically and mentally.

To give an idea of how I do this, let me summarise my weekly regime: I cycle every second day, waking early to meet Nelo, and we do a brisk fifteen-kilometre ride to a coffee shop, where we stop for a steaming mug of Portugal's finest espresso. We cycle another fifteen kilometres back home along a beach path with a view of the Atlantic shimmering in the morning sun. It's not a bad way to start the day.

On non-cycling days, I do a moderate run-walk for about eight to ten kilometres. As my heartbeat is elevated, I use Dr Phil Maffetone's MAF method to maximise aerobic function. Even without training particularly hard, I find my running speed is starting to get back to what it should be at my age.

I then swim for three kilometres, about an hour, three times a week. Although some people find it boring, I love swimming and it's a great all-round aerobic workout.

I also do CrossFit three times a week. CrossFit is a HIT (high-intensity training) programme – a mix of aerobic exercise, callisthenics and Olympic weightlifting promoting strength, conditioning and overall fitness. A crucial aspect is that it increases my paddling power.

The best of all is when the wind blows and I take my surfski down to the beach. I usually paddle between twenty and forty kilometres, but on really good days I will go as far as sixty. I hardly consider this exercise, not only because I love it so much, but because after all these years of downwind paddling it's a joyride surfing one swell after the next.

This busy physical regime is paying dividends health-wise. Plans are in the pipeline to do the 2023 Molokai, now sponsored by Shaw and Partners, this time in a double-ski with Fernando Fernandes, an exceptionally inspirational Brazilian wheelchair paddler. I am also eligible to compete in the Transplant Games, following my stem-cell operation, so that too is something to consider.

I also find it perversely inspiring that so many paddlers still want to beat me on the water, despite my cancer. I love it – and I never forget that these were the same great guys sending me magnificent messages of hope and inspiration when I was at my lowest physical ebb. This, to me, is what it's all about, and I often joke if I pass them, shouting, 'Hey, what's wrong with you guys?'

My first proper race after stem-cell surgery was in Portugal, May 2021. Organised by the Portuguese Canoe Federation, it was a two-lap course, eighteen kilometres out and back, and a tough contest for me with little wind. Despite that, I was very happy to win the Over-50 category in an overall field of more than two hundred racers.

Six weeks later I flew to Lanzarote in the Canary Islands to compete in the ICF World Surfski Championships. It was a tremendous race, well organised and thankfully with the usual strong Atlantic winds blowing. I ended up forty-first overall, losing about twenty positions on the flat water and the run up the beach. Most encouraging was that I came second in my age category after one guy kamikaze-dived over the line to beat me by a few hundredths of a second. He was booed by his teammates.

To add to my schedule, I do regular motivation talks combining sport, business and fighting cancer and have started CoachChalupsky.com, an online training platform. So far I have 2 000 paddlers on my growing mailing list, and judging by the responses, many are finding these sessions useful in improving their skill sets. I also advocate the keto way of eating to lose weight and am happy to say I have had success – particularly among men, for some reason.

On top of that, I am consistently testing new ideas, improvements, innovations and designs for Nelo Kayaks. Without fail, every paddling session involves fine-tuning techniques and equipment. I have also been coaching

Portugal's surfskiing sensation Bernardo Pereira, the 2021 world junior champion, and plan to help him become the best surfskier in the world. I have no doubt this will happen, and it will be done in a Nelo design.

One of our most exciting ventures is Nelo Kayak's pioneering expansion into Brazil, which has some of the best downwind surfskiing conditions in the world. The country also has a massive water-sport community, with enthusiasts ranging from kayakers deep in the Amazon jungle to surfers risking life and limb on mutant point breaks, such as the aptly named 'Shock' on Rio's Itacoatiara Beach. Today the world's best surfers, led by reigning world champion Gabriel Medina, come from Brazil, while the biggest wave ever surfed, measured at 24.38 metres, was ridden by Rodrigo Koxa. Both are from São Paulo. This is remarkable as barely two decades ago few Brazilian surfers were even known, let alone highly ranked on the world circuit.

It's not only surfing. Just catching flights around the country and seeing travellers clutching SUPs (stand-up paddleboards), windsurfers and, to a lesser extent, surfskis is testament to the astonishing Brazilian beach-sport revolution. Surfskiing is destined to be an integral part of it.

I have always known that Brazil is a water-sport nirvana, but even I was astounded by the sheer magnificent extent of it when invited to compete in the 2021 Molokabra race. The four-day contest is more of a downwind festival than anything else as surfskis, outriggers, windsurfers, kitesurfers and SUPs all compete along the country's north-eastern shoreline. It's indisputably one of the best venues for wind sports anywhere in the world.

The day after I finished my last round of chemotherapy in Portugal, Clare and I flew out to Fortaleza, the capital of Ceará state, for the start of the race. My doctor shook his head and said, 'Are you crazy? You should be in bed recovering!'

Molokabra is named in homage of the Molokai race with the suffix 'bra' short for Brazil, but perhaps equally appropriate is that 'bra' is also the iconic surfer slang for 'brother'. As much as I love the Molokai, I now believe that the Molokabra is going to be the next epicentre of downwind racing. It's impossible to manufacture more ideal conditions: hundreds of miles of coastline where winds seldom blow below twenty-five to thirty knots, no gnarly shore breaks hampering launches, no bluebottles – and no sharks. The translucent turquoise ocean annually averages about twenty-eight degrees Celsius and almost makes the Caribbean look murky. It's surfskiing heaven.

The fact that there were 350 contestants at the start of a race that has little, if any, global publicity backs that up.

The Molokabra actually consists of two races: the eighty-two-kilometre Molokabra Downwind, which lasts three days, and the fifty-kilometre Super Molokabra on the fourth day, giving a total of 132 kilometres of superb surf-skiing.

It was a tightly fought event, and I was ecstatic to cross the finishing line first in both races with a cumulative time of five hours and nine minutes. To give an idea of the intensity of the contest, Luiz Wagner Pecoraro finished seventy-five seconds behind me, with fellow Brazilian Alexandre Ferreira a minute or so behind him.

However, the truism that if something seems too good to be true it usually is had me worried. Was I singing the praises of Brazil too loudly? Was I putting too much in store in saying this was the best downwind paddling in the world on the basis of a mere two-week trip?

There was only one way to find out, and that was to do it again. This time I took Nelo for an expert second opinion and we would paddle from Fortaleza to Jericoacoara, about 250 kilometres up the Ceará coast. They already have kitesurfing safaris along that stretch where the warm Atlantic winds never die, but we would be doing the first organised surfski safari.

It was the trip of a lifetime. Nelo and I have never enjoyed paddling so much. Every day was a roller-coaster in conditions so perfect I had to pinch myself to make sure it was true.

Here we were, me in my late fifties and Nelo in his early sixties, behaving like excited schoolboys. One had been stricken by polio in his childhood, the other was currently fighting cancer. Neither of us has for one moment let that stop us. The fact that we were on a glorious downwind safari when so many other people stay cooped in the confines of their minds is in essence what life choices are all about.

When not paddling, I gave coaching lessons on the beach. Here guys who had paddled in the Amazon River estuary told me that when the wind blows in one direction and the tide surges in the other, the runs are more spectacular than on the Columbia River Gorge. I shook my head in amazement. This country was even better than I thought for paddle junkies.

Nelo Kayaks is going to increase its operations in Brazil. We will be at the forefront of the water-sport revolution and I cannot believe how lucky I am to be involved. I helped pioneer thriving paddling communities in Hong

Kong, Mauritius, Dubai, Tahiti – even Holland, of all places. But Brazil is a bit more special because it already has a strong water-sport culture. There are so many paddling communities dotted along the beaches that are starved for cutting-edge equipment and coaching. Their eagerness and thirst for improvement and better techniques are unrivalled. I love being connected to such energy, and as they are so enthusiastic and passionate about our sport … why not help them to do it correctly?

One thing is for certain: I will be back. Next year I hope to defend my Molokabra title. Entry is by invitation, so hopefully no more hotshots than necessary will get invited. That way I can keep on winning it!

LESSON LEARNT

NEVER SIT BACK and do nothing. By some people's criteria, Nelo and I are 'handicapped'. That is the last thing on our minds. Life is not for the lethargic, or at least not if you want to relish it to the fullest. Get out there, keep moving and keep doing positive stuff.

If you do that, you will, in the words of Bob Dylan, stay forever young.

32

The hundred-footers

Just off the coastline of a small northern Portuguese town called Nazaré lies one of the largest underwater canyons in the Atlantic Ocean.

It stretches for 227 kilometres and plunges to 5 000 metres – a giant hole in the bottom of the sea nearly three times deeper than Colorado's Grand Canyon and with even steeper slopes.

When fierce winter storms brew, large mutating swells are funnelled down this vast submarine chasm. As they speed towards the coast, the rising seafloor at the canyon mouth forces the deep-water monsters upwards into towering cliffs of water, overtaking waves coming from the shallower continental shelf and tripling them in size. Legend has it that on perfect storm days, when giant rollers being spat out the canyon sync perfectly with incoming continental-shelf combers, some waves crest at more than thirty metres – the magical 100-footer, as surfers call it.

The astronomical power needed to generate waves soaring to 100 feet is so immense it's almost impossible to imagine. And the focal point of this meteoric energy is a rocky headland on Nazaré's Praia do Norte (North Beach) under a centuries-old lighthouse that is now immortalised in surfing folklore. And it's not far from where I live.

The Nazaré canyon has always been dreaded by local fishermen and is littered with wrecks. Most old-timers have at least one relative lost at sea. There is even a German U-boat lying on the ocean bed. But few surfers knew about the winter swells thundering up the gorge, especially as the tiny country of Portugal was not by any stretch of the imagination considered a big-wave cauldron. Monster-surf riders were all at Waimea, Cortes Bank, Mavericks or Jaws.

Then, on 1 November 2011, a Hawaiian big-wave junkie named Garrett McNamara rode the tallest wave ever surfed in the world. He and his jet-ski tow-in partners, Andrew Cotton and Al Mennie, were alone in the water, but it was recorded on video and measured at 23.8 metres (78 feet).

Overnight, the former fishing village of Nazaré became a global sensation.

The photo of Garrett, a speck on an Everest of raging water, was shown on almost every news bulletin in the world. Garrett said later he didn't sleep for forty-eight hours, not only amped from the fizzing adrenaline of the big ride but also because requests for interviews never ceased.

The effects were electrifying, not least for the bemused people of Nazaré. Big-wave riders flocked to a sleepy town they had never heard of before to ride the now legendary Godzillas of the deep. The big guns wanted a 100-footer – and to be the first to surf it.

But even so, Garrett's record stood for six years until Brazilian surfer Rodrigo Koxa rode a 24.38-metre (80-foot) foaming giant in November 2017. It was massive – but not a 100-footer. He described the experience as 'dancing with God'.

Before Rodrigo broke Garrett's record and long before hordes of surfers turned the town into a winter congestion zone, I decided to have a look at Nazaré, which is only a two-hour drive away from Vila do Conde. I was suffering from the same adrenaline rush afflicting Garrett, Rodrigo and Andrew Cotton – a British surfer who would break his back in a Nazaré wipeout in 2017. Nothing excited me more than the thought of riding a wave higher than 100 feet. But not on a surfboard. I wanted to do it on a surfski.

I sent several emails and texts to Garrett, who spends most winters in Portugal, but he didn't reply. I think even he thought it was too crazy to ride Nazaré on a surfski. So on 27 October 2015, Clare and I, joined by Gonçalo Tomás and his partner Sara, who at the time ran the Douro Marina Surfski School owned by Nelo Kayaks, drove out to see the monster surf ourselves.

At first sight it looked disappointing. The waves didn't seem that big, and from the now famous lighthouse that stands sixty metres above the ocean, they looked even smaller.

I decided to do a test run, but it was impossible to launch from the beach owing to the power of the shore breaks. I tried for about an hour to paddle out along the calmer south side, but even that was impenetrable – which should have been a warning of what was actually out there. I didn't know it at the time, but on that day the waves were so big and shifty that they were breaking 500 metres north of the lighthouse, which locals say only happens when swells tower more than fifty feet.

Eventually, I ran to the sheltered harbour wall and launched from there. As I reached the surf zone, I thought, 'What the hell is going on?' These waves were at least ten times bigger than what they seemed to be from the lighthouse – some peaking between sixty and eighty feet. I had never seen anything like it. They were also the most difficult breaks I have encountered, with walls of water charging all over the place, proving far trickier than anything I had surfed before. I've ridden big waves around the world, including Hawaii's Waimea Bay, Teahupo'o in Tahiti and Dungeons in Cape Town. But this was something else, all right.

Equally astonished at the deceptive size and power were Clare, Gonçalo and Sara. Seeing me out there, they had a proportional measurement of how big the surf truly was. Clare later said that when I paddled over one rising twenty-five-metre swell as a tiny insignificant blip on a fluid mountain, the enormity of it all was suddenly put in terrifying perspective. Whenever a set came thundering through, she had to look away. Much of the time they couldn't see where I was, and being in a grey boat among all the foam and spray didn't help. All three were praying that I didn't catch a wave, either deliberately or accidentally.

I had no intention of surfing those monsters, as all I had on was a wetsuit and a lightweight life jacket that I race in. It would have provided no buoyancy whatsoever in that oceanic warzone. Equally concerning was having to look continuously behind me. If I got sandwiched between two eighty-footers, I most likely would not have resurfaced. But despite the fear, I was exhilarated – particularly while watching German surfer Sebastian Steudtner ride a seventy-one-footer that morning, which won him the prized XXL Biggest Wave of the Year Award.

After about an hour and a half, I paddled ashore and Clare and Gonçalo rushed up, saying that Garrett McNamara was at the lighthouse.

Garrett was not happy, fuming about how I should never have been out there in those dangerous conditions. I then introduced myself, and coming from Hawaii he recognised my name from the Molokai races. When I told him I had been sending him texts and emails asking about Nazaré conditions without response, he mellowed a bit. We then had lunch together, but he was non-committal about giving me assistance. I assume he gets lots of those requests, and as he's such a legend, I didn't pursue the matter.

Three days later we returned, and this time I hoped to ride some waves. Looking out from the lighthouse, the surf seemed pretty small, and Clare reluctantly agreed that I could go out, although she claims that the size of the waves would have made no difference to my decision. Barbara and Rene

Appel, who previously managed the Epic dealership in Hong Kong, were with us and dropped me off at the harbour.

Once again, judging the surf from the lighthouse bore no resemblance to reality as it was breaking at between thirty and forty feet. Not small at all. Once again, Clare could barely look, as seeing me as a speck on a wall of water was somewhat unsettling. I still didn't have a proper life jacket, so I only took off on a few experimental waves to get a feel for the conditions. Barbara, a photographer, snapped some photos from the lighthouse, a vantage point that tends to diminish the size of the waves. But even so, contrasting my 5.6-metre surfski with the actual height of the swell gives a good idea. I don't know if a bigger wave has ever been ridden on a surfski, but that ride made up my mind that with the right equipment, I could catch much bigger ones. Even a 100-footer.

Obviously I will need state-of-the-art safety gear, such as the triple-buoyancy life jacket pioneered by my friend and champion big-wave rider Twiggy Baker, who is also from Durban.

I will need a surfski specifically designed for big-wave riding as well – it has to be fast, extremely manoeuvrable and stable, as I want to catch a 100-footer as a purist and not be towed in. With the right surfski, I believe I can paddle fast enough to catch these liquid mountains. To do so, I will need to be hitting at least twenty-five kilometres an hour, and if it's windy it'll give me an even faster run. Once I catch it, I will be screaming down an almost sheer wall of water, eight storeys high, at speeds of up to sixty kilometres an hour. The fastest speed I have recorded on a surfski is fifty-six – so it's going to be a lot of fun. It could also kill me.

These plans I made before my cancer shock. They are on the back burner at the moment, although still vividly seared in my mind. But it goes deeper than that. Cancer is a metaphorical 100-footer that I am already riding, and so far I have not been wiped out. On the contrary, on most days I am on my surfski paddling the ocean, rather than any sickbed. There has been no retreat, no surrender. The magical 100-footer is still out there in the cavernous canyon of Nazaré. It's waiting for me. I hope to catch it.

Of all the lessons life has taught me – from youthful endless summers on the beach and racing surfskis around the world to surmounting business problems – the most important is to live every day as intensely as you can.

Life is a 100-footer. Ride it.

Notes

CHAPTER 18

1. SeaKayaker User Archive, 'The Race to 10 Molokai World Surf-Ski Championship', SeaKayaker, 22 February 2004. Available at https://seakayaker.org/race-10-molo kai-world-surf-ski-championship/ (accessed 11 February 2022).

CHAPTER 20

2. Rob Mousley, 'Oscar Chalupsky: Surfski.info's 2006/2007 World Champion!', Surfski.info, 12 July 2007. Available at https://www.surfski.info/latest-news/story/ 205/oscar-chalupsky-surfskiinfo%C3%A2%E2%80%99s-2006/2007-world-cham pion.html (accessed 11 February 2022).

CHAPTER 21

3. Rob Mousley, 'Perth World Cup 2007 – Drama Galore', Surfski.info, 8 December 2007. Available at https://www.surfski.info/latest-news/story/346/perth-world -cup-2007-%C3%A2%E2%80%93-drama-galore.html (accessed 11 February 2022).

CHAPTER 23

4. Mike Booth cited by Joe Glickman, Surfski.info. Available at https://www.surfski .info (accessed 14 February 2022).
5. Matt Bouman cited in Rob Mousley, 'Molokai: Chalupsky makes it number 12!', Surfski.info, 21 May 2012. Available at https://www.surfski.info/latest-news/story/ 1406/molokai-chalupsky-makes-it-number-12.html (accessed 11 February 2022).

CHAPTER 29

6. Joe Glickman, 'Mauritius & Durban: Don't Drink Gas with a Chalupsky', Surfski .info, 2 August 2009. Available at https://www.surfski.info/reviews/item/840-mau ritius-durban-don%C3%83%C2%A2%C3%A2%E2%80%9A%C2%AC%C3%A2 %E2%80%9E%C2%A2t-drink-gas-with-a-chalupsky-**-videos-**.html (accessed 11 February 2022).

Index